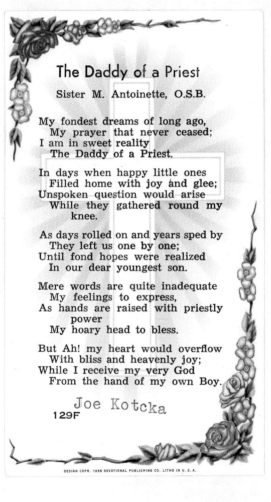

The Daddy of a Priest

Sister M. Antoinette, O.S.B.

My fondest dreams of long ago,
  My prayer that never ceased;
I am in sweet reality
  The Daddy of a Priest.

In days when happy little ones
  Filled home with joy and glee;
Unspoken question would arise
  While they gathered round my
    knee.

As days rolled on and years sped by
  They left us one by one;
Until fond hopes were realized
  In our dear youngest son.

Mere words are quite inadequate
  My feelings to express,
As hands are raised with priestly
    power
  My hoary head to bless.

But Ah! my heart would overflow
  With bliss and heavenly joy;
While I receive my very God
  From the hand of my own Boy.

Joe Kotcka

129F

DESIGN COPR. 1955 DEVOTIONAL PUBLISHING CO. LITHO IN U.S.A.

THE SCOPE OF THEOLOGY

THE SCOPE
OF THEOLOGY

Edited by Daniel T. Jenkins

The World Publishing Company
Cleveland and New York

Published by The World Publishing Company
2231 West 110th Street, Cleveland 2, Ohio

Copyright © 1965 by Daniel T. Jenkins

Manufactured in the United States of America

Library of Congress Catalog Card Number: 65–25777

Contents

Abbreviations

CC	Christianity and Crisis
CS	Christian Scholar
ER	Ecumenical Review
JP	Journal of Philosophy
JR	Journal of Religion
JTS	Journal of Theological Studies
PH	Philosophy
PQ	Philosophical Quarterly
RGG	Die Religion im Geschichte und Gegenwart, 3d ed.
SR	Stanford Review
ST	Studia Theologica
TH	Theology
TWNT	Theologisches Wörterbuch für das Neuen Testaments, ed. Kittel
VC	Verbum Caro

Introduction

This book is an introduction to the study of theology. To many people in these days, theology appears as one of the most remote and obscure of subjects. It has become a form of speech to refer to the general principles lying behind a political movement or a subject of study as their "theology," with the implication that these are so general that they can be taken for granted and not worried about by practical men. It must be admitted that the study of theology, like that of other subjects, has its share of false academicism and unnecessary obscurity, but we hope that this book will show to any who might hold such ideas that theology is very much alive, practically important, and closely related to other intellectual activities.

Theology might be defined in a preliminary way as systematic discourse concerning God and His ways. It arises in the first instance on the basis of specific religious experience which appears in a particular context. The religious experience with which the authors of this book are primarily concerned is Christian. This controls their approach but does not mean, as Professor Smart reminds us in his essay, that Christian theology can be adequately studied without reference to other theologies based on different kinds of experience. These other theologies certainly exist and demand to be taken into account by Christians.

What gives Christian theology its point of departure is the faith that Jesus Christ reveals the true God. Whether this means that this theology can be studied effectively by an unbeliever is a question which has been much debated. That it can be studied after a fashion by someone who professes unbelief is obvious. But more than that, one of the things which the well-instructed student of theology has to learn is that it is very hard for him to say at any one point whether, in his mind, he is a believer or an unbeliever. Faith always exists in tension with its contradiction and achieves the understanding which is its intellectual goal only when it reckons seriously with the possibility that its contradiction may be true. All that can safely be said here, therefore, is that theology cannot be studied very well except by those who see that it tries to deal with questions which have meaning because they arise out of a body of experience which demands explanation. No one is likely to make much of Christian theology unless he has some awareness of what worship, prayer, the sense of sin, moral constraint, atonement, forgiveness, gratitude, love, and obedience signify, and unless he has some imaginative understanding of the peculiar nature of the compulsion exercised by the figure of Jesus Christ. This is one reason why Christian theology has nearly always been undertaken as an activity of the Church, as a response to what members of the Church believe to be a revelation of God made human in Jesus Christ and as an attempt to work out the intellectual implications of that revelation. The fact that theology normally arises in the life of the Church does not mean, however, that it has no place in the life of the university, since it cannot achieve understanding of its own subject matter without some effort to define itself in relation to other departments of knowledge. This is demonstrated by the essays in the second half of the book.

Even when theology has been limited to the study of specifically Christian theology, it remains a very large field, with many considerable subdivisions. So much is this the case that, since the days of the Enlightenment the study of these subdivisions, known as theological encyclopedia, has itself been treated as a subdivision in its own right. In these days there is no universal agreement as to what these subdivisions should be. In America, with its lively experimentalism, many highly original schemes for theological education have been devised, and frequently changed. But, as might be expected, most schemes have certain constant and indispensable elements. Thus, a broad distinction is discernible between what can be described as historical and as normative or constructive studies. In the former, the approach is very much in accordance with what is commonly known as scientific scholarship, where the aim is the isolation, definition, and classification of facts and ideas and their exposition in an appropriate order. In the latter, the approach is broadly philosophical, where the aim is analysis, synthesis, and evaluation.

Historical studies in the theological sphere are normally divided into the general and the specifically Christian. The former are the history of the various religions and the science of religion, which is itself subdivided into important sections, including the comparative study of religions, their psychology and sociology. The specifically Christian historical studies are those of the Bible in both Testaments and Church history. The latter frequently includes the history of Christian doctrine, although that is sometimes included as part of the study of systematic theology.

The normative disciplines can similarly be divided into the general and the specifically Christian. The characteristic general discipline is the philosophy of religion. This, in its turn, has been divided in various ways, of which perhaps the most common is into the epistemology and the ontology of religion. Occasionally the psychology and sociology of religion are studied under the heading of its philosophy. Apologetics, which tries to answer objections to belief in divine existence and to the truth of Christian revelation is sometimes considered a part of the philosophy of religion and sometimes as a part of systematic theology, although there is some debate as to whether it should properly be considered a separate subject in its own right.

Systematic theology, which tries to state the major Christian doctrines in relation to one another on the basis of Scripture and the history of theology and in the setting of our own time, is the specifically Christian normative discipline. In his great work of systematic theology, *Church Dogmatics*, Karl Barth has incorporated Christian ethics as part of dogmatics, which is another name for systematic theology as I have defined it. Not everyone would agree with him, although there would be widespread agreement that Christian ethics should be studied in close relation to systematic theology. A part of Christian study which does not fit easily into the historical and normative categories but which is of great importance is practical theology, sometimes more narrowly defined as pastoral theology. This deals with the care of souls, the craft of preaching (whose study is formalized as homiletics), Christian education, and Church organization and administration.

This book follows the normal patterns of the arrangement of theological courses to only a limited extent, and a word of explanation of our procedure is necessary. The first part deals with those subjects which are basic in most courses, with three essays on different aspects of biblical study, two on Church history, and one on systematic theology. If space had permitted, essays on the history of the Church in the Middle Ages and on the history of creeds, confessions, and theological systems might well have been added.

In dealing with those aspects of theological study which impinge with particular directness on other subjects, it has seemed best not to fit them into a very closely defined framework. Instead, people who are very familiar with the borderline between theology and other subjects have written essays on the relation between them. The reason for this is that, in these days even more than in the past, the frontiers between them are rapidly shifting, and new possibilities are frequently emerging. We hope that this approach will convey something of the flexibility and the vigor of the present state of the conversation.

Two warnings must be given. The first is that this series of essays does not cover the whole ground. The absence of one subject in particular cries out for explanation, especially in modern America. There is no essay which deals in detail with the relation between theology and psychological studies. A great deal of attention has been devoted to this relationship in recent times, particularly with reference to psychiatry, where its practical importance is obvious. The omission of an essay on this theme should be noted, therefore, but no dark and devious reason for it need be sought by the psychologist. It is simply due to the kind of situation which arises in a book of this kind. Difficulties arose about obtaining an essay, and—especially as Professor Winter's essay deals with some of the issues which are common to all the human sciences—it seemed best not to hold up the production of a book already delayed in order to repair this omission.

It is, indeed, hard to avoid omissions in a book of this kind if it is not to become unwieldy. Thus many people particularly involved with these subjects might complain that the theology of Christian missions and ascetical theology, dealing with prayer and spiritual discipline, and liturgical theology, and the theology of the Christian nurture of the very young have been overlooked, although they are all of considerable practical importance. We can only reassure those of our readers who are familiar with theological education that we know that these subjects exist and remind those of our readers who are not that they are important.

The other warning which must be given is this: not only do the essays in this book fail to cover the whole field; they are also no more than introductory to those parts of it with which they deal. The approach of the essays is academic, since they are intended primarily for students, but they do not purport to be "digests" of the subject matter of theology. Their aim is to whet the appetite, to give some idea of the scope and range of the subject, and to indicate what the outstanding issues are which invite further inquiry.

It has been customary for many years to talk of the importance of making theology intellectually respectable. This is not an altogether improper matter to be concerned about, since certain aspects of the study of theology have been allowed to fall into disrepute, although some of the disrepute may be due as much to the ignorance and prejudice of their critics as to the failings of theologians. But beyond a certain point, theology cannot really live if it is only respectable according to the current conventions of respectability. It must also be intellectually disturbing and stimulating, raising questions we prefer to leave dormant and stretching our minds to their limits. And as the greatest of modern theologians has reminded us, it should be beautiful, an exercise in which our minds find true delight. We hope that these essays will help those who are new to the study of theology to see how all this could be.

DANIEL T. JENKINS

THE SCOPE OF THEOLOGY

1. The Study of the Bible

J. Davis McCaughey

Why the study *of the Bible*? Several factors—linguistic, literary, and historical—make it appear as though the study of the Bible consists of two separate disciplines. Few men have equal skills in work on both Testaments, and distinguishable skills have to be imparted to students. The distinctions between Old Testament and New Testament are now embodied in a number of institutions: professorial chairs, learned journals, and learned societies all bear witness to the tacit assumption that Old Testament studies and New Testament studies are not only distinct but also essentially separable disciplines.

The distinction, if not the separation, must of course be accepted; but the serious student is not finished with the question of the Bible when he has completed his studies in the Old Testament and in the New Testament. Indeed he may not have carried through his studies in either Testament in their correct context if he drives far the notion of the relative autonomy of either discipline from the other. A separate essay on "The Study of the Bible" in a volume which also contains essays on the Old Testament and the New Testament must try to demonstrate why this should be the case. The justification of the very phrase "the study of the Bible" lies in a fact which may be stated in a number of ways, of which we must be content with one: that the Christian Church has as a datum of its historical and dogmatic life the canon of Holy Scripture, the Bible. Our task is to try to begin to discern the significance of that fact.

I

What is the significance for the study of theology of the existence
of a canon of Holy Scripture? From its earliest days the Christian
Church had a problem concerning which Scriptures she was to
regard as authoritative. The history of the canon has often been
told. To this day there are differences between the Greek, the
Roman, the Protestant, and Anglican Churches over the books
which may properly be said to belong to that canon; but the
differences are of marginal significance, and even in a day of
ecumenical conference they scarcely warrant lengthy discussion.
That is not to say that the historical questions about the formation and acceptance of the canon are closed. Far from it: the discovery of the Gnostic library near Chenoboskion and the fuller
knowledge of Gnosticism which is flowing from this discovery
have sharpened our awareness of the circumstances in which the
canon of the New Testament won recognition in the Church.[1]
It could scarcely be said, however, that it is only from this source
that the question of the canon is being thrust once more into the
forefront of theological debate, important though these studies
may yet prove to be. The question of the canon has become "a
special problem"[2] today very largely because of the impact upon
our consciousness of modern literary-critical study of the biblical
documents.

First we might observe that the criteria for canonicity which
were for long acceptable in the Church are no longer so. Profes-

[1] See W. C. van Unnik, "The Gospel of Truth and the New Testament,"
in F. L. Cross, *The Jung Codex* (New York: Morehouse-Gorham Co.,
1955); R. M. Grant and D. N. Freedman, *The Secret Sayings of Jesus* (New
York: Doubleday & Co., 1960), esp. chap. VI, "The Gnostics and Our
Gospels"; B. Gärtner, *The Theology of the Gospel of Thomas*, Eric J.
Sharpe, trans. (New York: Harper & Row, 1961), esp. chap. VIII, "The
Gospel of Thomas and the Gnostic View of Scripture"; and R. McL. Wilson, *Studies in the Gospel of Thomas* (London: Mowbray & Co., 1960). In
none of these, however, nor in any other literature which has come to my
hands, has the question been discussed fully and systematically. On the other
hand, Søren Giversen's recently published "Nag Hammadi Bibliography
1948–1963," *ST*, Vol. 17, Fasc. 2 (1963 [Aarthus, Denmark]), has forty-five
pages of titles of books, studies, and reviews; and one would be rash to
assume that among them the matter has not received extended treatment.
[2] Kurt Aland, *The Problem of the New Testament Canon* (Westminster,
Md.: Canterbury Press, 1962 [paperback]).

sor G. S. Hendry rightly objects to the way in which the Westminster Confession isolates inspiration as the hallmark of canonical
Scriptures:

When the Church had to decide which books were to be received
into the canon of the New Testament and which to be excluded,
it did not confine itself to the question, Which are inspired? The
principal test it used was that of apostolic origin, just as the test
for the Old Testament had been that of prophetic origin (both
taken in a somewhat broad sense). The distinctive feature of the
apostolic writings is that their authors were actual participants in
the revealing events; they were themselves *in* the truth of which
they wrote, and it was on this account that they were commis-
sioned to be witnesses to it. (Acts 1:8, 21–22.) The inspiration of
their writings ought not to be isolated from their own relation to
the truth; in other words, it should not be thought of as something that happened to them only when they wrote, but rather as
something involved in their being apostles.[3]

That is well said, and would gain fairly general acceptance. Its
particular application is more difficult. For instance, "apostolic
origin" has to be taken in a *very* broad sense, much broader than
that given to it by the New Testament documents or the early
Church, if it is to cover many books in the New Testament. Apart
from the letters of Paul (and of his authorship we can speak with
reasonable certainty only of six or seven), is there any recognizable sense in which we can speak of apostolic authorship of any
document in the New Testament? Much used to be made of the
place of eyewitnesses in the formation and preservation of the gospel tradition. Few scholars would now wish to defend the view
that the author of any of the four Gospels was himself an eye-
witness; and many scholars, admitting the validity of the work
of the form critics, would go further and suggest that the form
of the traditional material used by the Gospel writers was already
conditioned more by community needs than by personal reminis-
cence.[4]

[3] G. S. Hendry, *The Westminster Confession for Today* (Richmond, Va.:
John Knox Press, 1960), p. 33, n. 2.
[4] See the important articles by D. E. Nineham, "Eye-Witness Testimony
and the Gospel Tradition," *JTS*, New Series, Vol. IX (1958), pp. 13–25,
243–52 and Vol. XI (1960), pp. 253–64.

A critical view of the authorship of the books of the New Testament and of the pressures by which traditional material concerning Jesus was handed down has made it virtually impossible to regard the term apostolic origin as a meaningful way of describing the hallmark of a canonical writing, unless "apostolic" is used in what would indeed be a very general way. Even supposing these critical judgments could be shown in this or that respect to be erroneous—supposing a few more letters could be attributed to Paul, or that Petrine reminiscences could be shown to have influenced the writing of Mark—the authority of the canon of the New Testament would not be substantially strengthened. Its authority cannot be made to depend upon conservative conclusions as to the authorship of individual books.

It must be conceded, however, that apostolic origin never meant simply authorship by an apostle. Dr. Aland has usefully remarked that "if one wanted to sum up in a formula the external principles which played a part in the choice of the canonical Scriptures, one can only speak of the principle of 'having no principles.' From the Muratorian Canon, e.g., we can see how every emerging principle on which the choice has professedly been made is expressly repudiated again in words."[5] He speaks too of "the freedom with which the early Fathers (as also the reformers) judged as to whether a writing did or did not belong to the Canon." They pointed to the *regula fidei* or the *kanōn tēs alētheias* by which everything is measured, even the books of the New Testament. When the Church, ecclesiastically organized, recognized (not created) the canon of Scripture, that canon henceforward provides the guiding posts between which is to be found the faith and teaching by which the Church lives. There can be little doubt that through many subsequent centuries that faith and teaching was assumed to be a coherent whole, one part of which was (if properly understood) entirely consistent with all other parts.

Here the problems confronting the student of today are considerable. Literary and historical scholarship has shaken free from their context in the whole the individual books of the New Testament; and when we look at the individual books we are con-

[5] Aland, *op cit.*, pp. 14–15.

fronted by a bewildering variety of viewpoints, and are given an introduction to many differing Church situations. There is far less uniformity of doctrine, morals, or Church life than was at one time supposed. This point has been made with some force in recent years by Prof. Ernst Käsemann in a number of essays;[6] and while his Lutheran colleague Prof. Hermann Diem[7] and his Roman Catholic colleague Dr. Hans Küng[8] take him up on a number of points and in particular challenge Käsemann's view of what is to be done about this state of affairs, neither of them seems disposed to differ from him radically on the fact that there is a wide diversity of doctrine and practice in the churches of New Testament times. The period of harmonizing seems to be over.

The appeal to the New Testament concerning the proper ordering of the life of the Church is instructive in this regard. Until relatively recently it was widely assumed that there was an order in *the* New Testament Church which could be taken as a precedent for the reordering of Church life in later generations. Pursuing this method of appeal to precedent, it is not altogether surprising to discover that Presbyterians find conciliar government in the New Testament, Congregationalists the church meeting, and Episcopalians episcopacy. Apparent inconsistencies could, it was assumed, be easily harmonized. It was, for instance, once widely believed and taught that the terms *presbuteros* and *episkopos* were used indifferently of the same office. At the end of the nineteenth century Bishop Lightfoot in his commentary on Philippians could write: "It is a fact now generally recognised by theologians of all shades of opinion, that in the language of the New Testament the same officer in the Church is called indifferently 'bishop' (*episkopos*) and 'elder' or 'presbyter' (*presbu-*

[6] E. Käsemann, *Exegetische Versuche und Besinnungen*, I (Göttingen: Vandenhoeck & Ruprecht, 1960), particularly the essay, "Begrundet der neutestamentliche Kanon die Eiheit der Kirche?"

[7] H. Diem, *Dogmatics*, Harold Knight, trans. (Philadelphia: Westminster Press, 1959), esp. chap. VIII.

[8] H. Küng, S.J., *The Council in Action*, Cecily Hastings and N. D. Smith, trans. (London and New York: Sheed & Ward, 1963), esp. Part 4. 1. (Published in England under the title, *The Living Church*.)

teros)."[9] This opened the way to attempts to achieve a synthesis not only of New Testament order but also of terms. That such a harmony cannot be found within the New Testament is now apparent to many. The Jerusalem Church and the Gentile Mission develop along very different lines; and by the time all documents which make up the New Testament have been written, many forms of Church life are apparent in its pages. Within its spectrum we have everything from the Johannine Church—with sacraments but without any marked interest in ministerial order, and with perhaps some antagonism toward it—to the pastoral Epistles with their highly developed preoccupation with discipline and order.[10] It is now clear that there can be no simple appeal to the precedent of the Church of the New Testament in order to solve our problems of Christian disunity. Whatever function the canon is to perform it is not intended to provide us with a manual of Church order, as was certainly at one time believed.

If the unity of the New Testament cannot be found in a high degree of uniformity of teaching on the part of the various New Testament writers, and if it cannot be found in more or less uniform practices in the churches of the New Testament period, wherein can it be found? Up till relatively recently, many would have been happy to answer: "In the apostolic preaching." A whole generation of English-speaking students has owed much in its understanding of this matter to two little books, important out of all proportion to their size: A. M. Hunter, *The Unity of the New Testament*;[11] and C. H. Dodd, *The Apostolic Preaching and Its*

[9] J. B. Lightfoot, *St. Paul's Epistle to the Philippians* (London and New York: Macmillan & Co., 1894), note on "The synonymes 'bishop' and 'presbyter,'" pp. 95–99.

[10] Among recent literature on all this see H. Fr. von Campenhausen, *Kirchliches Amt und geistliche Vollmacht* (Tübingen: Mohr, 1953); E. Schweizer, *Church Order in the New Testament*, Frank Clarke, trans. (London: SCM Press, 1961), E. t. of *Gemeinde und Gemeindeordnung im Neuen Testament* (Zurich (Stuttgart): Zwingli Verlag, 1959); M. Goguel, *The Primitive Church*, H. C. Snape, trans. (New York: The Macmillan Co., 1964), E. t. of *L'Eglise Primitive* (Paris: Payot, 1947), Vol. III of the author's *Jésus et les Origines du Christianisme* (1932–1947); G. Bornkamm, "Presbuteros," in *TWNT*, Bd VI; C. F. D. Moule, *The Birth of the New Testament* (New York: Harper & Row, 1962), chap. IX, "Variety and Uniformity in the Church."

[11] London: SCM Press, 1943.

Developments.[12] These books enabled many to see that there is a message which belonged to the primitive Church and which, through many developments, can be found expressing itself in a variety of circumstances within the New Testament documents. This was the apostolic kerygma. Here was an attempt, still influential and still valuable, to find a canon within the canon, a message within the New Testament by which to judge the relative merits of different books and parts of the whole. At the end of his survey Professor Dodd could claim that "the farther we move from the primitive modes of expression, the more decisively is the central purport of it affirmed. With all the diversity of the New Testament writings, they form a unity in their proclamation of the one Gospel."[13] Yet even though Dodd had chosen his words carefully, doubts crept in which suggest that some readers of Dodd's work were assuming a uniformity of affirmation both about the person and the work of Jesus and about the New Testament teaching on eschatology which neither the New Testament nor the earliest message which can be discovered in its pages ever possessed.

A series of articles which appeared in quick succession in the *Journal of Theological Studies* must suffice to indicate ways in which earlier confidence was shaken in the possibility of recovering the kerygma as providing the framework of New Testament theology as a whole. Professor C. F. Evans, following Martin Dibelius, called in question the validity of using the early speeches in Acts as evidence for primitive Christology.[14] He certainly makes it less easy to assume that we can easily discern the kerygma: "a hub from which spokes radiate in all directions, or, to change the metaphor, a skeleton which can still be seen here and there under the flesh, holding the flesh together." Dr. J. A. T. Robinson followed this with an attempt to disentangle the primitive kerygma from Luke's own theology in the early speeches in Acts,[15] but the result of his work is to demonstrate that Acts 2

---

[12] New York: Harper & Brothers, 1960 (London, 1936).

[13] *Ibid.*, p. 74.

[14] C. F. Evans, "The Kerygma," *JTS*, New Series, Vol. VII (1956), pp. 25–41.

[15] J. A. T. Robinson, "The Most Primitive Christology of All?" *JTS*, New Series, Vol. VII (1956), pp. 177–89.

and Acts 3 contain two different and mutually inconsistent Christologies, each of them with the claim to be regarded as primitive:
one was to win out to a wider recognition, the other (Acts 3)
"lies embedded in the book of Acts like the fossil of a by-gone
age." Dr. R. P. Casey's attack on the very idea of an apostolic
kerygma was more complete.[16] The speeches in the early chapters
of Acts are a misleading starting point. It is better to start with
the few certain affirmations about Jesus' sense of divine vocation,
and to observe how "the mind of Jesus became historically the
mind of the cosmic Christ and then of the Catholic Church." In
the reliability of this development, Casey has the utmost confidence: "Its earliest illustrations indicate a line of progress in which
there was no erratic departure but a steadily increasing insight in
the New Testament which led consistently to later, fuller, and
more precise conciliar formulations."[17] Although Casey's attack on
the apostolic kerygma is complete, although he will have nothing
to do with the suggestion that there is a biblical theology of the
person of Christ or of any other tenet of the faith, he emerges
from the whole discussion the most confident Catholic—and perhaps by implication most satisfied with the little which the documents inside the New Testament canon have to give us. He
appears to make fewer claims for the New Testament, and he is
content with less from it in the way of illumination of the Faith.
The New Testament is for him but a moment, a historically
formative and critical moment, in the life and faith of the Church.
The canon of the New Testament no longer stands, as it were,
over against the Church, with the kerygma as a yardstick by
which to measure her preaching. It marks the first stages of the
Church's formulations of the faith, going back to Jesus' sense of
divine vocation. The Church's faith develops and grows from that
moment and from that historic person.

What has been gained from this long and as yet inconclusive
discussion about the apostolic kerygma? We cannot obtain agreement about how the kerygma is to be defined; but we may register
two interrelated points, the first of which is that the search for

[16] R. P. Casey, "The Earliest Christologies," *JTS*, New Series, Vol. IX
(1958), pp. 253–77.
[17] *Ibid.*, p. 277.

what may be called a canon within the canon is inescapable. Commenting that since Semler (1725–91) the canon of Scripture had, especially in Protestant theology, undergone constant critical investigation, Dr. Lukas Vischer writes: "This critical work leads to a fundamental readiness to distinguish qualitatively the separate writings in the canon on the basis of their content and in some measure to determine a narrower canon in the traditional canon."[18] But we must take the matter further than the separate writings; for within each book distinctions are to be made. As Prof. W. C. Kümmel puts it: "Human limitations and human error are to be taken into account in *all* writings of the New Testament; and not only their apostolic authorship or particular antiquity but the actual nearness to or distance from the basic proclamation of the New Testament decides the significance as norm of a New Testament writing or a part of it."[19] To adopt the critical method at all means that of any biblical author, at any point in his writing, we must ask the question: "Is he right?" But this in turn only raises more acutely the question of the standard by which we pass this judgment.

The second lesson to be learnt from the discussion concerning unity and diversity in the New Testament witness is that this question is intimately related to that concerning continuity and discontinuity in the Church's life and message. Dr. Casey is surely right in insisting that the really important question is not in the relationship between the supposedly early preaching of the speeches embedded in the early chapters of Acts and later developments at the hands of Paul, John, and others. The really important question is that of the relationship between the message and purpose of Jesus and the message and purpose of the early churches. Certainly there is discontinuity. It is becoming more and more clear that Jesus did not claim for himself all the titles which were afterwards ascribed to him and are to be found in the gospel tradition. It is equally clear that in no simple sense can Jesus be said to have founded an institution which is lineally descended from him. Whatever Loisy's intention may have been when he stated that "Jesus announced the Kingdom of God and

[18] "Kanon II," *RGG*, 3d ed., Bd. III, col. 1121.
[19] "Bibel II B," *RGG*, 3d ed., Bd. I, col. 1138.

the Church arrived," the statement in itself is one of fact. There is a critical point of discontinuity between Jesus and the Church, and it can be fixed chronologically at the crucifixion and the resurrection. The relation between Jesus and his disciples was radically altered by that event. The old relationship of Master and disciples was not simply continued or restored after the tiresome interruption and the unfortunate ignominy of the cross. The cross and resurrection create a radical discontinuity between what Jesus said and did in his earthly ministry and what the disciples and the Church were to do this side of those events. But there is also genuine continuity, not in a straight line but a projection of what happened in one time and place in Palestine into a new series of situations, Jewish and Gentile, marked by a new dimension: the imperatives of the Risen Lord, the leading of the Spirit, and the prospect of the universal mission. The table-fellowship which Jesus had had with taxgatherers and Pharisee alike now becomes the type of the fellowship which Jew and Gentile together would have at the table of the Lord. The calling not of righteous but of sinners within Israel became a call addressed to every man. The twelve who by word and existence were to announce to Israel that the last hour had come, now became proclaimers of the fact that the new age had dawned in the resurrection of Jesus, that the judging act had been performed and that all men were called to repent and await the hour of restoration of all things. No doubt the overwhelming reality of the risen and living Lord caused many and various statements to be made about him in different parts of the Church; but the statements did not create the reality, they were no more than attempts to serve it. No doubt many and varied attempts were made to provide a Church order through which the risen Lord could put his followers into a true relation of faith in him, love for one another, and hope for the coming Kingdom. But again the various forms were not designed to create but to serve the reality of the new relationship in the gospel; they were (in very different ways) to embody the new life in Christ. There is in the New Testament a continuity from Jesus into a variety of affirmations about him and of Church "orders" (if that is a permissible term). All of these affirmations seek to set forward in practice the truth of Paul's dictum that *God is not a God of confusion, but of peace.* Note that Paul uses not the word "order," but "peace" which is an evangelical word.[20]

II

The argument so far has been around the problem raised by the canon of the New Testament. The question is complicated but not essentially altered when we remind ourselves that the canon of Holy Scripture for the Christian Church consists of Old and New Testaments.

What has been said about variety of viewpoints within the canon is immediately apparent when we turn to the Old Testament. The narrow nationalism of the Book of Esther and the universal sympathy of the Book of Jonah stand in more than contrast to each other. Their outlooks would seem to be mutually exclusive. Within the Book of Psalms are to be found varying attitudes to God's judgment and his mercy which cannot be regarded as consistent one with the other. The Pentateuch, as we have it, is the work of the returned men of the exile and appears to cover inner contradictions, which become more apparent the more we learn about the sources on which it is built and the purposes to which its parts were put during the oral period which preceded any writing. Whatever may be the case with the New Testament, it has long since been impossible to regard the Old Testament as equally in all in its parts the vehicle of God's Word to man.

Thus the search for "a canon within the canon" at first seemed more urgent in the case of the Old Testament than the New. A generation or two ago it was still popular to try to solve this puzzle by speaking of "progressive revelation," as though the teaching of Old Testament writings led to ever clearer insights into God's will and nature until the climax is reached in the person of Jesus Christ. It is now easy to see how such an interpretation was influenced by the optimism of the times in which it prevailed. The objection lay not only in that Old Testament writings do not fall neatly into a sequence wherein the later are manifestly

[20] I Cor. 14:33.

nearer to Christ than the earlier, but more significantly in the observation that the Old Testament has built into its writings its
own criteria for detecting God's redemptive purpose operating
in history. Hence the revival of an old term *Heilsgeschichte* (history of salvation or salvation-history)[21] to designate those events
in which God's sovereign and gracious action cuts across or
through the course of observable history, and which provides the
clue to the meaning of surrounding history. Thus it is not necessary to say that all Israel's history was the sphere of God's revelatory dealing with Israel. At least the reader need not look in the
first instance at this untidy mass of events. The biblical writers
have brought the events into a coherent relationship one with
another in certain decisive instances. Indeed the really decisive
events were already interpreted in their relation to one another
before the writers as such started their work. Thus Professor von
Rad's analysis of the earliest forms of Israel's confession of faith
reveals a way of understanding Israel's own tradition and history
which, with great variety and complication, remains the basic
pattern of the vast corpus which is the Hexateuch.[22] Israel's story
of salvation is basically that of God's election of Israel in Abraham
and the patriarchs, of his delivery of Israel at the Red Sea and
of his triumphal leading of Israel into the Promised Land.[23] Like
the kerygma in the New Testament, this story of salvation has its
central point in the exodus from Egypt, of which it has often
been remarked that what the cross is to the New Testament, the
rescue from the hands of Pharaoh is for Old Testament faith.[24]
To this proclamation of God's mighty acts the Psalms and the
wisdom literature are specimens of response; and the prophetic

---

[21] For a brief account of the history and meaning of this term see O. A.
Piper, "Heilsgeschichte," in *A Handbook of Christian Theology* (New
York: Meridian Books, 1958), and the literature there cited.

[22] See Gerhard von Rad "Das formgeschichtliche Problem des Hexateuch,"
now available in his *Gesammelte Studien zum Alten Testament* (München:
C. Kaiser, 1958); and Part 2 of his *Old Testament Theology*, Vol. I, D. M.
G. Stalker, trans. (New York: Harper & Row, 1962).

[23] As is well known, the passages from which this early Credo is derived
are chiefly: Deut. 26:5–9; 6:20–24; Josh. 24:2b–13; Pss. 136, 105, 78; and Jth.
4:6 ff.

[24] See, most recently, D. Daube, *The Exodus Pattern in the Bible* (London: Faber & Faber, 1963); but the literature on this topic is immense.

literature is a reorientation of that basic faith in such a way as (it was hoped) to enable Israel to discover the true rhythm of its life as the recapitulation of that story of salvation in contemporary history: Israel now moves again through election, judgment, and deliverance toward the consummation of her existence in the hour of fulfillment of the divine promise. Israel now looks to the future and awaits the coming salvation.

The difficulties of resting content with the *Heilsgeschichte* as the clue to the understanding of the Old Testament are similar to the difficulties experienced in a constant preoccupation with the kerygma as the foundation of New Testament theology and as the unifying point in the canon. In both cases the question of the relation of the faith confessed or proclaimed to the events of which it purports to speak requires clarification.[25] If faith is said to have proceeded from certain revelatory events, then faith's account of those events which can be given by other means must not be too sharply divergent. Certainly if it could be shown that the biblical writers have brought about "an antihistorical transformation of the course of history into a fairy tale or a poem" (Eichrodt), the matter would be extremely serious, for the writers themselves claim to proceed from a previously given history. The integrity of the Bible depends upon its being demonstrable not only that its unity derives from one way of talking *about* hypothetical or actual events, but also that those events themselves to which it points can be shown to be laden with the issue of belief or unbelief which the action of the living God always precipitates into the affairs of men. In other words the focal points which provide unity to the canon of Scripture are the covenant-making events in which God engages Israel in his worship and service, and the renewed covenant in the death and resurrection of Jesus Christ.

Hence there is something to be learned about the unity of the Old Testament as well as about the unity of the New from Casey's onesided attack on the kerygma. Both Testaments pro-

[25] On this and a number of other points, see Eichrodt's criticism of Von Rad in W. Eichrodt, *Theology of the Old Testament*, Vol. I, J. A. Baker, trans. (Philadelphia: Westminster Press, 1961), "Excursus: The Problem of Old Testament Theology," p. 512–20.

ceed from God's dealings with human persons and their consequent awareness of divine vocation. Discussing the inadequacy of
the term *Heilsgeschichte* as an account of Paul's view of God's
dealings with men, Prof. C. K. Barrett writes: "Paul sees history
as gathering at nodal points, and crystallizing upon outstanding
figures—men who are notable in themselves as individual persons,
but even more notable as representative figures. These men, as
it were, incorporate the human race, or sections of it, within
themselves, and the dealings they have with God they have rep-
resentatively on behalf of their fellows."[26] The canon of Scripture
then encloses these typical figures; and they in turn give us the
moments by which to judge all God's dealings with men in every
time and place. With these qualifications—that God's dealings
with men are always within the texture of observable history,
and that it is with men that God deals—we may see in *Heilsgeschichte* and kerygma useful ways of speaking of the canon
within the canon of Scripture. For, of course, the qualifications
are themselves amplifications of the proclaimed message. In these
streams of history which flow from such decisive dealings is to be
found the continuation of God's dealings with subsequent generations in Israel and the Church. Confronted by such traditions
of faith and hope there is kindled a like response on the part of
men of other ages and places.

III

The canon of Holy Scripture constitutes a problem and at the
same time a challenge to the Christian conscience, and in particular to the Christian intellectual conscience, the mind of the theologian. I have only touched on some aspects of that challenge,
but enough perhaps to encourage us to pursue the study of Scripture as a whole and not merely as a chance collection of separate

---

[26] *From First Adam to Last* (New York: Charles Scribner's Sons, 1962),
p. 5; cf. A. J. Fridrichsen: "An Israelite prophet or Jewish Messiah cannot
be understood solely in terms of Western thought in the nineteenth century. The man of God is never isolated. He is always the centre of a circle
taught by his words and example, in which his manner of life and teaching
continues after his death. What is taught and written in this circle is ultimately derived from its founder and embodies his life and character." From
his "Jesus, St. John and St. Paul," in *The Root of the Vine* (New York:
Philosophical Library, 1953).

documents; enough too perhaps to warn us against any facile solution to the problem of the unity of Scripture. Thus any conclusion must also be a call to further study and reflection.

1. First, the canon of Holy Scripture is one of the given elements in the Christian tradition. It shares the "scandal of particularity" with the events of which it speaks. The books of the Old and New Testaments stand in a ring around certain nodal events and persons; and to the Christian the answer to the question "Why these books?" is no easier and no more open to unrefutable demonstration of its truth than that to the question "Why Israel?" or "Why this man Jesus?" And those questions are always with the theologian.

2. While the history of the canon may sometimes have been written in such a way as to suggest that the important thing was the boundaries which it defined, both historically and theologically the important thing is the center of which its various parts speak. Here our problem is at its most acute. The message of the books of the Bible cannot on any really important topic—such as the person of Christ, the relation of grace to law, the proper ordering of Israel or the Church's life for the fulfillment of its mission—be said to speak in unison. Neither is any conventional harmony always audible. But for those with ears to hear, the same message may be frequently heard not only transposed into different keys, but even presented in different tonalities.

Yet in all its diversity the conclusion is inescapable that the same God is dealing with his children, whether believed on in the world or misunderstood and misrepresented; but whether in true or false statements the biblical writers are men engaged by the God of Abraham and Moses, the Father of Jesus Christ. The search for some internal criterion of judgment is inescapable. It is also extremely difficult. In particular the Christian theologian may not allow the question of the unity of Scripture to dissolve itself into two questions, one about the unity of the Old Testament, the other the unity of the New Testament. To begin with, the very terms Old Testament and New Testament are (strictly speaking) meaningless apart from the fact that they belong together in Holy Scripture. The Old Testament is only *old* Testament to the Christian Church. These writings are not properly described as such either by the Jew or by the student of comparative religion in the ancient Middle Eastern world (the *religionsgeschichtliche* school). Similarly, *New* Testament has no significance except to those for whom it is new in relation to what is old. It is not simply a collection of documents about Christian origins, although much has been learned from those who have regarded it as such.

It is impossible for the Christian scholar to escape the question of the relation between the Testaments. This relation is extraordinarily difficult to define; but it operates as the true and full context of work in either Testament from an early stage in the work of exegesis. It is not good enough for the Christian scholar to say that Old Testament and New Testament must each be allowed to speak for themselves before any attempt is made to relate them. The unity of Scripture is not imposed from without; it springs up from within. Neither the Old Testament nor the New can speak for itself without presupposing and speaking of the other.[27]

Attempts to describe *how* this unity makes itself apparent cannot be altogether evaded. No one way will be regarded as satisfactory to every thinker, but all point to a real connection. According to Prof. Paul Minear there is a unique "angle of vision" which is characteristic of the biblical writings;[28] and he has argued further that "the content of Scripture demands of the historian a methodology different from that which he is accustomed to operate."[29] Others prefer to speak in terms of a *Heilsgeschichte*—history of salvation. So, for instance, Prof. B. W. Anderson: "Thus the Old and New Testaments are inseparably related, not like the child to the mature man, but like the acts of a drama which press forward towards the denouement and finale. The Bible is essentially *Heilsgeschichte*—the history of divine revelation which reaches its crowning climax and fulfilment in Jesus

[27] See in this connection two recently published symposia: Claus Westermann, ed., *Essays on Old Testament Hermeneutics*, J. L. Mays, trans. (Richmond, Va.: John Knox Press, 1963) and B. W. Anderson, ed., *The Old Testament and Christian Faith* (New York: Harper & Row, 1963).

[28] *Eyes of Faith* (Philadelphia: Westminster Press, 1946).

[29] Summary of Minear's article on "Christian Eschatology and Historical Methodology" in *Neutestamentliche Studien für Rudolf Bultmann* (Berlin: A. Töpelmann, 1954) to be found in J. D. Smart, *The Interpretation of Scripture* (Philadelphia: Westminster Press, 1961), pp. 287 f.

Christ."[30] This way of stating the matter has been particularly attractive to Protestant thinkers, but not only to Protestants; for it stresses the distinctive, unique, unrepeatable, and definitive character of the revelation in God's acts in Israel's history culminating in Jesus Christ. Distinction between the biblical revelation and subsequent doctrinal formulation is thus guaranteed, while at the same time it is affirmed that the same God drew near to men in both Testaments and draws near to men of subsequent ages as the Word spoken in Scripture is preached and the evangelical sacraments of baptism and the Lord's Supper are observed.

Others again will wish to state the matter in different terms. Some will claim, with Dinkler, that "the Bible does not require a special hermeneutics, but is rather an instance of a general hermeneutics"; and that the open-mindedness of the scholar requires that he should beware of employing "such conceptions as 'Word of God' or 'justification by faith' or *Heilsgeschichte* as exclusive principles."[31] But few will deny that the task of the Old Testament exegete and that of the New are the same in kind: a constant dialogue with the text, issuing in preaching. The result of these biblical events, reproduced in word and sacrament, is the faith of the Church. The material with which the dogmatic and systematic theology has to do is not (as with the Old Testament or New Testament scholar) the actual text of Scripture but the faith and teaching of the Church—the revelation as once given, received, repeated in various forms, and seeking its coherent statement in our day. His task is not so much exegesis as such, but reflection and construction upon the results of exegesis; and the systematic theologian has the right to expect to hear from the biblical scholar elucidation not simply of single texts or books or Testaments, but of the Word of God contained in the Scriptures of the Old and New Testaments.

3. I have spoken much of the canon within the canon, and little of the boundary of the canon. While the center is more important than the circumference, the circumference can never be neglected. The arguments used by Irenaeus for accepting only four Gospels are not likely to commend themselves to us (that

---

30 "Bible" in *A Handbook of Christian Theology*.
31 Erich Dinkler, "Hermeneutics," *ibid.*

there are four zones of the world, and four principal winds, and so on[32]); but yet the more we know of second-century Gnosticism the more subtle appears the temptation to allow the borders of what was permissible to be set widely. If, as is widely believed, the recently discovered Valentinian *Gospel of Truth* is that referred to by Irenaeus, we at once admire his perception in judging it unworthy of canonical authority and wonder at the wisdom which was given to the Church to separate from itself such a subtle and lofty religious spirit.

Our interest in the breadth of the canon is today likely to be of a more positive character. Professor Edmund Schlink has spoken of the apostles (holding and setting forth the gospel, the authoritative Christian message) as "the paradigm for the extent and limits of Church unity."[33] The phrase might be applied to the canon of the Scripture. It is clearly possible, according to the New Testament, to be a Christian in a variety of ways: to make a number of Christological affirmations, to order the Church's life in a number of ways. The sharp awareness of the variety of expressions of faith and life within the New Testament which we owe to modern scholarship should strengthen the ecumenical recognition of fellow Christian as fellow Christian. We must recognize those whom the New Testament recognizes. The limits cannot be placed more narrowly without denying the canon. But so far our interest is still somewhat negative. More positively still the existence of great diversity within the canon enables the Church to lay hold anew on the fullness of her faith and life. It may be well enough for the individual Christian to have a preference for one presentation to be found within Scripture. He may prefer the faith and Church of the Fourth Gospel to that of the pastoral Epistles, or if he is an ecclesiastical administrator he may even prefer the world of the Pastorals to that of the apostle Paul. He may prefer the prayer of a psalmist to the indictment of a prophet. But such private preferences will not do for the Church. The canon of Scripture not only describes the extent of what is

---

[32] *Against Heresies* III, 11.11.

[33] In a paper on "Apostolic Succession" made available to a section of the Fourth World Conference on Faith and Order at Montreal, 1963. This paper has been published in French in *Verbum Caro*, No. 69 (1964).

to be recognized, it also sets forth the fullness of what is to be learned. Its many-sidedness warns the Church to look again at her language concerning her Lord, at her order and disorder; the scope of her message, its cosmic dimension, and its psychological depth. Varied as the ways were in which men of many ages spoke of their faith and their life together, there was no colorless neutrality in their language or attitude: they were speaking of God's ways of dealing with his people.[34]

4. The canon of Scripture is then, in its diversity, that witness (or those witnesses) from which the Church preaches. It has sometimes been said that one difference between the first generation of the great reformers and their successors, the scholastic Lutherans or the Reformed scholastics, was that for Luther and Calvin the Scriptures were to be expounded and preached; for their successors the Scriptures were source books for doctrine. Luther and Calvin were above all great exegetes. The judgment is no doubt too simple; but it points to an important situation from which literary and historical criticism has delivered us: preaching can once more be based upon biblical exposition, rather than on popularized morals or doctrine. As such, it treats the Scripture as Scripture itself intended. There are only a few documents in the Old Testament, and none in the New, which were not written to convict, to convince, and to heal. It is as men in the Church in other ages listen in to the prayer of the psalmist, the preached laws of Deuteronomy, the sermons of the prophets, the confession of faith of Mark or John or Paul, that their faith is kindled and worship and obedience become possible. The word of the biblical writer is not so much addressed directly to the man of today. It is directed to his own audience. The task of the exegete

[34] In connection with the point made in this paragraph see the long section in small print in Karl Barth, *Church Dogmatics*, Vol. I, Part 2 (New York: Charles Scribner's Sons, 1956), pp. 599–601. Barth states with great sensitivity the case of the man, every man, who receives the canon of Holy Scripture from the Church, but it "can be used by us only in part"; he speaks of the thankfulness with which we acknowledge that one part speaks to us, and of the determination to go on in the awareness that the limitation may be in ourselves rather than in the scriptural witness. He ends with the important observation that "out of modern biblical criticism which has been so radical in the sphere of private opinions and discussions the desire for a new confession in relation to the canon has not emerged."

is to make clearly audible that conversation about the faith which took place in Old Israel or in the early Church. In that conversation of prophet or apostle with people, God was entering into controversy with his people. From the axis of that conversation may be kindled the spark which brings God into controversy with men in other days.

2. The Old Testament

James Barr

Our first task is to discuss the basis in principle upon which we affirm that the study of the Old Testament is a quite essential part of the study of Christian theology.

The first answer which may be suggested lies on the level of history and the history of ideas. If we look to the life and work of Jesus Christ as the master model for theological understanding, we also recognize that this model existed in a particular historical situation; and this situation, that of Judaea in the first century A.D., has a particular historical past which can be traced back well into the second millennium B.C. The reasons for the special place which Judaea had within the Roman Empire, and for the fearful conflicts into which it threw itself so soon after the time of Christ, lie in the ways in which the ancestors of the Jews over centuries had reacted to situations within this same land. And, in particular, this is so not simply because the history had taken place; rather, people were especially aware that it had taken place, since a sacred Scripture, which was the basis of religion and culture, narrated it to them and formed their consciousness through the telling.

In the realm of ideas, however, the historical inheritance is even richer. The work of Jesus was done in a situation in which certain great truths could be taken approximately for granted: that there was one God, living and personal, who had called, delivered, judged, and restored a people of his own; that he had communicated to them a corpus of verbal assertions of his will and requirements, so that the knowledge of these was not derived primarily, if at all, from the mental searchings or reasonings of man; that the world in which we live was created good by God, in such a way that God was not part of the world nor the world of God; and that God had in store for his people a transformation to a new state or era, including the coming of a new David as ruler in this final period. Ideas such as these, even allowing for variations here and there, were normal currency among the Jews, and the combination of them was such as to furnish a high degree of peculiarity among the cultures of the known world.

This combination and the development of it is the work and achievement of the Old Testament. It is because this complex of thought was taken for granted that certain questions of the relation of man and God could be raised within it with an unprecedented intensity; the crisis in the Gospels is the clash, within this idea world as it stood in its late-Jewish development, between the will of men whose minds, in good or in evil, were attuned and related to this system and the will of God from whom it itself came. It should be observed that in this complex almost everything in the Old Testament plays a certain part. Certain leading ideas and formulas can indeed be isolated; these are the points where the most overt conceptualization takes place. But these themselves have their base in a complicated mental shape in which certain ideas can be identified as primary but in which the manifold details of an ancient tradition had some part, so that the removal of any part might make some change in the impact of the tradition as a whole. Thus the Old Testament forms the mental matrix in which the work of Christ is cast.

These are perhaps sufficient reasons in themselves for the importance of Old Testament studies, and at any rate there would be some fair degree of agreement about them. But most Christian scholars would also hold that some further *theological* affirmation has to be made. The Old Testament does not constitute only an historical and mental framework for God's communication through Christ; it is itself a part of his communication. The revelation basic to Christian belief has more than one side or aspect, and to the side or aspect embodied in the New Testament Gospel it is theologically essential that another side or aspect should exist and precede. The Scripture for Christianity is not the New Testament, with the Old as an historical background; it is the whole Bible, with two Testaments. The relation between the two sides or stages in revelation is, however, a complex one, and no simple statement can be satisfactory. Such contrasts as those of Law and Gospel, of Promise and Fulfillment, of Old Covenant and New, are found in the Bible. In each of these cases, for the contrast to have full theological validity, it is essential that some real revelatory value be ascribed to the first stage: to the Law, to the Promise, to the Old Covenant. The God of the Gospel, of the Fulfillment, of the New Covenant, must have been active also in the first stage in reality. Contrasts such as these have to evaluate the Old Testament aspect positively and not only negatively. This is true even if we assess the Old Testament primarily as Law; for in St. Paul's treatment the Law, for all its weakness in comparison with the Gospel, is a true assertion of the holy will of God. The approach of Bultmann, under which the Old Testament functions primarily as a story of failure and disaster, should be regarded as stimulating but one-sided. In general, for the Christian it is true and essential that God made himself known to Israel, and that our destiny and our faith are linked with the destiny and faith of Israel. Over the definition of the exact mode by which this general assertion is to be related to the variety and detail of the Old Testament text there is room for a great deal of discussion, and some considerable difference of opinion would be found.

If this will suffice to establish the importance of Old Testament study within the theological disciplines, we may now look at some of the perspectives and approaches which Old Testament study uses.

We may begin by mentioning the study of the history of Israel, with its correlate in the historical criticism of the Bible. For this we still operate very largely on the basis of the work of the nineteenth-century scholars, among whom particular prominence belongs to the name of Julius Wellhausen. The study of Israelite history requires an evaluation of the date, nature, purpose, and tendency, and thus of the general historical reliability, of the sources. On investigation it soon became clear that no satisfactory result could be attained if the documents were given the dating and authorship which traditional Church custom had attributed to them; thus if the Pentateuch were assigned uniformly to the date and authorship of Moses, only a poor and contradictory result could be obtained from its use as a historical source. After a certain amount of scholarly trial and error a much better solution was made available. Deuteronomy, or most of it, came from about the seventh century B.C., and was associated with the reformation of Josiah. Other elements in the Pentateuch, isolated as the "Priestly Document," were even later, and these had formed a general framework within which much older materials had been fitted. On the basis of such an hypothesis a history could be written which would arrange in chronological series certain different conceptions of institutions such as the priesthood or the sanctuary. Similar methods would serve to state the relation between other parallel narratives, such as those of Kings and Chronicles. In this way the history of Israel, the historical criticism of the biblical books as historical sources, and a certain amount of history of the development of Hebrew religion are closely interrelated.

Undoubtedly, as we have come to recognize, this kind of scholarship is not infallible. Scholars of the early twentieth century often exaggerated the precision with which sources could be distinguished; moreover, and perhaps even worse, they often wrote as if the distinguishing of the sources completed the work of commentary and removed any outstanding problems. It was possible for a complicated historical situation, or a subtle religious relation, to be too quickly assessed by a scholar as a "contradiction" leading inevitably to a "solution" through source division. Moreover, the rise of newer methods, of which I shall speak shortly, brought about a lower degree of emphasis on source criticism. Nevertheless, when we compare the position of the Wellhausen view with the older traditional approach to the Bible, it is clear that the results of historical criticism in a general sense form an accepted plane to which almost all modern studies relate themselves. That Deuteronomy comes from a time several centuries after Moses, or that chapters 40–66 of the Book of Isaiah did not come from the eighth-century prophet of this name, are positions which find very wide acceptance today.

Moreover, the existence and acceptance of opinions such as

these has been a chief factor in the reorientation of Christian attitudes to the Bible. Today we may feel that, if revelation and the relation between God and man had been understood properly, this itself would have brought about a certain freedom in handling the Bible as a historical document. Historically, however, in a very large number of cases it was not pure theological considerations but the impact of biblical criticism which led or forced people to a new assessment of the Bible. Today, when we acknowledge the Bible to be the Word of God, we also understand it to be a human product open to historical questions of date, authorship, purpose, and accuracy. Most modern theologies have done something to formulate some such picture of the Bible. Fundamentalism on the other hand has felt it necessary on theological grounds to reject the application of critical methods to the Bible, or else to argue that if they are used they do not lead to antitraditional results in respect of authorship, accuracy, and so on. In any case there is no doubt that the rise of historical criticism, and this especially in the Old Testament, has had a very great effect upon the conceptions of the Bible held in the Church. It is doubtful if anyone who has not faced the fact of historical criticism has begun to see the point of modern theology.

This whole area of history, history of literature, and history of religion is, however, much more rich and complex than I have thus far indicated. In order to illustrate the starker effects of source criticism I have taken some outstanding and fairly clear examples. But the Old Testament literature itself contains much more complex and uncertain problems; and the whole field of study has been enriched by knowledge coming from three main directions: archaeology, the study of ancient Near Eastern literature and culture, and newer approaches to the Old Testament itself.

The earlier scholars had very little to go on beyond the Old Testament itself, along with late Jewish sources and some materials, mostly fragmentary, in Greek; to this may be added Arab sources, which of course mainly come from the Islamic period. But through the late nineteenth century and increasingly in the twentieth there has been a great increase in exact knowledge of ancient cultures, gained directly by archaeology. Through the years archaeology (if a layman like the writer has a right to judge) has become increasingly detailed and scientific; the work is not designed for the spectacular recovery of outstanding items, but for the patient building up of a great network of cultural data interrelated by the stratification. This work now takes up the attention and the energies of many scholars. Historically it is of the utmost importance in that it gives us an independent check, additional to that provided by literary analysis of documents, on the historical traditions. Thus when we consider the story of the conquest of Palestine by the Israelites we have to weigh the archaeological evidence of city-destructions and cultural changes within the relevant strata against the picture which would seem to emerge from a critical use of the literary sources.

Equally important has been the study of the literature and culture of Israel's neighbors. Scholars like Wellhausen were much influenced by Arab culture, with which they had a good acquaintance; but more recent scholarship has been increasingly occupied with the more ancient cultures, known from inscriptions and documents discovered in the course of archaeological research.

Extensive literatures are now available from Egypt, Mesopotamia, Ugarit in northern Syria, and the Hittite empire; and important evidence in inscriptions exists for Palestine-Syria generally and for other significant areas like ancient South Arabia.

All this roughly contemporary material, while it does a great deal to fill out the picture of the world in which ancient Israel lived, produces for the theological student a number of new and difficult problems. At certain points, for example, it shows that a practice or institution of the Old Testament has apparently close parallels in the Oriental environment; for example, there are several points at which the laws of Hammurabi come very close to the legislation attributed to Moses. At other points comparable documents show a very considerable diversity, as for instance between the Israelite and the Babylonian creation stories. This whole series of relations, whether close or remote, has inevitably raised the question of the distinctiveness of Israelite thinking and religion in comparison with its environment, and, not unnaturally, it has become customary to attach theological significance to the answer. Whether this has been wise or not is another matter. This is a rapidly moving area in which methods and results change constantly, and it is probable that some of the simple formulations which seem to give quick theological satisfaction, such as the idea that the distinctiveness of Israel was given by its historical centeredness, will not stand careful examination. But at any rate the material and the questions are there and will continue to be a center of study. Unfortunately the various areas (Egyptology is a marked example) are now becoming very specialized, and the linguistic requirements alone are formidable, so that on the theological scene much will have to be received by mediation rather than by direct contact. Fortunately, up-to-date works of reference are being provided for this need.

Thirdly, we have to consider the rise of newer methods of studying the Old Testament literature itself, and in particular the so-called form criticism and tradition criticism. Though form criticism has become famous for its use on the New Testament, it was used even earlier by Gunkel on the Psalms, and scholars are still making significant progress with its use in the Old Testament. If generalizations may be offered here, it may be suggested that the form-critical approach produces particularly useful results where we have (1) fairly numerous examples of a *recurrent* literary form, and (2) considerable doubt whether we can identify a historical situation which is specifically associated with the production or use of the passages under study. In these circumstances it is worth noting that form criticism is not necessarily to be associated with the degree of historical scepticism which has often gone along with it in some types of New Testament study. These are circumstances in which the attempt to assign a date or source, which was so often the central interest of the older historical criticism, can be quite precarious, so that it is more fruitful to study the function of the form and its situation in life. Meanwhile, however, many problems remain in the use of form criticism and in the relating of it to other approaches to the material.

With the emphasis on tradition we partly overlap with and partly go beyond form criticism. The older source criticism gave a certain impression that the sources were written documents which had been stitched together, and which could be taken apart

and restored to their original form, sometimes almost intact and
complete, once the identification of the distinctions had been carried out. There was also a tendency to suggest that the oldest
documentary source had a quite exceptional historical and religious priority in comparison with later sources, and a corresponding tendency to neglect the development in the tradition, and its
biases, before the formation of the earliest source. The newer
emphasis on tradition has attacked this position in several ways.
One way has been to question whether the "documents" were
written sources at all, and to argue therefore that they were still
in comparatively fluid oral form when they were welded together; and from this a somewhat inconclusive debate on the
respective roles of oral and written tradition has followed. In more
extreme cases it has been argued that the whole picture of the
older source criticism could be completely replaced by one based
on the study of tradition. More commonly the study of tradition
has accepted, and based itself upon, some literary source, or division. A particularly influential piece of work has been the attempt
by Noth and Von Rad to trace the various elements of interest
which served to integrate the detailed materials of the Pentateuch.
These elements are not documents or sources but themes or mo-
tifs. The theme of "wandering in the wilderness," for example,
served to bring together a number of stories relatable to this locus
by setting or by the type of incident narrated, while the theme
of "promise to the fathers" likewise served to assemble in an apparently temporal series the figures of tribal patriarchs who had
existed somewhat independently in traditions associated with
identifiable places.

There are two regards in which the emphasis on living tradition
may prove helpful to theological students. First, it may do something to soften the rather stark contrasts between the sources
detected by the older historical criticism. Second, in so far as the
living tradition was motivated by theological considerations in
selecting and resetting the materials, the study of this process may
give helpful leads for the theological use of the Old Testament;
this approach has been used especially by Von Rad. It may be
expected that the emphasis on tradition will lead to further new
insights in the future.

We can now turn to some discussion of the text and language of the Old Testament. For the text, an interesting contrast may be made with the position in the New Testament. The Greek text of the latter displays a great variety of readings, many of them making some considerable difference to the meaning, but almost all of them making sense. In comparison with this, the Hebrew text of the Old Testament, as transmitted in the medieval manuscript tradition, is impressive for its high degree of uniformity. Variant readings in manuscripts do of course exist, but are for the most part of slight importance for the meaning. In many cases, however, though a uniform reading is offered by the manuscripts, it seems to scholars to make poor sense. The ultimate difficulty here is the fact that biblical Hebrew is known only in a very restricted corpus, so that many words and expressions are found for which no certain and standard parallels are known. It may be that these are rare or abnormal expressions (abnormal in relation to what is frequently encountered and therefore registered as a usual linguistic habit). On the other hand, the text may have been transmitted wrongly.

Thus within the Hebrew text the task of textual criticism does not lie mainly in the choosing between two or more available readings. Where there is difficulty, therefore, the possibility of conjectural emendation plays a much greater part. This brings us however to the most important parting of the ways in Hebrew textual criticism. Conjectural emendation was a favorite resort of the earlier scholars. Many such treatments, of which examples are common in the apparatus of Kittel's text, were arbitrary rewritings of a difficult text into a simpler or more obvious one; enjoyed no supporting evidence other than the existence of the difficulty in the first place; and suffered from the new difficulty of explaining how an originally simple text had been lost and a more harsh or peculiar one preserved. Clearly in such cases the production of a clarification which will successfully explain the transmitted text is fatal to the emendation. The way which many more recent scholars have taken is to retain the text but to explain it as an unusual locution, heretofore unknown indeed in biblical Hebrew, but evidenced from the cognate languages, Accadian, Arabic, Ugaritic and so on. This choice, then, between conjectural

emendation of the Hebrew on the one hand and resort to explanations from comparative philology on the other, is perhaps the
most pressing one in modern textual criticism. It is a matter, however, on which decision has to be made on the merits of individual
cases and not on general principles. It is probable that wild guesses
from the cognate languages have caused as much trouble as arbitrary conjectural emendations.

While the medieval Hebrew manuscripts, as I have said, differ
surprisingly little except in minor details, some exception has to
be made in this for the Qumran texts, some of which show important divergencies, and for the ancient translations, especially
those in Greek, Latin, and Aramaic. In thinking of these versions one must distinguish between the quality of the translation
and the value of the text underlying. Thus in the Septuagint one
can find places where the translation is poor, wooden, or inaccu-
rate (and this differs from book to book), but where the text
underlying can be perceived to have been good and is supported
from Qumran or another source. It is important for the beginner
to understand that the versions cannot be used intelligently without a knowledge of the translation techniques applicable for the
passage in question.

The study of Hebrew language is a recurring problem in theological education, because of the time spent on learning and the
poor degree of retention commonly achieved. Yet there is no
good reason in principle for this difficulty, for Hebrew is not a particularly difficult language. One of the commonest troubles is that
students, though they find an elementary course in grammar rather
easier than they had expected, do not go on to achieve any degree
of familiarity or fluency in the language before they have to work
on biblical texts which are chosen for their theological interest
and which are often bristling with linguistic obscurities and un-
certainties. In these circumstances, since their knowledge does not
give them any faculty of discrimination between one thing said
and another thing said, students use their Hebrew merely as a kind
of equipment for decoding the text in correlation with translations, grammars, lexicons, and commentaries. It is not a discrimi-
nating channel of communication, and its life soon dies away.
Among other causes of trouble may be mentioned: poor descrip-

tion of Hebrew in many standard grammars and other works; failure to orientate students, many of whom have no good linguistic background, in methods of handling linguistic material; and poor organization of theological curricula, in which too often linguistic knowledge is "got" at an early stage rather than used in practice throughout, with the result that students have already forgotten it a year or more before they graduate.

Yet the case for learning Hebrew is a very strong one, and the loss occasioned where it is abandoned is evident in those large areas of the Church which have neglected it. It means a ministry unable to respond to the elementary discriminatory signals transmitted in the text; and from this there follows an unhappy dependence on secondhand sources and a loss of proximity and intimacy with the Old Testament scene.

On the scholarly level the study of Hebrew has become much more complicated through the attention given to the cognate Semitic languages and their literatures; the importance of these has already been partly indicated. Even the student who does not learn any of these languages will recognize the influence exerted upon scholars by evidence gained from them. This evidence is the main basis upon which a historical treatment of the grammar and the lexical stock of Hebrew can be built. Moreover, as we have seen, important results are to be expected from the study of Near Eastern literature with comparison of form and content with biblical materials. Nevertheless it is possible that there is also an important and neglected task to be done with Hebrew itself, and that comparative study has too often had a distracting effect, especially where comparative statements are mingled indiscriminately with descriptive statements about Hebrew. Much more could be done to describe Hebrew usage clearly and accurately, and to help students to attain some discrimination in evaluating the rather heterogeneous data from comparative language study which often reaches them.

We now turn to questions of religion and theology. The statement about historical criticism above has already indicated how this method almost necessarily involved some kind of developmental history of certain religious institutions, practices, and beliefs—in other words a reorganization in a reasonable or probable

historical sequence of a body of data which within the text itself
were otherwise disposed. Thus for example the total constitution
of the priesthood in the Mosaic legislation is reorganized in a historical sequence with several stages, each represented by a certain
body of data. This in turn may involve the question whether there
is some generally probable sequence in the development of religion which could be used in assessing the probability of a historical reconstruction. In other words, historical criticism of the Bible
may have to make contact with general theories of the history of
religion.

The stock example here is the idea of ascending development.
People sometimes have a respect for the "higher" religions (mono-
theistic, ethical, more rational, less magical) and also a body of
observations (rather poorly organized) about the practices and
beliefs of "primitive" peoples. Used as a scheme in biblical study,
this has meant that various elements in the Old Testament would
stand at various stages; one passage would be a "survival" from
animism, while another would be a first step on the way to "ethical monotheism," as the highest stage was often called. It is not
true to say, as is often said, that an ascending development or
evolution was the only model used by the nineteenth-century
scholars; for they were also well aware of degeneration, legalism,
hardening, and loss of energy and applied these terms freely to
certain areas in the Bible. Nevertheless the evolutionary model
has been a very prominent one. Today it is not widely accepted
by scholars, and the contrary position, that "high" gods were
there at the beginning and that a religion at any time might include elements both "primitive" and developed, has been elo-
quently advocated. There remains a great deal to be done in the
correlation of Old Testament studies with the general history of
religions.

There are some who dislike this idea on theological grounds,
feeling either that the biblical witness should not be lumped together with a general concept of "religion" or that general concepts of religious history cannot be legitimately applied to the
Bible. It is difficult however to accept this objection. If it were
accepted strictly, all that would happen is that an important task
would remain undone. First, the Bible does not supply us with

regulative concepts for the history of religion. Second, the scholar has to consider and evaluate not only the religion approved or accepted in the Old Testament, but also the rejected "opposition" religion or religions and the religious prehistory which lies behind even the earliest texts, the names of God, and the like. If there were no correlation with history of religion, historical criticism of the texts would be lamed from the beginning. The important work which remains to be done in this area has, however, to some extent been overshadowed by the rise and/or revival of Old Testament theology, to which we must now turn.

The impression made by the older historical criticism in its union with religious history was above all a fragmented one. The Old Testament seemed not to speak with any one voice, but each text made sense only when located as a stage in a process. This seemed unsatisfactory theologically, unless one was content to regard the progressive refinement of religion as the revelation of God. The great need felt was for a synthesis, which without denying historical development would bring together the unity of Old Testament thinking. The rise of Old Testament theology in its modern form (from about 1930) took place largely in answer to this need. Of most of the modern Old Testament theologies, in spite of their considerable variety, it can be said that they work to provide a statement of a central emphasis which can be distinguished fairly clearly from peripheral elements within the Old Testament and from the master pattern of other religions even where other individual elements are shared. It is also widely held that this central emphasis provides the chief link with the New Testament.

Many questions however remain unsettled. Eichrodt, one of the greatest pioneers, holds that Old Testament theology is a descriptive study, belonging in principle with historical study rather than with dogmatic theology. Others like Vriezen have argued that its methods must be truly theological. There has also been much discussion about the principle of organization to be used in an Old Testament theology. It is my own belief that we should not try to prescribe any one organization, and that the variety of perspectives offered by different scholars has been fruitful and desirable. The complex of Old Testament thinking can be cut

with sections in many different directions, and none of them alone
will be final.

A significant move is made with the work of Von Rad, who,
arguing that the witness of the Old Testament is to the acts of
God and not to the structure of its own thinking, moves away
from the interest in a synthesis toward a theology based on the
intention of the different streams of tradition. This may solve
some old problems of Old Testament theology and create some
new ones. In general it may be said that modern Old Testament
theology has come of age. The worry about fragmentation of the
biblical witness, and the corresponding drive toward some syn-
thetic approach, is no longer present in the same degree. An analytic approach is no longer regarded as something to be feared,
and the task now may be to produce some kind of "Old Testament theology" of the individual and detailed text rather than to
look for a general synthesis to which the particular text may be
related.

The question of relation to the New Testament has already
been mentioned. It has prompted much study of the typological
and analogical methods by which the New Testament interpreted
the Old, along with the question of how far such methods can
be used by us today. This question is of much importance for the
homiletical use of the Old Testament in the Church. The subject
is a delicate one, for typology is capable of infinite abuse, and
there is much suspicion of it; on the other hand, it is certainly
present in the New Testament, and some serious discussion of it
seems to be necessary in any attempt to consider how the Church
should use the Old Testament. Since the war, English and especially German scholars have published important studies of the
problem; a volume of essays edited by Westermann has recently
provided in English the salient points of the German discussion.

In any case one cannot relate the two canonical Testaments,
whether typologically or otherwise, without giving emphasis also
to the literature of late Judaism: the so-called Apocrypha and
Pseudepigrapha, the Qumran texts, the remains of Jewish literature in Greek, and the Rabbinic literature in Hebrew and Aramaic.
The recent and salutary emphasis on the unity of the two canoni-

cal Testaments has sometimes had bad side effects in producing a failure to attend, for example in matters of linguistic evidence, to the extracanonical literature, rather as if the early Christians had no linguistic and mental experience outside the usage and ideas of the biblical canon. Within the late texts, it is of course the Qumran texts which have recently had greatest attention, and very considerable further understanding is to be expected from the continuing study of them. For the beginner they are in some ways difficult to study, for many texts have still to be published, while the novelty of the field has called forth a very large literature in articles along with no small number of extreme or highly experimental theories. The Rabbinic texts, though longer known, also suffer from lack of satisfactory editions and from lack of the volume of critical work which has been done on the canonical literature.

Another subject of importance for the assessment of the Old Testament in theology is the investigation of Hebrew mentality and ways of thought. This is at present a fairly controversial area. The approach which has become so familiar as to achieve a sort of dogmatic status in some kinds of theology, namely, the contrast of Greek and Hebrew mentalities, is really an enlargement of a few rudimentary philosophical distinctions within later culture, and is historically full of weaknesses. Theology has to consider how it can extricate itself where it has become unwisely entangled with this particular cultural assessment. But it is probable that a good deal of further discussion will be devoted to the subject. Historically it should not be impossible to give much better pictures of what the various kinds of Greeks and the various kinds of Jews were like within the relevant periods. Exegetically, the question is how far the things actually said by the biblical writers have to be associated with an underlying mentality in order that the texts may be understood; how far reliable methods exist for the identification of a tacit mental structure of this kind; how far this affects the use of linguistic evidence; and how far theological authority should be sought in such structures. The answer depends in particular on the development of competent linguistic and anthropological methods within theology, for nothing can be hoped for from the mixture of old-fashioned historical philology with scraps of philosophy which has so much characterized this movement in the past.

One final theological point. Though the Old Testament is part of the Church's life and faith, it is not the exclusive property of the Church. The Church still lives alongside the Jewish people, whose own tradition the Old Testament is and for whom also it still serves as a sacred book. According to St. Paul this is, I think, not accidental; the linking of our destinies with those of Israel after the flesh is part of the plan of God. If this is true, and I believe it to be true, it adds a yet further dimension of meaning and interest to the study of the Old Testament. Israel is not a reality in the past only. The difficult questions concerning the relation of the Church to the Jews of today are finding new and active interest among theologians today. The study of the Old Testament is something we share, at least in part, with Jewish scholars, and indeed with secular scholarship also. The fact that this work can be carried on in this setting is of great significance for the nature and constitution of the Church.

3. The New Testament

G. B. Caird

Week by week millions of Christians, in making an affirmation of their faith, repeat the name of Pontius Pilate. A minor official in the Roman provincial administration during the first century might seem to have very little to do with religion in the twentieth century. But Pilate properly retains his place in the creeds of the Church to remind Christians that their faith has its roots not in philosophical argument, nor in Church dogma, nor in religious experience (important as all these are), but in historical events, which happened once for all "under Pontius Pilate." Christianity has a number of characteristics in common with the other great religions of the modern world. All religions declare that man must live his life in a spiritual environment as well as a material one, and all undertake to reveal to man the nature of his spiritual environment and the demands it makes upon him: all, that is to say, have both a theology and an ethic. But Christianity does not start with ideas about the origin, nature, and destiny of human life; it starts with facts. In the first instance it is not a view of life but a gospel, and gospel means news.

For this reason the study of the New Testament is central to Christian theology. The New Testament is the record of those creative events from which the Christian faith and the Christian Church took their origin. By "events" I do not mean bare, uninterpreted occurrences. Countless occurrences happen every day which nobody bothers to write about or even to remember, because nobody considers them significant. Occurrences are noticed, remembered, and ultimately written down as history only when they enter into the experience of some observer who is able to relate them to other facts of his experience in a system which is meaningful not only to himself but also to his audience or readers. The facts of the gospel story were from the first experienced by the witnesses as an act of God and recorded against a background of theological interpretation. Nor was this interpretation something that existed only in the minds of those who told and retold the story in the early Church: it was part of the stuff of the events through which they had lived. For Jesus himself would not have acted or spoken as he did unless he had been impelled by a sense of divine vocation and mission. Some sort of theological interpretation created the events and is inseparable from any truly historical study of them. The early Church set aside as canonical Scripture the twenty-seven books which we call the New Testament, and distinguished them from all other literature, because they believed that in the life, death, and resurrection of Jesus, and in the impact he made on those who knew him, God had given a complete and final revelation of his own character and purpose; and they declared that these books contained the only reliable record of those events and of the authentic interpretation of them which must be normative for all subsequent Christian teaching and practice.

The study of the New Testament is an historical discipline. The task of any historian who is worthy of the name is not simply to accumulate facts about the dead past, but so to relive the past that it becomes relevant to the conditions and needs of the present. The New Testament scholar, by using all the resources of modern critical scholarship, projects himself back into the first century, entering by sympathetic imagination into its life, its feelings, and its ways of thought, and learning to some extent at least to see the world through the eyes of the New Testament writers; and then comes back to the present to share with his contemporaries what he has discovered. What he discovers will be both the chief source and the norm of all theological thought. Others indeed must take up the task where he lays it down, tracing the development of New Testament teaching through the centuries, relating it to modern patterns of thought and conduct, and making it credible to the contemporary mind; and every Christian must make the gospel a personal possession which controls the inner springs of his being. Every Christian, and certainly every theologian, is in some sense a student of the New Testament, but we must not allow that fact to obscure the distinction between the historical study of the New Testament and any superstructure of theology or faith that may be built upon it. If we approach the New Testament with our minds dominated by Church dogma, modern problems, or personal experience, we shall find in it only what we already expect to find, instead of listening to what it has to say to us. We may believe that in Jesus Christ God has spoken a Word of truth that is relevant for all ages, and that the record of this Word is in the New Testament; but we do not begin to put ourselves under the authority of that Word unless we allow the writers of the New Testament to speak for themselves, and unless we recognize that what they say is spoken to their own contemporaries in the language and thought forms of their own age. It is true that sometimes, when I read the Scriptures, the words I read will conjure up in my mind ideas which never occurred to the original writer. I may, if I think fit, ascribe such ideas to the guidance of the Holy Spirit, but I have no right to treat them as part of the message of that particular passage of the Bible. If God spoke through Paul, he spoke through Paul's mind, and I put myself under the authority of *this* Word only by exploring the mind of Paul with all the resources at my command.

The belief that the New Testament is an historical document which yields its full and true meaning only to the most meticulous historical criticism is open to attack on two sides. On the one hand, it must be admitted that in the past the probing of the New Testament by the methods of the secular historian has led not to deeper understanding but to complete scepticism. There are still sceptics who will tell us that the historical element in the Gospels is so thoroughly overlaid with legend and myth that it is impossible to make any trustworthy reconstruction of what actually happened, and there are others who will add that in any case this does not matter, since the Church's faith is not in the Jesus of history but in the living, heavenly Lord. On the other hand, there are Christians who point out that the Bible is a book about God and that no amount of antiquarian delving into the past enables a man to find God. Religion, they say, consists not in amassing information about a past age but in personal encounter with God in the present.

We are bound to treat such arguments with respect. Yet neither of these attacks on the historical method can be sustained. Historical criticism of the New Testament ends in scepticism only when it starts with scepticism as one of its presuppositions. More than sixty years ago W. Wrede argued that, once we have recognized the hand of the early Church at work in the formulation of the whole gospel tradition, and not just in problematical corners of it, we ought not to attempt to isolate within the tradition an authentic core, which could reliably be attributed to Jesus, as long as any alternative explanation of the evidence could be found—a principle which no secular historian would dream of applying to the documents he was studying. Others have since adopted Wrede's procedure without always copying his candor. The way forward beyond scepticism lies not in the abandonment of the historical method but in a stricter application of it and a stricter examination of the prejudices of those who apply it. As for the attempt to have faith in the living Lord or to have a personal encounter with God, apart from a knowledge of the historical Jesus, is not this the oldest of heresies—the Docetic heresy which denies the reality of the Incarnation? And is it not denounced in the New Testament as the great lie, springing from the spirit of Antichrist?

The historical approach to the New Testament has one very important corollary. History, just because it involves the activity of unpredictable men, has about it an element of contingency and arbitrariness. If it be true that God was in Christ, then it follows that God committed himself to this realm of particularity, embracing it as the necessary medium of his self-disclosure. Against all idealists who identify truth with universals, the New Testament asserts that the truth of God is to be found in a particular man, who lived in a particular place at a particular time and addressed himself to the problems and needs of his own age and his own people. The trouble with ideals and principles is precisely that they never do come down from heaven. Plato was conspicuously unsuccessful at politics when he was given his chance to found his ideal republic; and the French, who embarked on a revolution with high ideals of liberty, equality, and fraternity, have in fact contributed far less to the political progress of mankind than the irrational and pragmatic British. We have no right to take the gospel story and distill out an essence of pure, eternal truth, leaving aside a residue of historical accident belonging to the first century. The life and teaching of Jesus are relevant to other ages and circumstances just because, in their totality, they were first relevant to his own situation. It would likewise be an affront to Paul to attempt to force his ebullient thought into a rigid system of eternally valid theology. Having escaped from the fetters of Judaism, Paul consistently refused to turn the gospel into a new legalism. The Christian way, which he both taught and superbly exemplified, was to know "the mind of Christ" and to apply that mind to all problems of belief and conduct. The gospel in the hands of anyone who really understands it always displays a rich vitality and the power to adapt to new needs and new situations. The music of the New Testament choir is not written in unison but in a counterpoint of many voices.

It is sometimes said that the one indispensable qualification for the understanding of the New Testament is faith. There is a profound truth in this to which we shall return at the end of this essay. But it is a truth which can be dangerously misrepresented, both by the enemies and by the friends of Christianity. It might be taken to mean that the Christian cannot be a scientific historian, since he is already committed to his conclusions before he has even begun to examine the evidence; or that Christian history belongs to a realm apart, forever secure from the erosion of sceptical criticism, since the secular historian a priori lacks the qualification to deal with it. Christianity has appealed to history, and by history it must be justified. It simply is not true that one man is precluded from understanding another unless he shares his creed. If it were true, all who professed themselves Christians would understand the New Testament better than any Jew, which is demonstrably false; and no Christian scholar would have any right to be heard on the subject of Islam or Buddhism. It has been plausibly argued that Athanasius understood the beliefs of

Arius, which he detested, better than Arius did himself. The New Testament scholar is an historian, and the historian is under no obligation to share the beliefs of the people about whom he writes. What he needs (besides a basic training in the tools of his trade) is an ability to identify himself sympathetically with others, to get inside their minds (an exercise more closely akin to love than to faith). It is precisely at this point that the New Testament scholar faces his biggest difficulty. For the New Testament was written by men of widely different gifts and temperaments, and he is unlikely to achieve an equal rapport with all of them. If Luke is his friend, Matthew may be a comparative stranger. If he is at home with Paul, he will find the Fourth Gospel full of surprises. If the Pastoral Epistles are congenial to him, he is likely to be out of his depth in the Revelation. Yet this is his task, to attune himself as best he can to the many voices of the chorus, so that together they may bear their different but consentient witness to the one Christ. But if he is to do that, he must first master the techniques of his calling.

All the books of the New Testament were written in Greek. Excellent modern translations exist, and the humble believer may justifiably be content with them. But the serious student must read the Scriptures in the original tongue. To understand a man's mind one must know his language. Anyone who has ever attempted to translate anything but the simplest of statements from one language to another, and particularly from an ancient language to a modern one, knows that the art of translation is always difficult and frequently impossible. Words which denote physical objects may have exact equivalents in another language, but not words which denote ideas. Such words commonly cover a wide variety of more or less closely related meanings, and it is comparatively rare for two words in different languages to coincide over their whole range. The Greek *pneuma* and the English "spirit" have a considerable area in which they overlap, but *pneuma* also means wind and breath, and "spirit" also means mettle, vigor of mind, courage; while the French *esprit* has a flavor of its own which makes it different from both of them. The Greek *sarx* and the English "flesh" are not exact synonyms, for Paul reckons envy and hatred among the sins of the flesh. Even when we are able accurately to render a word's meaning, it may have associations or evocative power which elude us. For example, Paul and Silas were accused at Thessalonica of teaching that "there is another *basileus*." *Basileus*, one may say, is the Greek for king, and so it is. But it was also the title for the Roman emperor in those provinces where Greek was the official language. We do not think of the emperor as king, because in Rome, for emotional reasons deep-rooted in early Roman history, *rex* was a forbidden word. If then we render *basileus* by "king," we miss the full force of the accusation that the apostles were guilty of treason. But if we render it by "emperor," we miss the point that this false charge was only a distortion of what Paul actually believed about the kingship of Christ.

The precise force of words depends not just on their dictionary meaning, but on the whole thought-world of the user. The New Testament scholar therefore must not only know Greek; he must be able to ask what sort of Greek he is dealing with. There are four very different types of English spoken in London, Glasgow, New York, and the South Seas. A French translator, faced with the sentence, "I'm mad about my flat," would need to know whether the speaker was an Englishman delighted with his residence or an American furious at his punctured tire. Similarly there is a world of difference between the Greek of the Septuagint, of the Egyptian papyri, and of the philosophical schools. The word *doxa* in classical Greek means either opinion or reputation; but in the Septuagint, through being used as a translation of the Hebrew *kabod*, it comes to mean honor, or the radiance of the divine majesty. In the New Testament it is used with its Septuagintal meanings. But how often has this sort of transformation happened? Is *aletheia* in John's Gospel the truth as understood by the Old Testament or the truth as understood by the Greek philosophers? Is the *Logos* of the same Gospel the divine reason of the Greeks or the word of God which came to the Old Testament prophets?

Thus the study of language sooner or later involves us in the study of the whole historical setting of early Christianity. Yet even with the most comprehensive knowledge we still have to beware. The New Testament writers were describing events and experiences without any parallel, and had to convey their new ideas in such terms as were available to them. They had to pour the new wine of the gospel into old linguistic bottles. The words stretched even to breaking point under the strain. Many of them took on new shades of meaning which can be determined not by a study of linguistic origins and history, but only from the new contexts in which they are used. We may begin by thinking that we need to know Greek to read the New Testament, but we end by recognizing that it may take a full study of theology to make us certain of the meaning of a single word.

A second preparatory discipline is textual criticism. There are in existence, as far as we know, some 4,700 manuscripts of the New Testament, ranging from complete vellum codices to small fragments of papyrus, but in no case has the autograph of any New Testament book survived. The earliest manuscript is a tiny fragment of John's Gospel, written at approximately A.D. 150. The text of all these manuscripts varies considerably, because the scribes who did the copying made mistakes, whether from fatigue, inadvertence, poor eyesight, or some quite inexplicable reason. (Even in this age of printing misprints still occur.) The task of textual criticism is to get behind the multiplicity of readings in the surviving manuscripts to the original text written or dictated by the author, and it is a complicated task which calls for the exercise of a highly trained critical judgment. One cannot just count the manuscripts in favor of each reading and decide by majority vote, for many of the manuscripts, including most of the complete ones, are late products derived from a common source—a scholarly edition produced at Byzantium not earlier than the fifth century; and therefore their combined evidence is not necessarily equal in weight to that of a single fourth-century codex, such as Vaticanus or Sinaiticus. On the other hand, the date of a manuscript is not a certain indication of its worth, since a late manuscript may have been copied directly from a very early one which has since disappeared. If we had the pedigree of all the manuscripts that have come down to us, we could arrange them all in a huge genealogical table, which would provide at a glance an accurate index of their relative worth. As it is, the most we can do is to classify them in four main family groups:

1. The Byzantine text, subsequently adopted with only slight changes by the English translators of 1611;

2. The Alexandrian text, represented by the fourth-century codices, Vaticanus and Sinaiticus, and by the third-century Chester Beatty papyri;

3. The Western text, represented by the fifth-century Codex Bezae and the Old Latin translation;

4. The Eastern text, divided into two subfamilies, the one represented by the Koridethi manuscript, the other by the early Syriac translations.

The last three text families must have been already in existence by the end of the second century, and we have no reason to suppose that any one of them is invariably superior to the others, nor even that any combination of them is always to be preferred to the remaining one. When Westcott and Hort produced their text, on which the English Revised Version was based, they treated the Alexandrian text as "neutral," i.e., as the main stream of textual tradition from which the other types were divagations. The modern textual scholar has great respect for the two great Alexandrian codices, supported as they are by the Chester Beatty papyri, but he does not regard them as infallible. He is more inclined to rely on internal evidence to help him decide between readings—the style or theology of the author and transcriptional probability, i.e., the principle that the reading is to be preferred which explains how the other readings arose.

When Westcott and Hort had finished their work, they declared that they remained in real doubt over only some fifty-five readings. Some of the instances which they left in doubt have been settled by new evidence, and some of the questions which they regarded as settled forever have had to be reopened. The fact remains, however, that textual scholars can be more confident about the text of the New Testament than about that of any other work of ancient literature. In any case the vast majority of doubtful readings do not substantially affect the meaning of the passage in which they occur. But there are exceptions.

One of the most important exceptions is found in Luke's account of the Last Supper (Luke 22:14–20). Almost all the manuscripts have what is known as the "longer version," but the Western text has the "shorter version," omitting verses 19b–20. If we accept the longer version, then Luke's account, apart from the mention of two cups, is closely parallel to those of Mark and Paul. If we accept the shorter version, we are at once immersed in problems, for we have an account in which the distribution of the cup precedes the breaking of the bread, and in which nothing is said to connect the sacrament with the cross. What source was Luke using? Was he freely rewriting Mark, or had he an independent tradition? If he had an independent tradition, was it a purely historical recollection of the upper room, or was it embodied in a liturgical form? That is to say, was there ever in the first century a form of eucharistic celebration in which the cup preceded the bread and no mention was made of the cross? Did Luke's hypothetical source, like the Marcan setting into which he inserted it, identify the Last Supper with the Passover, or did it agree with John that the Passover was still to come on the Friday night? And why did Luke, who certainly knew Mark's Gospel, omit the important Marcan saying over the cup?

In spite of the difficulties it raises, and in spite of the admittedly impressive weight of manuscript authority against it, most scholars believe that the shorter version is what Luke wrote. For there are other places in the closing chapters of Luke's Gospel where the Western text has a shorter reading which is demonstrably preferable to the longer reading of the other manuscripts, and where the longer reading can be shown to have been borrowed from another part of the New Testament. In this passage the verses omitted by the Western text look like a clumsy insertion from I Corinthians and Mark. The words "and the cup likewise after supper, saying" are pure Paul; an independent tradition might have preserved a saying of Jesus word for word the same, but hardly a narrative sentence without a verb. And the phrase "which is poured out for you," which in Mark's account qualifies the word "blood," is here awkwardly attached to a sentence from Paul, so as to qualify the word "cup." In addition to all this Luke's theology and transcriptional probability are in favor of the shorter text. Here then is one case of textual variation where a great deal turns on our choice or reading, where there are powerful reasons for accepting the less strongly attested text, and where there is still a difference of opinion among experts. Textual criticism is part of the prolegomena to New Testament study, but this does not mean that its work must be complete before literary, historical, and theological study can begin. Many of the questions it raises can be settled only in the light of all these more advanced disciplines.

We turn then to literary criticism, the study of authorship, date, and sources. Within this area, though perhaps no questions ought to be regarded as finally closed, there are many on which, thanks to the massive labors of earlier generations of scholars, there is very general agreement: that Mark's is the first Gospel, that the authors of the first and third Gospels used Mark and another documentary source called Q, that the third Gospel and Acts form a two-volume book, that Paul did not write the Pastoral Epistles, that the John of Revelation is not the author of the Fourth Gospel. But there are other questions, such as the authorship of Ephesians and the date of I Peter, on which opinion is deeply divided; and others again, such as the authorship of Hebrews, where the evidence is too meager even to provide a basis for disagreement. In recent years there has been a tendency to make virtue of necessity and claim that, after all, very little depends on our ability to answer such questions as these. Those who have denied that Paul wrote Ephesians have urged in extenuation that, so far from diminishing the stature of Paul, they have added to the apostolic firmament a new star of the first magnitude. Certainly we should be unwise to tie the permanent value of the New Testament too closely to the solution of critical problems. Yet there are some critical questions which make a great deal of difference to our interpretation of the New Testament as a whole.

There are, for example, two schools of thought about the composition of Luke's Gospel. Those who hold the Marcan hypothesis believe that Luke, like Matthew, used Mark's Gospel as the framework into which he inserted the material he derived from his other sources; and those who hold the Proto-Luke hypothesis believe that he had already combined his non-Marcan material in a first draft of a Gospel before he came across Mark. Before we are tempted to dismiss this debate as an academic parlor game, we must look more closely at its implications. If we accept the Marcan hypothesis, we commit ourselves to the view that Luke rewrote his sources with such a degree of editorial freedom as to cast serious doubt on his claim to be a reliable historian. According to the Proto-Luke theory, not only was Luke remarkably faithful to his sources, but he used for much of his Gospel a tradition independent of Mark, by which Mark's evidence can be corrected or corroborated. Our estimate of the historical value of the Gospels is therefore inseparably bound up with this critical question.

Again, there are some scholars who have denied that Paul wrote II Thessalonians, largely because of an apparent discrepancy between I and II Thessalonians in the matter of eschatology. The first epistle reminds its readers that the day of the Lord is to come, suddenly and without warning, like a thief in the night, and the second epistle tells them not to get excited, because it cannot happen yet; other world-shaking events have to happen first. If, with most modern scholars, we persist in the traditional belief that Paul wrote both letters, this is bound to affect our attitude to eschatological language wherever we find it in the New Testament; for no man could have written both these letters in a short space of time, as Paul must have done, if he expected his readers to take with pedantic literalness the two very different statements he was making about the day of the Lord. Moreover, the second epistle contains a difficult passage (2:3 ff.), which gives a mythological portrayal of the Roman Empire, similar to that of Revelation. If Paul wrote this, it would form a considerable qualification of his teaching on Church and state in Romans 13:1–7.

Literary criticism has suffered some neglect during the past forty years because attention has been concentrated on oral tradition. Before any of the New Testament books were written, there was a period during which a tradition of preaching, teaching, and Old Testament exegesis was formulated and handed on by word of mouth. The pioneers of research into this period were the form critics, whose interest was in those traditions which in the end gave rise to written Gospels. They believed that sayings of Jesus and stories about him circulated at first as isolated, atomic units, which were molded by use into a small number of stereotyped forms, each of these forms being the product of some need in the life of the Christian community. They went on to claim that not only the form but much of the content of the tradition was created by the needs of the Church and attempted to provide criteria by which authentic tradition could be distinguished from later accretion. Like the historical criticism of an earlier age, form criticism has petered out into scepticism, not because there was anything fundamentally wrong with its method, but because of the unexamined presuppositions with which it was applied.

The study of oral tradition, however, is relevant not only to the Gospels but to the Epistles. Many of these show striking similarities of language and doctrine, which the literary critics used to explain as an indication of literary dependence. Not only Ephesians and the Pastoral Epistles, but Hebrews, I Peter, James, and even Revelation were "deutero-Pauline": their authors must have read the letters of Paul, and the books must have been written after about A.D. 90, the probable date for the publication of the Pauline corpus. Nowadays such similarities are more plausibly explained by the supposition that the authors of all the books, Paul included, were drawing on a common stock of early Christian tradition.

There remains one further preliminary discipline before we are ready for the main task of New Testament study. We cannot hope to understand any man's mind unless we know something of the world of thought in which he was at home. The threefold inscription on the cross in Hebrew, Greek, and Latin reminds us that Christianity took its origin at a point where three great streams of ancient culture met.

Jesus was a Jew, and so were most of the men who wrote the New Testament. From the start Christianity presented itself to the world as the fulfillment of the promises and aspirations of the Old Testament. Its Bible was the Septuagint, and one of the indispensable tools for the study of the New Testament is a concordance to the Greek Old Testament. But it is no easy task to give an accurate picture of Judaism in the time of Jesus. The Rabbinic literature comes from a much later date—the earliest document, the Mishna, was compiled about A.D. 200—and it is by no means obvious how far these writings can be treated as evidence for first-century thought and practice. They certainly contain a considerable amount of early tradition, but we cannot now follow a former fashion and regard the Judaism of A.D. 200 as identical with a "normative Judaism" of A.D. 30. Quite a different Judaism, and one which undoubtedly influenced the New Testament, is found in the apocalyptic writings—the literature of a passive (or not so passive) resistance to the encroachment of paganism during the three centuries between the persecution of Antiochus Epiphanes (167 B.C.) and the destruction of Jerusalem by Hadrian (A.D. 135). Further evidence of the vitality and variety of Judaism is provided by the documents of the Qumran community, which belong to approximately the same period. It used to be thought that Palestinian Judaism was a phenomenon quite distinct from the Hellenistic Judaism practiced in the synagogues of the Dispersion, but even this long accepted assumption has now had to be queried. For the Jews of the Dispersion are known to have maintained close links with Jerusalem, and there were Hellenists (Greek-speaking Jews) residing in Jerusalem and worshiping in their own separate synagogues. On the other hand, our chief knowledge of Hellenistic Judaism comes from the voluminous writings of Philo of Alexandria, who was roughly contemporary with Jesus, and it is an open question to what extent his work was known in other parts of the Mediterranean.

The Greek converts to Christianity came out of a background even more heterogeneous than that of their Jewish fellow Christians. Not many of them can have been adherents of the great philosophical schools, but most of them would have been familiar with the popular philosophy of the itinerant preachers—a large dose of Stoicism with a dash of Plato. Yet in this strange twilight of the Greek genius, not even philosophy had remained totally Greek. When the campaigns of Alexander had broken the barrier between East and West, Oriental ideas and practices had flooded into the Greek world, and in particular astrology. Our detailed knowledge of ancient astrology comes from sources of a later period, but even before the Christian era we can detect its all-pervasive influence, especially in the development of the popular form of Stoicism. Religion, too, had become cosmopolitan and syncretistic. The Olympian gods had declined along with the city-state, and thereafter people had found an anodyne for their failure of nerve in a multiplicity of mystery cults. Classical Greece had had its indigenous mysteries at Eleusis, at which initiates could see the annual re-enactment of the death and resurrection of the earth-maiden Persephone, and already in Socrates' time the cult of the Thracian goddess Bendis had reached the Piraeus. Before long Cybele from Asia Minor and Isis from Egypt were to spread their influence across the sea. New cults could always be sure of a hospitable welcome, for after all the new mother-goddess was only the old, familiar one with a new name and an unfamiliar ritual. By New Testament times an international trade in religions was well established. It is true that our knowledge of the mystery cults, like our knowledge of Rabbinic Judaism and astrology, comes largely from sources that are later than the first century, but there is no reason to suppose that these cults changed appreciably across the years. The same is true of what has been called "the higher religion of paganism." This is found most clearly in the Hermetic writings, which were written in the late second or early third century, but which undoubtedly contain earlier ideas. They are dedicated to the Greek Hermes, who has been identified with the Egyptian Thoth, and they present a highly spiritual religious philosophy which has some remarkable parallels with the teachings of the New Testament, partly no doubt because they too had been influenced by the Septuagint.

It is of course one thing to recognize that all these religious and philosophical movements were part of the background of early Christianity, and quite another matter to treat the New Testament as though it were simply the product of this environment. The more one reads in the Rabbinic writings, the Qumran documents, the commentaries of Philo, the fragments of the Stoics, or the tracts of the Hermetica, the more one is bound to be impressed not only by the unity but by the sheer vitality and creative vigor of the New Testament. The early Christian preachers had to address Jews and Gentiles in language they could understand and therefore had to clothe their message in the thought-forms that were already familiar; but whatever they touched, they transformed.

The Romans were content to derive their intellectual ideas and culture from the more imaginative Greeks, and left little impression on the religious or philosophical thought of the ancient world. But in one sphere they were originators. There can be no proper understanding of the New Testament without some knowledge of Roman law and provincial administration. Christians benefited from the Pax Romana and suffered under Roman persecution. We need, then, to know something about Roman imperial policy, and in particular their policy in dealing with foreign religions, if we are to understand why, even in the New Testament period, Church and state came into conflict.

The object of all this preliminary study is to enable us to read the New Testament as though we were members of those congregations to which the books were initially addressed. No New Testament writer ever took his pen in hand in order to leave a permanent record of his faith for the benefit of future generations. He wrote to meet the immediate need, perhaps the desperate need, of his friends. The New Testament is a book of answers, and to read it is rather like listening to one end of a telephone conversation. ("Don't you remember?" says Paul, "I told you all about this when I was with you.") If we are to read intelligently, we need to read between the lines, to fill in the questions which called forth these particular answers. But we should not suppose that, by submerging ourselves in the world of the first century, we shall find the gospel any more congenial or easy to believe. It is a common modern fallacy that the development of scientific knowledge had made Christianity harder to accept. The evidence is that the preaching of the cross was from the first "a stumbling-block to Jews and foolishness to Greeks." It shattered the fondest hopes and transcended the wildest dreams of Jew and Gentile alike. There were indeed Christians in the first century who succumbed to the temptation of accommodating the gospel to the *Zeitgeist*, of making it popular and attractive by omitting all that was demanding and all that was shocking. "They belong to the world," said John of his opponents in the province of Asia, "and therefore the world listens to them." The Church has to face a similar danger in every age, and this is one reason why the historical study of the New Testament will always be vitally important. Without this as our standard of judgment when we try to translate the gospel into twentieth-century terms, we should certainly produce something too deeply imbued with the spirit of our own age. Only if we have the skill and the patience to discover why the gospel was a shock to men of the first century, shall we be able to use it to shatter the complacency and lift the vision of our own generation.

When all the work of preparatory study has been done, historical research offers to us the acquaintance of a group of witnesses who in many different ways testify to the centrality of Jesus for their own lives and the life of mankind. Their testimony consists partly of historic event, partly of an affirmation that these events were from start to finish an act of God. Nowadays we might feel compelled to treat the one part of the testimony as material for the historian and the other part as theology; but the New Testament writers did not make that elementary mistake. They knew that the historical part of their evidence could not be credible to anybody unless their interpretation of it was true. Why should anyone believe the miracles of Jesus unless in him God's Kingdom had become an earthly reality? How could Jesus have taken upon himself the burden of the world's sin and suffering unless God was in him, reconciling the world to himself? How could it be true that Jesus had left the tomb unless the resurrection was God's great act of vindication and victory? They knew too that they had been convinced of the truth of the gospel because God had sent his Spirit into their hearts to confirm their faith. They could believe that God had been in Christ, perfectly and completely, because in some small and imperfect fashion they had experienced him at work in themselves.

A large part of the New Testament consists of ethical instruction, but this is always firmly related to the history of Jesus. The imperative of moral demand rests on an indicative, and not just on the past indicative of God's act in the earthly life, death, and resurrection of Jesus, but on the present indicative of his continuing action through the Holy Spirit. The early Christians were convinced that the transformation and triumph which they experienced in their own lives and observed in their fellows and in the corporate life of the Church was not their own achievement but God's handiwork. "They have conquered him [Satan] by the blood of the Lamb and by the word of their testimony." "Let us run with perseverance the race that is set before us, looking to Jesus the pioneer and perfecter of our faith." "I am sure that he who began a good work in you will bring it to completion at the day of Jesus Christ." "Beloved, we are God's children now; it does not yet appear what we shall be, but we know that when he appears we shall be like him, for we shall see him as he is." "You yourselves are our testimonial . . . written not with ink but with the Spirit of the living God."

The certainty of the New Testament writers, then, had a double foundation, the eyewitness testimony of those who had known Jesus and the confirming testimony of personal experience. But such conviction was not open to everybody: there were qualifications. "He who has ears to hear, let him hear." "To him who has more will be given; and from him who has not, even what he has will be taken away." The qualifications are not intellectual, but moral. "My teaching is not mine but his who sent me; if any man's will is to do his will, he shall know whether the teaching is from God." "Solid food is for the mature, for those who have their faculties trained by practice to distinguish good from evil."

At this point the historian lays down his pen. His task is to describe, to bring the past to life, and in this case to bring to life the convictions of the men who gave us the New Testament. Whether their testimony is true it is not for him as an historian to say. That is something that everyone must decide for himself. There is nothing in the New Testament to coerce belief; for Jesus himself is recorded to have refused proof to those who asked for it, and to have spoken harshly of their request, on the grounds that the word of God carries its own credentials, so that anyone who is prepared to accept and obey it can freely recognize the source from which it comes. All history is what we make of our past; and by what we make of this piece of our past our faith is formed, our future is determined, and our lives are judged.

4. Early Church History

Alec Graham

In his inaugural lecture on the study of history which he delivered at Cambridge in June 1895, Lord Acton discussed the view that "Modern History is a subject to which neither beginning nor end can be assigned. No beginning, because the dense web of the fortunes of man is woven without a void; because, in society as in nature, the structure is continuous, and we can trace things back uninterruptedly. . . . No end, because, on the same principle, history made and history making are scientifically inseparable and separately unmeaning."[1] The early history of the Christian Church is equally a subject to which neither beginning nor end can be assigned: it is impossible to understand the history of the Christian Church without some knowledge of the history of the Jewish people and of the place of Jesus of Nazareth within that history, and without some knowledge of the early history of the Christian Church it is impossible to understand the later history of both Church and state. Nevertheless there is "an evident and intelligible line"[2] which marks off the years before A.D. 70 from those after: in that year Jerusalem fell to the forces of Titus, its population was scattered and its temple destroyed: Judaism was deprived of its focal point, and the Christian Church no longer ran the risk of being controlled by the strongly conservative Jewish Christianity of the Church in Jerusalem. There is another "evident and intelligible line" which nearly four centuries later marks off the years

[1] *Lectures on Modern History* (London: Macmillan & Co., 1907), p. 1.
[2] *Ibid.*, p. 3.

before 451 from those after: in that year the Council of Chalcedon agreed on a declaration which, over the greater part of Christendom, came to be accepted as the definitive statement of Christian belief concerning the person of Jesus: by this date the classic expressions of Christian belief about God, man, Jesus, and the Holy Spirit had been formulated and generally accepted. The period of history which we shall consider falls between these two dates, 70 and 451.

While the Christian Church in the period is woven "in the dense web of human fortunes," and while there are strong elements of continuity which connect it at either end of the period with its own uninterrupted life, the Church itself makes a claim that a discontinuous element has entered history; this is the conviction of all the New Testament writers: they all believe that in Jesus we see one who is both continuous and discontinuous with human life and history. This conviction is shared by all Christians throughout the period which we are studying; to some extent the faith of Christians in every age may be taken to support the claim of the New Testament writers, for the existence and faith of the Christian Church are themselves a part of the evidence which has to be evaluated in any consideration of the Christian claims about Jesus. In the history of the Church itself, however, we see a strange mixture of the continuous and discontinuous: heroism, devotion, sanctity (which may be interpreted as evidence of supernatural influence at work in the Christian society) side by side with unscrupulous ecclesiastical power politics, misuse of spiritual privilege for selfish ends, human weakness and stupidity, which all indicate that members of the Christian Church are continuous with the rest of humanity.

Besides pointing independently to these elements of continuity and of discontinuity in Christian origins and in Christian history, the New Testament and the early history of the Church also illuminate each other, for to a certain extent they overlap in time. The evidence of the Didache, for example, is useful in considering the history of the Synoptic tradition of the sayings of Jesus, and the policy of the Roman authorities with regard to Christians in the first century and in the early second century is an important factor in helping us to interpret the attitudes of Paul, Peter, and Revelation towards the imperial power. Conversely, it is impossible to treat adequately questions such as, for example, the reconciliation of lapsed or immoral Church members, the emergence of the monarchical episcopate, or the development of Christian worship without a careful study of the evidence from the New Testament, part of which may well be later than the earliest patristic evidence.

It would also be equally artificial to pretend that this period (or indeed any other period) of Church history can be properly studied without some knowledge of the secular history within which the Christian Church has its own particular history. The development of the Church in this early period has to be considered against the background, for example, of imperial government: the prosperity and relative security of the Antonine age, the rapid succession of assassinated emperors and military *coups d'état* in the third century, the consolidation of imperial power under Diocletian and Constantine, the division of the empire in the fourth century, and the eventual extinction of imperial rule in the West in the fifth century, all affected the fortunes and development of the Christian Church. Conversely, the Christian Church itself may well have played at least a contributory part in the decline of the Roman Empire in the West.

Economic, social, and administrative developments within the empire certainly had a strong influence on the course of Christian history: it is not a coincidence that the rise of the fortunes of the Christian Church in the fourth century took place at exactly the time that members of the middle classes were securing positions of greater influence and importance in the imperial service: the growth of monasticism in the fourth century is not entirely unconnected with the financial plight of the curial class: the boundaries of ecclesiastical provinces in Gaul coincide with the provincial boundaries of the Roman administration.

Furthermore, no study of the fortunes of the Christian Church in this period would be complete without serious attention being paid to other religious and philosophical movements: they often deeply affected the course of Christian history, and they were themselves influenced by the spread of Christianity. The biography of Augustine of Hippo illustrates the impossibility of considering Christianity as an isolated religious movement: brought up in North Africa on a simple Catholic piety, he was to become a Manichaean auditor for some years before he was reconciled to the Church and was baptized, and the influence of Cicero on him in his youth, and later the influence of Neoplatonist writers, cannot be exaggerated. Similarly, it is impossible to understand the spread of Christianity in the first century without some knowledge of the mystery religions to which in some ways it must have seemed so similar; or the problems of the Church in the second century without some appreciation of the nature of Gnosticism, which itself had a strong Judaeo-Christian element in its own origins; or the situation in Rome toward which Constantine and Ambrose adopted different policies in the fourth century, without some awareness of the support which the pagan state religion still received there throughout the century.

As important as each of these political, economic, social, and religious factors which have to be considered in any study of the history of the early Church was one further factor: the presence of barbarian armies either on the borders of the empire or within the empire itself. For the greater part of our period the presence of the Persians on the eastern frontier of the empire also had marked repercussions on the life of the Church. In the fourth century, for example, when the policies of the emperors Constantine and Julian deeply affected the fortunes of the Christian Church, Constantine died as he was preparing to campaign against the Persians, and Julian was mortally wounded on an eastern battlefield. Beyond the limit of our period, the refusal of many Eastern Christians to accept the Chalcedonian Definition as orthodox teaching about the person of Christ may perhaps be attributed to an unconscious desire on the part of some of these Christians to be theologically as well as politically independent of the Roman Empire.

The presence and pressure of the barbarian forces on the Rhine had been a cause of constant concern to the imperial authorities in the second century: in the reign of Marcus Aurelius, about 170, some Teuton bands even penetrated into northern Italy. It was in the third century, however, that the Teutons' attack became more

threatening: Teutons were followed by Franks, Franks by Vandals and Goths; by the end of the third century the attack was
on the frontier of the Danube as well as on that of the Rhine. The
empire in the fourth and fifth centuries found itself obliged to
employ Franks to fight against the Goths and then Goths to stave
off the Huns. The repercussions which these attacks had for the
Christian Church in the latter half of our period varied very much
from century to century. In the mid-third century the emperor
Decius launched an attack on Christians and tried to recall his subjects' loyalty to the traditional beliefs and cults of the empire: this
was a desperate attempt to consolidate the ideological basis of the
empire so that the barbarians might be faced by a united front.
Little more than a century later, Christian emperors were leading
Christian soldiers into battle against Arian invaders, and by the
middle of the fifth century the prestige of the Catholic Church
in the West stood higher still: in 452 Pope Leo I led an embassy
to Attila the Hun in an attempt to dissuade him from advancing
on the city of Rome. Roman forces had suffered a defeat as severe
as Cannae, at the hands of the Goths at Adrianople in 378; Rome
itself had fallen to Alaric the Visigoth in 410; the emperor in
Ravenna became increasingly ineffectual in the course of the
fifth century until the empire in the West came formally to an
end in 476. Its place was taken by numerous barbarian kingdoms;
many of the new rulers were Arian in belief and rejected the
Nicene faith. But the Church in the West dependent on Rome
remained the haven wherein were preserved humane values, classical learning, and Christian orthodoxy: above all, the Church inherited some of the prestige of the vanished empire, for she alone
was a supranational society transcending the tribal, racial, and
national divisions in western Europe.

If the Church at the end of our period was one of the few unifying forces in western Europe, at the beginning of our period
she was suspected by the state on the grounds that she was disruptive of the very basis of society. The standard charges which
were regularly brought against Christians throughout the first
three centuries of the Church's history were that Christians were
atheist, immoral, and unpatriotic. It is easy to understand how this
impression was given: Christians often met for their worship in

the evening or very early in the morning in the house of one of the members of the local Christian community: any closed society which meets in the hours of darkness, which has its own rite of initiation and its own teaching, discipline, and organization known only to its members, is bound to cause resentment and suspicion. This suspicion was, in the case of the early Christians, fed by rumors about worshipers who consumed their savior's body and blood and who loved one another. To many people outside the Christian community it seemed that Christians were cannibals and loose livers. It was known that they generally did not attend games in the arena and that sometimes they avoided service in the army: this gave the impression that they were unconcerned about the social and political stability of the empire, while their language about Christ, their king, could imply that they owed allegiance to an earthly sovereign higher than the emperor. It was also known that Christians refused to take part in harmless religious practices; these practices included those connected with local shrines and also those associated with acknowledgement of the emperor's divinity. This refusal could give the impression that Christians had no religious beliefs whatsoever: if they were atheists, they would probably be anarchists as well, and so they were thought to be dangerous to society. We can gather some impression of the attitude of many educated pagans to the Christian Church from several sources—from the letters of Pliny (c. 112), for example; from the works of the Christian apologists (who were seeking in the mid-second century to establish the harmlessness and antiquity of the Christian religion); from the Octavius of Minucius Felix (who, c. 200, tried to rebut the charges most frequently made against Christians' morals); or from the reply to the philosopher Celsus by Origen (who, c. 245, tried to refute the charges made against Christians' beliefs).

It is impossible to be precise about the motives which led the Roman authorities in the first century to take proceedings against Christians: we do not know why Nero placed on Christians the responsibility for the fire of Rome, nor do we know for certain whether the Christians who were executed in Domitian's reign were executed because they were Christians. We cannot be certain about the reasons which led the imperial authorities to prosecute Christians, although it is very probable that Christians were haled before the magistrates sporadically in various parts of the empire. In general, however, the imperial regime at this time was tolerant and easygoing: provided that there was no disturbance of public order, the imperial authorities did not investigate the beliefs of the ordinary citizen, nor interfere with his behavior. The emperor Trajan insisted (c. 112) that Christians were not to be sought out; this provision was reinforced by his successor Hadrian: accusations against Christians had to be made in the proper form, anonymous accusations were not allowed, and those who brought unfounded accusations were punished. In fact, when Christians did suffer in the second century, they generally suffered in all probability not because they were Christians, but on the grounds that they were contumacious in refusing to do what any reasonable citizen would find no difficulty in doing, namely, to offer incense to Caesar or to swear by Caesar's genius.

As the second century wore on, however, we have evidence that the imperial authorities did not always show this same scrupulous respect for proper legal procedure: the account of the martyrdom of Polycarp (which may have taken place in 155 or about 167) and the account of the martyrdoms at Lyons in 177 both show that the pressure of the mob could cause the authorities to dispense with some of the judicial formalities. At this time it is probable that Jews were sometimes responsible for arousing or exacerbating hostility against Christians: Christians were claiming to be the true heirs of Jewry and so of the Jewish privileges in the empire, and the Jews were naturally eager to protect their own privileged position as a *religio licita*. It is not, however, until the reign of Septimius Severus at the turn of the century that we find any discriminatory legislation directed particularly against Christians or any breach in the official policy that Christians were not to be sought out. If the number of Christians who are known to have been martyred up to this time is small, there were in all probability other martyrs in some numbers whose names and martyrdoms have not been recorded: the spread of the cult of the martyr in the third century and Tertullian's fine phrase that "the blood of the martyrs is the seed of the church" both suggest that prosecution and martyrdom were among the hazards of being a Christian.

Before the Christian religion was officially tolerated at the beginning of Constantine's reign in 313, the Church did undergo three periods of persecution in which an attempt was made to break her leaders and to win back from her the support which in parts of the empire (for example, North Africa, Egypt, and Palestine) she enjoyed among some sections of the general population. Under Decius (249–51), Valerian (257–58), and Diocletian and his successors (303–13), a frontal attack was made on the Christian Church. The attack took a variety of forms: in each of these persecutions the leaders of the Church were in especial danger. Under Decius there was no attempt to extirpate Christians, but an administrative procedure was employed which had the effect of causing Christians, unless they wished to be considered treasonable, to deny their faith. Under Valerian, worship was forbidden: it was the practice of the Christian religion which was proscribed, not Christian belief. Under Diocletian and his successors, however, the attack was directed as before, at the leaders of the Church and its worship, also at its church buildings and sacred books, and before long the attack was extended in parts of the empire to include all Christians who could be discovered. Christians were not allowed to hold public office and were deprived of all civil privileges; Christian faith as much as Christian worship was proscribed. The disciplinary problems which faced the Church after the persecution under Decius show that considerable numbers of Christians proved disloyal to their faith, and Eusebius implies that there were many who "made utter shipwreck of their salvation" in the persecution under Diocletian and his successors. This last persecution was instigated by Galerius, who let loose such a reign of terror that, according to Lactantius, even the profession of letters was proscribed. At that time it would have been hard for Eusebius or Lactantius, who both saw persecution in progress, to believe that within a very few years Christianity would be officially tolerated in the empire, and that by the end of the century pagan public sacrifice would be forbidden in the empire's capital city.

The emperor Constantine was the most important figure in this remarkable reversal in the fortunes of the Christian Church. It is difficult to be certain about his religious convictions up to the battle of the Milvian Bridge in 312, but it is impossible to doubt his convictions after the battle. He had known Christians and had been impressed by them some years before he marched on Rome in 312: it is improbable that the support which he gave to the Christian Church from the very moment of his victory was motivated by a shrewd appreciation of the balance of political advantage. The most natural interpretation of the evidence is that Constantine's victory confirmed his tentative faith; after his victory he certainly took no trouble to conceal his Christian convictions. In his correspondence he addressed Christian leaders as brethren, he built and endowed Christian churches, Christian bishops were given positions of responsibility. Equally significant was the embarrassment evidently felt in 313 by the pagan panegyrist on the subject of the emperor's beliefs. During his reign he spent little time in Rome and felt ill at ease there, for Rome was the center of the pagan cultus which was still the official religion of the empire: this lack of sympathy with the pagan aristocracy and establishment at Rome may well have been the decisive factor which caused Constantine to transfer his capital to Constantinople, a new Rome in the East.

Even at the end of Constantine's reign in 337 Christians were still very much a minority group in the empire. The emperor considered himself as much responsible for the religious welfare of those outside the Church as of those within it. The fact that the emperor was not baptized until a few days before his death means that it is highly unlikely that he took a full part in Christian worship. His faith was probably of a fairly simple sort: if the Christians' god was the true god, then proper provision had to be made for this god to be reverenced and worshiped. Furthermore, recognition of the true god should be a means of promoting harmony within the empire: it is small wonder, then, that Constantine had little patience with Christian divisions—the Church should be a cohesive factor beneficial to the empire and not a divisive force within it. Concern for peace and comprehensiveness is the guiding thread in his policy with regard to both the Donatists and the Arians who in their different ways threatened the peace of the Church and of the empire.

Understandably the Church was completely unprepared for this change in its fortunes. Christians were amazed at the workings of providence which had so strangely led to their advantage: at first it was only to be expected that the leaders of the Church should welcome without reserve the patronage and protection of the emperor. Christians had no time to think out either the theory or the practice of their changed relationships with the civil power. Athanasius did indeed resist imperial policy in the course of the Arian controversy. He had, however, himself appealed to Constantine against the decisions of the Council of Tyre, but at a later stage in the controversy, in the reign of Constantine's son, Constantius, who was then an Arian sympathizer, Athanasius was the only Christian leader who refused to obey an imperial command to sign a profession of faith which was virtually Arian in content and has become known as the Blasphemy of Sirmium.

It is broadly true that the Church in the West regained its sense of proportion and its independence of maneuver with regard to the civil power more completely than the Church in the East. Toward the end of the fourth century successive youthful emperors in the West were of comparatively insignificant caliber beside such commanding ecclesiastics as Damasus, bishop of Rome, and Ambrose, bishop of Milan. Ambrose came from a family distinguished in the public service, and he had himself governed a province. In personality and in administrative experience he stood head and shoulders above the emperors Gratian and Valentinian II: Gratian had asked Ambrose for instruction in the Christian faith, and Valentinian II came to respect and rely on Ambrose after the bishop had successfully resisted imperial commands about making provision for Arian worship in Milan. Ambrose also exacted obedience to the law of the Church from the soldier-emperor Theodosius the Great: Theodosius himself was an outstanding personality, but he was a baptized Christian, and after the massacre at Thessalonica Ambrose could demand from him that he should submit to the Church's penitential discipline. Furthermore, once the Western capital had been removed to Ravenna, great ecclesiastical statesmen like Innocent I and Leo I, bishops of Rome, were the ablest and most commanding figures in the former capital of the empire: and after the collapse of the Western empire the Catholic Church in the West refused to accept dictation from Arian rulers and maintained its independence.

In the East, however, religious and ecclesiastical affairs were but one important part of the life of a large empire: imperial influence on the Christian Church was much greater than in the West, and imperial policy itself was often influenced by political, ecclesiastical, or theological factions. In the West, Ambrose emerged victorious from the conflict with the empress Justina: in the East, the empress Eudoxia was successful in securing the banishment of Chrysostom from Constantinople. No Eastern emperor, however, repeated the arrogant claim of Constantius, "What I will, let that be reckoned a canon," and few Christian thinkers went so far in their adulation of the emperor as did Eusebius of Caesarea with regard to Constantine himself. By the end of the century, the Church had largely adjusted itself to the changed situation: it was accepted on all sides in East and West that only the emperor could summon a general council, for this was a matter which deeply affected the life of the empire. Sometimes an emperor would force his policy on a reluctant Church, as did Justinian in the Three Chapters controversy in the mid-sixth century, but the results of such intervention were invariably reversed if in the long run they proved unacceptable to the general mind of Christians.

After the reign of Constantine and after imperial intervention in a variety of interests during the Arian dispute, the short reign of the emperor Julian (361–63) helped Christians to recover their balance. Julian was a fascinating character, dubbed "the Apostate," second only to Judas Iscariot and Pontius Pilate among the number of those execrated and reviled by Christians from his own time to the present day. He was philosopher, mystic, devotee of mystery cults, able general, and enlightened administrator. His policy of toleration was a subtle means of undermining the growing power of the Christian Church. The vilification which he suffered from contemporary Christians probably indicates that he succeeded in weaning many members of the Church from their Christian allegiance. To many pagans the policy of Julian must have brought fresh hope, but the altar of victory was removed from the senate house at Rome in 382, pagan sacrifice was forbidden by Theodosius in 392, and the defeat of the usurper Eugenius and of his pagan general Arbogast in 394 at the battle of the river Frigidus meant the end of pagan hopes. At the beginning of the fourth century Christianity had been persecuted: by the end of the same century pagan religious practices were proscribed. The Christian Church gained many new members, particularly toward the end of the century, but inevitably standards of Christian devotion and behavior declined.

The general decline in the observance of Christian standards which was the result of the increasing popularity of the Church during the fourth and fifth centuries was an important factor in the growth of Christian monasticism. Many Christian men and women held that to live apart from the secular world and from the regular life of the Church was the only means whereby they could lead a Christian life unimpeded by worldly cares. Moreover, their adoption of the monastic life demonstrated to the Church and to the world that they were living the Christian life in earnest. These two motives can be discerned in the earlier history of Christian monasticism. Christians went to live in the desert as hermits or in loose associations so that they might achieve spiritual perfection the more easily; often they hoped also to be able to demonstrate their devotion to their neighbors or even to outdo their neighbors in the austerity and rigor of their manner of life. The desert was not so much a refuge from persecution or from the responsibilities of life as a battleground where the devil might be met on his own territory and spiritual perfection achieved by vanquishing demons and diabolical temptations. Christians living as anchorites or in communities in the Egyptian or Syrian desert were spiritual athletes par excellence: they hoped to win spiritual purity of vision by hard struggle, and the prospect of achieving spiritual mastery to a higher degree than anyone else was an incentive to struggle all the more valiantly.

This spiritual struggle often took bizarre and extravagant forms: if love for God meant rivalry with and contempt for one's neighbor, then the monastic life may often have been self-defeating. By the middle of the fourth century the observance of a monastic rule was much more common in the East; Anthony of Egypt had exercised a paternal, supervisory role over his colony of hermits, but under the rule of Pachomius monks were organized in communities: ascetic austerities were curbed, each monk was under obedience to his superior, the work and worship of the monks were regulated. Basil, in Asia Minor, was the author of another famous monastic rule which eventually became generally accepted in the Eastern Church; it also considerably influenced Benedict and his sixth-century rule in the West. Obedience to the superior was an important feature of Basil's rule: emphasis was also laid on the value of work and also on usefulness to society by care for the sick and poor, but the principal motive in leading the monastic life remained the more perfect service of God and the achievement of pure spiritual vision.

Eastern monasticism had a strong influence on the development of monasticism in the West. Athanasius, who later wrote a life of Anthony, was exiled in Trier and in Rome, and the religious life developed there soon after his periods of exile. Hilary of Poitiers had been exiled in Asia Minor, and the monastic communities in central Gaul may well owe their foundation to his influence. Jerome had translated the rule of Pachomius and so made it available for Western readers. Augustine, who gathered a community of men in his episcopal house at Hippo in North Africa, had himself been much moved by the effect which an account of Anthony's life had on some of his acquaintances. John Cassian, the founder of the monasteries at Marseilles, had been a monk at Bethlehem, had lived in Egypt, and had studied both the writings of Basil and also the ascetic works of Evagrius Ponticus; and Honoratus, the founder of the monastery at Lérins, an island off the southern coast of Gaul, had also traveled extensively in the East. In these two monastic centers the austerities and rigor of Eastern monasticism were adapted to suit conditions in Gaul: the aim of the monastic life, as it was understood at Marseilles, remained the achievement of perfection and spiritual vision; at Lérins learning and scholarship were held to be equally important —at both centers, discipline and unrelenting effort were required of the monks. It is also possible that Eastern monasticism had some influence on the development of the monastic life in Ireland: here alone in the West were to be found ascetic practices as harsh as those of Eastern anchorites and hermits; we know that there were later some strong cultural and intellectual links between the eastern Mediterranean and Ireland, and it is possible that there were also links between Eastern monasticism and monasticism in Ireland.

Very often, in both East and West, there was suspicion and distrust between monks and bishops. The monks were often mistrustful of the worldliness of the ordinary Christian and especially of the ecclesiastical hierarchy. "Flee women and bishops" was not uncommon advice. The Council of Chalcedon tried, with only limited success, to subject monks to episcopal authority and supervision: in the West, Pope Celestine writing to some Gallic bishops in 428 had expressed his distaste for the monastic life. But however much dislike Celestine might feel for the uncouth living and anti-intellectual bias of many monks, it remains true that the monastery of Lérins in particular was a center of learning and credal orthodoxy at a time when Arian semibarbarians ruled the greater part of Gaul, and from this center came many of the most famous leaders of the Gallic Church in the fifth and sixth centuries.

Among the famous bishops from the monastery of Lérins was Hilary of Arles: he came into open conflict with one of the most amazing personalities who has ever been bishop of Rome. In the year 444 Hilary had deposed a neighboring bishop, who appealed to Leo I at Rome; his appeal led Leo to address to the bishops of the province of Vienne his celebrated letter which removed from Hilary his metropolitical jurisdiction, and this letter was reinforced by the imperial rescript *Certum Est* of 445. This rescript decreed that any bishop could be compelled by the secular arm to obey a summons to appear before the bishop of Rome. Imperial authority gave its sanction and support to the claims which Leo was making for papal jurisdiction throughout the Church. The claims themselves were formulated by Leo in the terms of Roman law of succession: Peter was the heir of Christ, and Leo, being Peter's heir, was also heir of Christ: the heir acted in all matters with the authority of the deceased person. Right at the end of our period, therefore, the papal claims were being made in terms which have varied little in essence ever since and which can be understood only against the background of late Roman testamentary law. The precise formulation of these claims and their endorsement by the rescript of Valentinian III stand, however, at the end of a long process of development.

In the course of the first three centuries of Christian history the see of Rome was accorded increasing honor and respect. Rome was the city where the apostles Peter and Paul had been martyred; the Roman Church had a long record of Christian orthodoxy and could boast several martyr bishops; it enjoyed the prestige of being the Church of the capital city of the empire. It may well have made an attempt under Pope Victor at the end of the second century to discipline Christians far outside Italy, in Asia Minor. The evidence does not allow us to be dogmatic about this, but it is certain that, whatever authority or prestige was possessed by the Church of Rome in the early centuries, this was enjoyed because the Church of Rome, rather than its bishop, was venerated. In the middle of the third century, during the course of the controversy about the validity of baptism performed by heretics or schismatics, it became clear that responsible leaders of the Church in both North Africa and Asia Minor were not prepared to follow the lead given by the Church in Rome. Firmilian, bishop of Caesarea, held that Pope Stephen, in threatening to excommunicate those who disagreed with him, was only excommunicating himself, and Cyprian, bishop of Carthage, held, in opposition to Stephen, that the commission given by Christ to Peter was the basis of episcopal authority rather than of the authority of the see of Rome.

During the fourth century, however, the influence and prestige of the Roman see greatly increased. At the very beginning of his reign Constantine entrusted to Miltiades, bishop of Rome, the presidency of the investigation into the Donatists' complaints; at the Council of Sardica in 343 limited appellate jurisdiction in episcopal disputes was conferred on the Roman see; and thirty-five years later, the Rescript of Gratian conferred on the see of Rome authority over metropolitans. These three examples of the growing prestige of the Church of Rome in the fourth century are all

instances in which authority is conferred either by the emperor
or by a council: they are not the recognition of rights or authority
already possessed.

The dealings of the North African episcopate with the Roman
see during the pontificate of Zosimus (417–18) concerning the
Pelagian controversy and during the pontificates of both Zosimus
and Celestine concerning the affair of the priest Apiarius show
that the Church in North Africa certainly did not recognize the
jurisdiction or the doctrinal authority of the Roman see. Within
little more than a decade, however, Catholicism in North Africa
had been almost eliminated by Arian Vandals: the church in the
West which had consistently resisted the claims of the Roman see
in respect of jurisdiction now ceased to have any influence, and
the way was now clear for the full statement of papal claims and
their general acceptance in the West during the pontificate of
Leo I. In the East, however, these claims were never accepted. For
instance, the Council of Chalcedon, which was predominantly an
Eastern council, acknowledged the pre-eminent dignity of the
Roman see and adopted the Tome of Leo as one of the touch-
stones of Christological orthodoxy, but it did not recognize any
authority or jurisdiction inherent in either the bishop or the see
of Rome. Ultimate authority belonged to the general councils of
the whole Church, and jurisdiction was properly exercised by
bishops, metropolitans, and local patriarchs.

This refusal to acknowledge Roman jurisdiction over the whole
Church reminds us that this period was often marked by dissen-
sion. Disagreements concerning the Roman see were, however, insignificant by comparison with the great heretical and schismatic
movements which were a feature of Christian history from New
Testament times onward. In the New Testament itself we can see
the Church's reaction, for instance, to both Gnostic and Docetic
doctrines; we can also see in the New Testament how, in the
first few decades of the Church's history, the unity of the Church
was endangered by personal differences, rivalry, jealousy, and
self-seeking as well as by theological disagreements. The Church
treated with extreme seriousness any teaching which denied
Christian affirmations about the goodness and uniqueness of God
or which undermined the Christian message of salvation. Gnosti-

cism and Marcionism in their different ways came into the former category; in the latter category came Arian teaching, which denied the divinity of Christ, and also later teaching about the person of Christ which did not do justice either to his complete humanity (Apollinarianism) or to the unity of his person (Nestorianism); and also Pelagianism, which inadequately treated the work of God in man's salvation. All these varieties of teaching and belief—and others besides—endangered proper understanding of the salvation which the Church existed to proclaim and to offer, and they all came to be regarded as heretical; very often these heretical groups formed separate, schismatic churches. In the formation and continuation of these separate churches many other factors apart from purely theological considerations played an important part: personal animosity, rivalry between sees, political influence, and linguistic misunderstandings all had their share. It is impossible, for instance, to study the course of the Arian controversy in the fourth century or the events leading up to the Councils of Ephesus and Chalcedon in the fifth century without being aware of the interplay of theological and nontheological factors.

This interplay can also be seen in the history of other schismatic movements which did not have a purely doctrinal basis for their origin. Many of these movements were concerned with disciplinary matters: the appeal of Montanism to Tertullian was certainly the strict line which it took about disciplinary problems; the origins of the Novatianist and Donatist churches and of the Melitian church in Egypt are to be found in the disciplinary problems which faced the Church at the end of the Decian and Diocletianic persecutions. All sides appealed to the New Testament, and they all found justification there for their positions about disciplinary matters on which the Church had come to no common mind by the end of the New Testament period. But however sincere was their appeal to the New Testament and to authentic Christian tradition, it is clear that personal rivalry as well as social, ethnic, and economic factors played important parts both in the origins and in the subsequent history of these schismatic churches.

Even after this brief sketch of the Church's early history it will be apparent that many of the problems which were to vex the

Church later in her history and which are still unresolved today
have their origin in this early period: in fact, the precise nature
of the problems is itself often part of our inheritance from the
early Church. The Church's relations with the secular power
were, for instance, a perennial difficulty throughout the Middle
Ages: this difficulty did not disappear at the Reformation. Nowadays we live in a predominantly secular era and in secular states:
in some countries there are still established national churches; in
others, there is still a strong alliance between the secular power
and a supranational church; in others, open hostility between an
avowedly atheist state or a Moslem state and the Christian
Churches; in others, the state is confessedly neutral. Christians
puzzled about their proper relationship with the state may be
helped by the Church's witness in the pre-Constantinian era and
by her mistakes in the centuries which followed.

Another problem which perplexes Christians today is the nature
of the Christian Church: what is the relationship of the Church
to the churches? The insight of Cyprian and Augustine may help
us toward a solution. What should be the place of the papacy, of
the episcopate, of general councils in the Christian Church? Our
study of early Church history may help us to see in their historical perspective the pronouncements made, for instance, by Boni-
face VIII in 1302 or by the Vatican Council of 1870, and also to
have a fuller appreciation of the work of the Second Vatican
Council on the subject of the episcopate. Again, how is the holi-
ness of the Christian Church and of its members to be understood
in the twentieth century? The history of early monasticism may
help us to understand the doctrine of the double standard which
dominated medieval thought on this subject, and to understand
how the medieval Church came to conclusions which are generally unacceptable today. Again, Christians are now trying to re-
state the gospel of salvation and the basic credal and conciliar affirmations about God and Jesus in terms which are meaningful
in the twentieth century; before any reinterpretation or restate-
ment is possible, however, it will be necessary to understand why
theologians in the patristic period used the particular words and
phrases which have become normative in the Church, and equally

necessary to discover what they intended to convey by means of this terminology: the study of early Church history will make this understanding much easier.

In this short compass it has been possible to mention only some of the more important trends and events in the history of the early Church. For a fuller understanding of the period it will be necessary to read both a general outline and also the documents and authors of the period.[3] No general outline of the Church's history, nor any collection of documents or Fathers, can present an absolutely unbiased, objective picture of the events of this or of any period. Any historian or complier must be interpretative and selective: Eusebius of Caesarea, the first historian of the Church,[4] was himself a patient collector of documents and information, but also a partisan as compiler and commentator. He saw in the Church's history the wonderful working of providence: a century later, Augustine in his *City of God* saw the guiding hand of providence in the fortunes of both Church and state. We may be less confident than Eusebius or Augustine in the possibility of discerning the finger of God in the history of our period or of any period, but, as we make our own interpretative assessment of the

[3] The most easily accessible outline is to be found in the first four volumes of the *Histoire de l'Église* produced under the general direction of A. Fliche and V. Martin (Paris: Bloud & Gay, [1934–]). These volumes have been translated into English under the titles: *The History of the Primitive Church*, by J. Lebreton and J. Zeiller, E. C. Messenger, trans. (New York: The Macmillan Co., 1949), and *The Church in the Christian Roman Empire*, by J. R. Palanque *et al.*, with the same translator (New York: The Macmillan Co., 1953). The most convenient selection of documents to the year 337 is in *A New Eusebius*, J. Stevenson, ed. (New York: The Macmillan Co., 1957), and until the appearance of the next volume of documents, which is planned to illustrate the Church's history from 337 onward, use may be made of *Documents Illustrative of the History of the Church*, Vol. II, 313–461 A.D., B. J. Kidd, ed. (New York: The Macmillan Co., 1923). The Fathers are available in a variety of translations and selections: among translations the "Library of the Fathers," the "Ante-Nicene Fathers," the "Select Library of Nicene and Post-Nicene Fathers," and the series of "Ancient Christian Writers" are all generally accessible, while among selections the "Library of Christian Classics" is especially useful.

[4] His *Ecclesiastical History* is easily available in the critical edition by H. J. Lawlor and J. E. Oulton, eds., 2 vols. (London: S.P.C.K., 1927–28).

Church's early history, we may with reasonable confidence of success have a more limited aim: to find there the clue to the understanding of the Church's problems in the twentieth century and also the clue to their solution. This aim may be less exalted and more prosaic, but if we study history for some practical purpose, this does not mean that we may not also find the study interesting for its own sake.

5. Modern Church History

Jerald C. Brauer

The division of church history into periods remains one of the most difficult problems confronting the discipline, and it is met most acutely in the division between medieval and modern. The traditional division of the field into three major parts has persisted, though it has long appeared unsatisfactory. The problem is confronted the moment one seeks to sketch out the area to be covered in modern Church history. Where does "modern" Church history begin? To state it more precisely, does it begin with the Reformation?

Early in this century, Ernst Troeltsch startled Church historians by turning Church history around and starting with an analysis of the contemporary age. He then moved backward to compare and contrast this reality with the Reformation, and on that basis he was led to certain conclusions concerning the affinities of the Reformation for the medieval world as over against the modern world. Setting aside the question of the accuracy or adequacy of Troeltsch's conclusions, this particular approach made a profound impact on the interpretation of the Reformation as the pivotal point between the medieval and the modern. Troeltsch compelled historians to rethink generalizations on this problem and made absolutely clear how difficult it was to place the Reformation within either the medieval or the modern period.

I shall leave it within the modern as a transitional phase between the two periods, but as an epoch in history with a distinctive genius of its own, which was probably never realized, even in partial form. The student of modern Church history must, then, be prepared to look seriously and in depth at the medieval period if he wishes to understand the modern. His point of departure is roughly 1300. At that point in history, numerous forces were at work drastically modifying the medieval West and radically questioning some of its basic forms and assumptions.

It will not do to judge these forces and changes simply as the morning star heralding the dawn of the Reformation epoch, which in turn ushered in the modern period. In a very profound sense, they were both the culmination and repudiation of the medieval. Dante, the symbol of this ambivalence, has been described as a horseman sitting astride the Middle Ages, driving in his spurs to make it move ahead, yet holding back on the reins.

I

The first phase of modern Church history is, then, the transitional period that begins around 1300 and culminates at the time of the Reformation. One should pay particular attention to the increasing complexity of factors suddenly brought into play within history and the subtle interplay of old and new forces as they slowly began to reshape history. Not that medieval life was so simple and uncomplicated, but rather the modern is defined, in part, by the emergence of new factors and an ever increasing complexity in all aspects of life. For example, the rise of the new national states did not await the Reformation. This was irrevocably under way long before Luther, and the new nationalism was born in the cradle of newly emerged forces and factors.

Within this circle of complexity, several things are to be carefully studied. The peculiar fortunes of the papacy, contrasting radically with its role and status in the high medieval period, are to be noted. For two-thirds of a century the chair of Peter was located in France, the most powerful nation in Europe and the most thoroughly modern of the rising nation-states. It is difficult to estimate the psychological shock of this Babylonian captivity on the mind of Europe. It must have been profound. Special attention should be given to the writings of Dante, Occam, and Marsilius of Padua as expressive both of the shock and the search for new political and religious forms. However, the student must be careful not to overlook some of the positive consequences of Avignon. Europe never had an opportunity to recover from that shock before it was confronted by a religious disaster—the Great Schism. For an additional third of a century, the Western world was shaken by another spectacle involving Mother Church.

It is at this point that the forces pressing for reform and for reunification find conciliarism as an instrument to achieve their goals. It is difficult to overestimate the significance of conciliarism not only for this moment in Church history but also for the role it was to play as an ideal in the entire modern period of Church history. It was a view to which the reformers were to appeal and to which various Protestant churches appealed as they struggled with the problem of extreme diversification in the Church.

The pre-Reformation period witnessed also the rise and development of one of the most significant intellectual and cultural forces in Western history: the Renaissance. The subtle interplay of interests and influences between Christianity and the Renaissance is to be carefully noted. It is not sufficient to mark the obvious, namely, that one segment of the Renaissance seriously questioned certain basic beliefs and assumptions of Western Christianity, and that another segment provided that same Christianity with invaluable humanistic tools. The consequences of the Renaissance are far more significant and subtle than such an obvious generalization. The intellectual, aesthetic, and moral forces and fermentation generated by the Renaissance are one of the keys to the entire modern historical development.

Though one should not overlook the economic, commercial, and political revolutions occurring in the pre-Reformation period, one should be aware of the fresh vitality expressing itself within Western Christianity. The efforts at reform within the religious orders, the rise of new forms of popular or mass religion, and the development of various types of discontent should not be ignored. A host of national reformers led by giants such as John Wycliffe, John Huss, and Cardinal Ximenez provide ample evidence of the various kinds and depth of discontent within the Church. They also reflect differing kinds of solutions to the problem of corruption.

This epoch witnessed one of the richest outbursts of mysticism

in Christian history, and it was a mysticism interested in reform.
The Brethren of the Common Life exhibit a remarkable combination of devotion, action, service, education, and reform. Names
such as Meister Eckhart, John Tauler, Henry Suso, and the famous document, the *Theologica Germanica*, remind us of the
vitality within the Church at this moment in history. The pre-
Reformation epoch also provides us with an opportunity to study
the sermons, and their consequences, of such great preachers as
Savonarola, Wessel von Gansfort, Geiler von Kaisersberg, and
others. Large numbers of humanistic scholars, Nicholas of Cusa,
Agricola, Reuchlin, Erasmus, Colet, More, and others, were calling
for reform and introducing methods of study into the universities
that were to provide a ready audience for the reformers and their
work. These are but a few of the men and movements to be
analyzed in accounting for the shift from the medieval to the
modern world through the Reformation. Already the presence of
numerous new forces and realities is obvious. Equally obvious is
the increasing complexity of interplay of these forces as history
works in and through them.

II

However medieval the reformers and the Reformation, they
were equally a step into the modern world. Judicious assessment
at this point is necessary if one is to evaluate the nature of the
Reformation and understand the dynamics of the emerging
modern world. There is no better point at which to dig in than
the life and career of Martin Luther. It is not by chance that so
much has been written in an attempt to evaluate, understand, mis-
understand, deify, and vilify Luther. He remains central to any
comprehension of the Reformation. Recent research has emphasized the point frequently forgotten in past polemics: Luther's
intention was only to reform the Church, not to break from it;
therefore a fresh appreciation of the Catholic elements in Luther
is now possible. Special attention should be given to Luther's
understanding of the nature of the Church and the authority of
Scripture, and to his conception of justification seen in a fuller
context of Christian thought. As the dialogue between Roman
Catholics and Protestants continues, special nuances in Luther's

theology will be brought to the foreground. This is not to be deplored but understood as an inevitable and salutary consequence of the Church seeking to understand her present in light of her past.

Luther was forced into many *ad hoc* decisions as the Reformation took root, and he was compelled to become Protestant. All students of modern Church history will note with interest how the Lutheran churches were organized, how the Reformation spread from Wittenberg, especially throughout Scandinavia, and how a special Lutheran tradition grounded in confessions of faith and forms of worship soon developed. The particular ways in which Lutheranism related itself to the state and to culture will be noted. Anglo-Saxon students require a special reminder to evaluate the Scandinavian countries at this point in addition to studying the developments in Germany. It is interesting to note that from the very first Lutheranism retained a close connection with the arts, particularly music, and it is possible to trace through modern Church history this special Lutheran emphasis among the Protestant churches.

To note adequately both the variety and the differences within the Reformation, the special emphases of Zwingli should be studied. He quickly found himself opposed to both Luther and the rising Anabaptists. Though there were many points of similarity between the two reformers, Luther was correct in stating a difference in spirit. It is this difference between Luther and Zwingli that marked the one as more Catholic and more ontologically oriented and the other as more Protestant and more moralistically oriented. Hence, the difference deserves careful study.

The work of John Calvin and the consolidation of Protestantism in the second generation can hardly be overstressed. All students of Church history must work through the *Institutes* carefully and study the experiment at Geneva. The former remains a basic resource for Christian theology to this day. The latter represents the first systematic attempt by Protestants to create a self-conscious community disciplined in its determination to fulfill the will of God in society in so far as this was possible in history.

Not to be overlooked by the student of the modern Church is the important but not as well-known work of the Rhineland

Reformation. Through men such as Bucer and Oecolampadius, Strassburg and other cities on the Rhine became centers for developing the famous "covenant theology" that was to sweep the Swiss Reformed, both Zwinglian and Calvinistic, transform Dutch and Scotch Calvinism, and pour into English Puritanism.

The English Reformation presents a special situation of its own, and therefore particular problems. The tendency for a long time was to view the Reformation in England in isolation from the Continental reform movement. There was just enough truth behind this to make it plausible. Recent scholarship has restored the balance between the English movement's continuities with, and discontinuities from, the Continental. In studying the English Reformation, the student should be prepared to look for different forms of religious expression or concern from those on the Continent, otherwise one might prematurely judge that there were no genuinely religious elements in the English Reformation. One cannot ignore the particularly close connection between crown and miter, culture and religion, in England. Neither can one deny its concern to be both Catholic and Protestant.

Of almost unique importance on the English scene is the rise and development of Puritanism. This can be viewed either as another stage in the English Reformation or as an attempt to reform the Reformation. In either case, it has no real parallel on the Continent. It cannot be understood as the counterpart of the Continental left wing, but only as a distinctive English movement which drew particular emphases from the Church-wide Reformation. Puritanism presents the student with an excellent opportunity to study the interrelation between Christianity and politics, a Protestant attempt at a total social ethic, and the first beginnings of the the denominationalism that comes to dominate the Anglo-American culture.

In recent years, the most creative reinterpretation in this segment of modern Church history has occurred in what has come to be called the left wing of the Reformation, and more recently the radical Reformation, as over against the magisterial Reformation. What the new Luther research has done for that segment of the epoch has now been done for the radical side of the Reformation. For the first time it can now be viewed, not as an ab-

horrent, schismatic Protestant malformation, but as an integral
part of the reform effort with its own distinctive genius as well
as its continuities. Attention should be given to the variety within
the radical Reformation, its rootage in humanism, its doctrines of
the Church, its concepts of ethics, and its special views on the relations of Church and state, religion and culture. Within the
radical Reformation, one encounters such diverse groups as the
pacifistic Anabaptists, the violent Millenarians, the "Spirit Mys-
tics," and the anti-Trinitarians.

Careful study of the role of the Reformation leads one to an
assessment of the Roman Catholic response to this effort. Once
the Roman Church had rejected the reforming efforts, there was
little alternative on either side but a radical break more drastic
than either wanted. Roman response to this break is frequently
designated as the Counter Reformation, a term disliked by Roman
Catholics. One question to be carefully investigated is the nature
of the Roman response and its consequences both for itself and
for Protestantism. One should be aware of the new spirit of Rome
that arises from the Council of Trent. Roman Catholicism's remarkable resurgence, led by the Jesuits and other new religious
orders, its newly defined dogmatic and doctrinal stance, and the
special role of the papacy cannot be overlooked. New forms of
piety, a vigorous battle to win back defected nations and to invade
Protestant strongholds, plus a fresh vital effort at missions to
heathen and heretics deserve careful analysis.

One consequence of these complex developments marking the
shift from medieval to modern Church history was a series of wars
and struggles between the Roman Catholics and Protestants, and
within Protestantism itself. For a century and a half, until 1648
on the Continent and 1689 in England, the world witnessed an apparently unending series of religious wars. It is important to study
these, both to understand the peculiar tie between religion and
culture at this moment in history and to note the replacement of
that tie by other and newer forces. The epoch of the religious
wars demonstrates the virtual impossibility of distinguishing between religion as the substance and as the form of culture through
much of the Middle Ages, right up through the Reformation. In
many ways religion *was* culture throughout this epoch. It was the

breaking of this all-pervading presence of religion that marks one of the major new emphases in the modern world.

III

Before moving into the distinctively modern segment of modern Church history, the student should study closely the settlements, both religious and political, which mark the end of religious wars. On the Continent, this provides a picture of religious alignment that remains virtually unchanged until past World War II. To be sure, the radical Reformation had no rights, or very limited ones, until the late nineteenth and twentieth centuries. But the external ecclesiastical map of Europe was drawn by the Treaty of Westphalia. Likewise the major theological confessions were all written by the end of the seventeenth century. In England, 1689 marks the point of settlement in the Church of England in its relations to the crown and to dissent. Henceforth the principle of toleration was to prevail, and dissent was to play a continuing role in English life. The shift from medieval to modern was complete.

Secularism is the broadest term used to convey the shift that has occurred in the modern Church. This is understandable, yet inadequate and even confusing. It is accurate in that it marks the demise of the Church-controlled or -dominated civilization and the passing of the identification of religion and culture as to both substance and form. But it is misleading in that it leaves the impression of a civilization in no way related to religion. This is the major problem of interpretation in modern Church history. There is no denying that religion remains vital and alive in the contemporary world. It has survived Fascism, Marxism, and bourgeois society, and will survive suburbia. But it is also obvious that Christianity is not now related to culture and politics the way it once was. This dilemma should attract the student's major attention.

It has been stated that the modern Church is marked by a complexity and interplay of innumerable forces not evident in the medieval Church. This fact presents special difficulties in the attempt to make sense of the modern epoch. The problem is not primarily a result of our identification with the period or the impossibility of getting all the pertinent facts. Both of these factors do present a difficulty, but the basic problem is the complexity of the forces at work and the lack of an idea or conception of the Church. This will be dealt with at a later point; here it illustrates the difficulty. The only fair approach to take in this situation is to point out the forces that appear central to even a preliminary understanding of the modern Church and that are encountered in all the nations and in the people of God in various modern churches.

The first basic factor that the student dare not ignore is the tremendous missionary outburst that marks the entire Western Church, Roman Catholic and Protestant. Professor K. S. Latourette thinks this is the major category of interpretation for the modern Church, and he has written its history from that point of view. Careful attention must be given to the origin, methods, and consequences of this activity. Especially instructive is a comparative study of Roman Catholic and Protestant efforts at missions. To trace through the story of missions from the seventeenth into the twentieth century is one way to write the history of the modern Church. Most of the major movements and influences at work in it are encountered, one way or another, in the mission development.

A cursory glance at missions reveals its intimate connections with Pietism, revivalism, and the reform movements that arose out of them. This history cannot be understood apart from Pietism. In fact, much of the strength and weakness of Protestantism, throughout the modern epoch, can be understood primarily through this factor. Unfortunately, a proper evaluation of the nature and role of Pietism has not been made; therefore the student must be very careful in his studies of this formative force. Pietism is of importance not only because of its relations with missions and reform; it is equally important because it reshaped the nature of the Church, its hymnody, Christian theology, and Christian ethics, both personal and social. It affected every segment of the Protestant Church and even found a counterpart in changing forms of Roman Catholic piety. In the American scene it shaped evangelical denominationalism, which predominates to this day. Pietism radically subjectivized the Christian faith and conditioned it in ways which ill prepared it for the modern world. These are issues which demand the closest scrutiny.

The radical change that beset the institutional Church in the modern period cannot be properly evaluated unless the politico-social revolutions that reshaped that world are seen in their dialectical relationship to the Church. The modern epoch has witnessed the discovery of the New World and the rediscovery of Asia and Africa; it has undergone an amazing surge in population that mounts in intensity each decade; it has passed through the industrial revolution with its accompanying technological revolution; it gave birth to the mercantile system, and then to laissez-faire economy. The modern nation-state built on family dynasties succumbed to democratic revolutions, while a new form of nationalism proved more potent than any particular political form. No sooner had the liberal democracies consolidated their gains than Fascism and Marxism arose to project still further revolutions in the political sphere. Meanwhile, aroused and potent Europe colonized throughout the world and brought vast areas under colonial control. This was hardly accomplished before two world wars and a fresh outburst of nationalism destroyed the colonial empires.

Meanwhile, the Churches were not unaffected by these world-shaking revolutions. At times they were in step to aid and abet the process. At other times they fought off the changes. In either case, the Church was both institutionally and doctrinally shaped and reshaped by these powerful forces. This is precisely what the student of Church history should expect to encounter, because the people of God are very much in the world, though ultimately not of it. The historian must seek to understand the subtle interplay of these forces in the life of the Church and in the lives of Christians. In the brief span of the modern Church, more drastic changes have occurred during any half-century than in the entire period from Charlemagne to Luther.

Equally profound and consistent with the increasing complexity and rapidity of change that mark the modern world is the series of intellectual revolutions that started with Bacon and Descartes and is still under way today. One ought never to underestimate the significance of the Enlightenment for the intellectual and institutional history of the Church. One might argue that, in part, the Church has been trying to come to terms with it ever since. This is especially true in that it first posed acutely the question of a radically different view of the cosmos. In some sense, the question of demythologizing is but the continuation of the same issue after history has moved through romanticism, idealism, pragmatism, and existentialism. Surely the intellectual revolution and its consequences for the formulation of Christian doctrine are not only not finished; they are barely under way.

Another way of stating this issue is to speak of the impact of science on the mind and on the day-to-day activities of modern man. Whatever the protests of innocence from both sides, neither science nor religion has really sought to understand the other or developed a point of view that permitted a creative interplay between the two. The temptation is always for one to swallow the other or ignore it. This remains one of the central issues confronting modern culture and one of the fundamental issues challenging the Christian faith. The Church has already learned that the answer does not lie in a simple surrender to the world view, methods, and presuppositions of modern science. She has tried that in a variety of ways. Many would question whether the answer lies in the simple assertion that Christian faith need not worry about such questions—that it must simply proclaim the gospel and administer the sacraments. The question is rather *how* the Church proclaims, witnesses, and embodies the gospel in a world that looks at reality in a certain way. Much of the modern history of Christian thought can be written and studied with this problem in the foreground.

Pluralism is an additional phenomenon that marks the modern Church everywhere today. It should be carefully investigated and analyzed. Its history and roots are complex, its influence incalculable. At one point it was thought that this peculiar situation marked only the American churches. Today it is obvious that it is the condition of the Christian Church throughout the world in all situations, even where there is an official establishment. In those nations, the pluralism arises from the fact that many other quasi religions compete for the loyalty of the people. In fact, Christianity now appears as a minority in most of these nations. Thus, pluralism is not simply a description of the condition of the

Church today; it is also a new situation, the special situation in which the Church is called to witness, and so a universal factor in the modern Church.

The rise and development of ecumenicity is another such major factor that calls for special attention. One cannot make sense of the contemporary Church, indeed of modern Church history, apart from the strenuous efforts to realize anew the oneness of the Church in the face of both its variety and its divisiveness. The ecumenical movement includes not only the history of the World Council of Churches, the various national councils, and the different denominational world federations; it especially reflects the movements and men who brought it into being and who sustain it. Above all, special care must be taken not to overlook the role of the laity. Also to be studied are the new theological emphases that have developed in the context of ecumenicity. Finally, the student notes the emergence of a new process in our age: the dialogue between Roman Catholics and Protestants and between Christians and Jews. All of this is to be understood in the wider circle of the ecumenical movement, which itself is a distinctive mark of the modern Church. It now appears that the calling of Vatican II by Pope John XXIII may be the most important ecclesiastical event in the twentieth century. Careful attention must be given to its achievements and possible consequences.

Particular attention must be given to Eastern Orthodoxy during the modern period. Large sections of Western Church history can be written with little or no reference to it, but this cannot be said of the modern period. From the moment that Western culture made an impact on Russia, and in the moment that Russia emerged as a great world power, the relationship between Eastern and Western Christianity achieved a new level. With the Marxist conquest of Russia, the eyes of the entire Christian world were turned east to note the consequences for Christianity. Thus, the modern period demands that the Church history student pay particular attention to Orthodoxy. Likewise, the participation of Orthodoxy in the ecumenical movement pulls the Western Christian out of the comfortable habit of ignoring the special genius of Eastern Orthodoxy. Its concept of the Church and of the relation of religion and culture, its liturgical life, and its monastic communities call for particular consideration.

Finally, the modern period confronts the theological scholar with a new challenge This is frequently spoken of as the post-Christian epoch. Nietzsche proclaimed that God is dead, and man could never be the same. In our own time, Tillich, Bultmann, and Bonhoeffer have persuasively argued that the world has come of age, so that earlier forms of religiousness are no longer adequate. These are but a few ways of saying the same thing: a drastic change has taken place in the modern age, and the Church is not sure how to cope with it. It is this new religionlessness that the student of modern Church history must assess with discernment and great care. This is where Christianity is today, and one must know how it arrived in this situation.

IV

It is a serious question what role Church history, in this case modern Church history, should play in the theological curriculum. Perhaps it could be dropped. Even though it never sought to be queen among the theological disciplines, Church history did have certain illusions about being a handmaiden of the Lord or at least a doorkeeper in his house of theological studies. There is question as to what role it plays in the preparation of theological students. The average student views it as a necessary hurdle to jump in order to receive a degree. Bible and theology are absolutely necessary; practical theology really prepares one for the basic activities of the ministry; the newer disciplines seeking to relate Christianity to culture appear interesting and relevant; but it is hard to appreciate the significance and role of Church history.

Much of this misunderstanding is due to the Church historians themselves. Theirs is a discipline which has frequently engaged in piling up more and more minute facts on the assumption that once all the facts were in, a generalization might be risked. Church history often has become chronicle rather than history, and to this degree divinity students are correct in rejecting it. Chronicle is necessary and of value to the disciplined historian, but hardly appreciated by the general theological student.

The heart of the problem appears to be a confusion as to the nature and method of Church history. In its efforts to achieve respectability and keep abreast of scholarship in general history, Church history has adopted the methods current in the field. This is always, in one sense, unavoidable. The various theological disciplines must be conversant with and use the methods employed in parallel disciplines in other fields of learning, in so far as these are appropriate. Nevertheless, it is seldom possible to adopt these methods outright without first discovering those points where the nature of theological inquiry—in this case Church history—calls for a different use of such methods. Shall we say a more dialectical use?

The Church historian cannot do his work independently of his fellow historians; he is very dependent upon them and, hopefully, contributes to them. In one profound way, his material and method are identical with those of historians in general. Both are concerned about the past and use special tools and a disciplined approach to get at it. All historians put questions to the past, because they think the past is of real consequence for the present. Even those who argue that the past is of value for its own sake are really saying that, for them, the past is of value for its own sake and therefore worthy of their study.

The concern for the past is usually rooted in the assumption that the past is our past and helps to explain who we are and how we got where we are. It is further assumed that, though this knowledge may not give us specific answers as to where we are going and how we should get there, it should provide us with a more realistic sense of the possible than we would otherwise have, and an awareness of the dynamics of movement toward our goals. The historian tries to find out what people have done, when they did it, where they did it, and why. To be concerned with anything less is not to be concerned with history. The better the historian, the more subtle his handling of these questions and the more eloquent his answers.

To respond to such questions, the Church historian uses the method of historical study. He tries to find out, in a carefully disciplined way, as much as he can about them. This is commonly referred to as collecting the data or gathering the "facts." The Church historian has no special method at this point and in no way modifies the basic methods of general historical scholarship. To be sure, even in this area of "fact" there are degrees of certainty, but the degrees are not dependent upon being a Church historian.

The other aspect of the historian's method is the framework of interpretation he employs as he attempts to answer the questions posed. Many contemporary historians are willing to admit that this framework of interpretation is equally important in their method, but others insist that to admit this is to reduce history to propaganda, in which facts are subjected to a shuffling around within the framework. But the facts should speak for themselves and provide their own interpretation if they are accurately discovered and described.

By definition, the Church historian cannot stand with those who take such a positivistic approach. Both his Christian faith and his knowledge of dialectics prevent it. Unfortunately, much of Church history is still written from a strictly positivistic point of view which assumes that if the author provides more and more knowledge of the "facts" of Church history, this will, in itself, provide answers to the questions put to it. Indeed, this view assumes that the facts will themselves determine the questions. There is, of course, some truth in both assumptions. But the truth resides in the correlation between framework and fact.

The Church historian assumes that the framework of interpretation makes a profound difference in the questions he asks, the nature and credibility of the facts he seeks, and the tentative answers he offers. The framework itself assumes a dialectical relation between the "facts" and the ultimate or comprehensive point of view of the historian. They enrich one another, contradict each other, sustain one another, and criticize each other. Many historians are willing to admit this as over against the straight positivists. The Church historian is distinguished finally from his other colleagues in the field of history by the content of the framework with which he works. In that the framework cannot be divorced absolutely from the search for facts and the construction of mean-

ing, there is, then, this difference between the Church historian
and other historians.

This can be illustrated by reference to a number of historical
problems. Take, for example, the origin of the *Book of Mormon*.
What the historian is prepared to accept as fact or as evidence is
not unrelated to the so-called framework or ultimate point of view
with which he works. After the acceptance or rejection of certain
evidence, the further problem of the interpretation of materials
remains. Both the total perspective and the evidence are brought
to bear at this point. Generally speaking, most historians, including Church historians, share a wide range of "fact" in spite of
differences of framework; however, there are degrees of difference in the acceptance of various so-called facts.

The total or final framework within which the Church historian
operates is some conception of the Christian faith; thus, he is at
this point a theologian. Furthermore, the Church historian has a
particular concern for the Church and for the meaning of history
as seen within the Christian perspective. It is not that he is unaware
of or disinterested in other Christian concepts. Rather, the truth
is that he cannot be deeply concerned with the Church or with
history unless these are in the wider context of Christian theology.
But granted this basis, he is especially concerned for the concept
of the Church and the nature and meaning of history.

As indicated earlier, modern Church history presents one with
an acute problem. It is difficult to locate the Church as it is
normally understood in Christian history. Up through the medieval period and through most of the Reformation, it appeared possible clearly to identify the Church and to write its history. This
traditional view breaks down in the modern period. Rather than
showing the Church as the central institution dominating culture
and society, the modern period confronts us with many churches,
each claiming a special role but none really expecting to be taken
as the final embodiment of God's people.

This has led some Church historians to argue that Church history cannot be written in the modern period—only histories of
individual denominations or a recounting of various religious
forces are feasible. Either the history of the Church—hence

Church history—is no longer possible, or it must await a special synthesis of the individual histories of all the denominations. Granted the traditional conception of Church history grounded on a particular view of the Church, such a position is consistent.

One of the central problems confronting all Church historians today, and the modern historian in particular, is the theological problem of the nature of the Church. It is indeed strange that many have not yet taken seriously the theological renaissance of the past thirty years, which provides numerous fresh ways of understanding the Church, so that it again becomes possible to write Church history. As Prof. Sidney E. Mead recently stated, "The beginning of the study is neither to identify, nor to prove the existence of 'the church' in the history-that-happens, but to assume that it is there all the time."

This assumption is part of the basic commitment or framework with which the Church historian operates. He believes certain things about God, man, and history. He views history as having a beginning, a middle, and an end; thus, he can speak of an historical process with unique meanings and an ultimate meaning. The new reality encountered in the Christ is believed to be the clue to history and its final fulfillment. Through this reality, the Church historian believes that the people of God are always in history, always taking shape or form; therefore one can pose serious questions about their community and its history. The people of the present are part of the people of the past and those yet to come. The particular form or shape of this community is likewise related, though it is not always identical in form. Thus, it is his view of the Church that enables the Church historian to risk writing Church history in the modern world, or confines him to the task of commenting on particular denominations.

V

Wide reading in modern Church history soon reveals certain glaring weaknesses. One of the most obvious is the almost total lack of knowledge of or concern with American Church history on the part of English and European historians. Attention will be paid to men or movements of purely local interest, but the New England theocratic experiment or the radical subjectivizing of Protestantism in American revivalism and its consequences for missions are completely overlooked.

Many of the leading features of modern Church life throughout the Christian world were first encountered in America, and it would be of great help to European Church historians if they would engage in a careful analysis of them. The full experiment with religious liberty is one such feature. Perhaps of greater importance is the reformulation of the Church into a new type in America—the denomination—which is neither the classical Church nor sect type. That which first emerged on the American scene is what has come to prevail throughout the European nations, yet their Church histories seem totally unaware of this fact.

These are but a few examples of the provincialism that still marks many of the modern European Church histories. They can no longer adequately understand themselves unless they understood what happened to the Christian community in America. On the American scene, an attempt was made to relate religion and culture in an utterly new way. Its successes and failures would be a great help in the process of self-understanding and reinterpretation now taking place throughout the Christian Church in the modern world. The American experience has ceased to be a curiosity or an anomaly, if it ever was. It has proved a prelude for what is happening in much of Protestantism in the Western world. Full churches in America should not mislead European historians into thinking that the American experience is unique; it is only uniquely modern.

Modern Church history could also profit if it were to use greater imagination in adopting methods and insights from other disciplines besides history. For example, the discipline of the history of religions has produced numerous creative works on the problem of methodology which would be of immeasurable help to the Church historian. Thus far, the Church historian has persisted in viewing his discipline only in the context of Western culture founded on Greco-Roman traditions. This is fully understandable. However, if a few attempts were made to view particular problems in Church history within the broader context of the history of religions, it might prove most exciting and stimulating. The contemporary history of missions cannot be written apart from this wider context. The study of the ascetic element in Christianity would appear quite different from its traditional treatment in Church history. These are but a few random examples.

Finally, the contemporary Church historian writing on modern Church history would do well if he were to view his discipline not simply as a scientific study but also as an art. History at its best is always an art, a creative achievement of the human spirit. It seems impossible for the Church historian to admit this. It is unfortunate, because it means he is not read by his colleagues. His task is to create a vision of the total life of the people of God at a given moment in history. He should do it with imagination, clarity, and precision. If he wishes to present but a portion of that total life, it will, nevertheless, help one to understand the totality. He should help himself and others to see and understand from whence they have come, where they are going, and wherein their freedom and their necessity lie.

6. Systematic Theology

Daniel T. Jenkins

I

The normative as distinct from the historical disciplines of theological study are themselves usually divided into two sections: those concerned with the status of religion in general and those concerned specifically with the Christian faith. The former are customarily gathered together under the heading of the philosophy of religion. This, in its turn, is divided in various ways, the most typical being that which separates the epistemology from the ontology of religion. Some people interpret the sociology and the psychology of religion in such a way as almost to make them a branch of the philosophy of religion. The subject of apologetics is difficult to place in any formal scheme. In some places it is studied under the heading of the philosophy of religion and sometimes it is more closely related to Christian dogmatics, depending on whether its main interest is in the justification of the independent validity of religious experience or in the answering of objections to the truth of the Christian faith.

The specifically Christian normative discipline is usually called systematic or constructive theology in English-speaking countries. Largely through the influence of Karl Barth, however, the practice has been growing of calling it by its old name, dogmatics. Some theologians, and again notably Barth, believe that this discipline is so central that Christian ethics should be included in dogmatics, and that whatever is valid in apologetics is part of the dogmatic task. We shall have occasion to look at these contentions later. "Dogmatics" is not a term which sounds attractive in most modern ears and it needs a little explanation. The average liberally-minded person takes a dogma to mean a sharply formulated statement of a belief, which rigidly excludes other beliefs and is imposed upon the mind from the outside, generally on the authority of a powerful organization which is able to make acceptance or rejection of this formulation a test of membership. Similarly, a dogmatic person is thought of as one who tries to commend his point of view not by demonstrating its inherent reasonableness in free discussion but by the force with which he asserts it and silences opposition. Such dogmatism is rightly regarded as an assault on human freedom, and when it is remembered how often churches and individuals have tried to enforce their views in this way in the past, people are naturally suspicious of a word whose associations appear to lend encouragement to it.

It must be clearly seen, therefore, that dogmatics and dogmatism are not the same thing. Dogmatics may or may not be a good word to use in these days, but it does not necessarily carry with it approval of irrationality or coercion. The nearest to an original meaning of the word *dogma* that can be readily reached is that it is the fundamental principle of a Greek philosophical sect. From this, it came to refer to the basic belief which united any group of people who lived in close fellowship as a distinctive community. Dogmatics is, therefore, the study of those fundamental beliefs which hold Christians together in the fellowship of the Church. It asks the questions, "What is the essential kerygma, that which those who first knew Christ proclaim concerning God to men; how have men understood it in the Spirit throughout the ages, and how are we to understand it as the Word of God in our own situation?"

Because it asks these questions, dogmatics must be seen as the climax of theological study, which depends on the other parts of it and in which these other parts are related to our present situation. It clearly must presuppose careful study of the Old and New Testaments, and of the experience of the Church throughout the ages as recorded in Church history. It has a particularly close relation to the history of the Church's doctrines, since it sees itself

as part of the ongoing conversation of Christian people in this
world about God and his ways. Unless a large part of its activity
is taken up with the study of the past in this way, it is likely to be
seriously misled. Yet its distinctiveness lies in its relation to the
present. It has to examine Christian ideas in relation to the thought
of its own time so that it can discover afresh what the lordship of
God in Christ means for its own time. Its preoccupation is, as Karl
Barth says in a famous phrase, with "the Church's concentrated
anxiety and concern about her own most intimate responsibility,"
that of seeking to ensure that the Word she proclaims is the veritable Word of God and not a mere word of man masquerading
as that Word.

It should be clear from this that in intention the study of dogmatics is the reverse of an obscurantist activity designed to ensure
that those who practice it remain undisturbed in "dogmatic slum-
bers." It is integral to a living Church, a declaration of that
Church's intention to keep herself open to the challenge of the
Word of God and her readiness to reform herself in order to
obey that Word in the ever-changing circumstances of life.

The first implication of this understanding of the work of dogmatics or systematic theology which deserves to be noted is that
it is a much more corporate activity than some people imagine it
to be. Karl Barth, in what is by far the most ambitious systematic
theological enterprise of our time, symbolized the departure of
most modern theologians from the individualism which had often
been characteristic of liberal Protestant thought, by renaming the
second edition of the first half-volume of his *Dogmatics*, which
was published in 1931, *Church Dogmatics*. The original edition in
1927 had been called *Christian Dogmatics*. The importance of this
may need underlining, especially in those Church circles where
the movement has been away from a pietism or revivalism which
has laid little emphasis on doctrinal formulation to extreme theological liberalism. In such situations, students often approach the
study of systematic theology with the expectation that through it
they are now going to discover their own personal theology or,
even more vaguely, to work out their own "philosophy of life." It
is true, of course, that systematic theology cannot be studied with-

out compelling the student to ask most radically where he stands in relation to its truth. Indeed, it is probably the best subject of study for the man with an intellectual vocation who wishes to make articulate and to define his faith. It is critical and constructive in its very essence. But this does not mean that the individual can properly approach it in isolation, wrapped up in his own peculiar problems. He cannot undertake the study of systematic theology unless he enters into the Christian community, in however provisional a way and with whatever reservations he may wish to make, and he cannot escape entering into a conversation with other men about the subject matter of theology. All subjects are co-operative enterprises, but this is true of theology to a peculiar degree. The concern of the systematic theologian is to discover what the Church as a community should believe and offer to mankind. He has an inescapable public responsibility. He cannot fulfill this without working through his own personal objections and difficulties, but he cannot even frame these aright while he remains primarily occupied with himself. Systematic theology is a Church activity; it is the servant of the Christian community's attempt to proclaim Christ to mankind.

This, in its turn, means that the student should approach systematic theology with a measure of humility. Not all the matters with which it deals will be immediately relevant to the interests of any one student; this should not make him assume that, therefore, they are necessarily irrelevant to the life of the Church. Similarly, any sensitive person approaching the study of theology today will be acutely conscious of many difficulties in the way of faith. It would be rash of him to conclude that similar difficulties have not presented themselves to others engaged upon the study, or even that, in different guises, they have not presented themselves to men in past ages. I have emphasized that dogmatics is a critical task in its essence, and no statement can be left unchallenged and no assumption can avoid fresh scrutiny. But the good student will realize, more clearly here than anywhere else, that the sternest criticism does not come from our own intelligence but from the Word of God itself, which is sharper than a two-edged sword.

II

The subject matter of Christian theology is God's relevation of himself in Jesus Christ. Systematic theology, therefore, is not an unfettered adventure in the realm of ideas, with no specific points of reference. The subject matter is severely limited to the events and the interpretation of them recorded in the Bible and the history of the community of the Church. It is this which Karl Barth is anxious to insist upon when, in the early pages of the first half-volume of the *Church Dogmatics*, he calls theology a science. By this he means that it is a human effort to study a definite object of knowledge, an effort which follows a self-consistent path and in which one is rationally accountable to anyone else who moves along the same path. It is open to doubt both whether this is an adequate definition of a science and whether it, in fact, adequately describes what theology tries to do. As Barth himself emphasizes in other places, God's revelation is not to be thought of as a *datum*, something given in the way in which the objects studied in the physical sciences are normally thought to be, but a *dandum*, something which is in process of being given, like the knowledge of another person in conversation with them. To call theology science may not, therefore, be the right way of putting the point, but it is right to maintain that it is not a merely speculative activity but one whose nature is defined by its object, Jesus Christ, believed to be the Word of God.

The term "the Word of God" is confusing because it is used in several senses. Its primary and controlling sense is that of God's revelation of himself to man, prefigured in the "Word of the Lord" which came to the prophets and reached its fulfillment in Jesus Christ, the incarnate Word. It is because it bears witness to this Word that the Bible is also called the Word of God. This can be misleading, because of the real dangers of bibliolatry, but it is at least right to speak of the Bible as the indispensable vehicle of the Word of God, because the Bible cannot be bypassed if men wish to hear what the God who was in Christ says to men and if they wish to check what they believe to be the Spirit's guidance to them at the present time. The Bible must inevitably be read selectively, in the light of its "assured central content, Jesus

Christ," but it must also be read with humility and vigilant attention because it is written to "make us wise unto salvation." A third sense in which "the Word of God" is used is that of the Church's preaching at a particular time. This can be thought of as appropriate in an even more qualified sense than the Bible can. Indeed, it is wrong to speak of the preacher in the highly stylized activity of delivering sermons as "proclaiming the Word," as Protestants are apt to do. It is the Church, and not merely the ministry, which proclaims. The function of the sermon is to help the people hear the Word more clearly in their own midst, so that they may the more effectively proclaim it in their lives. The preacher is the servant of the Church's service of God in the world. It is only when he sees this that his ministry can be spoken of as that of the Word of God.

Why is the complicated apparatus of systematic theology necessary in order that God's Word may be declared to men? Is not the study of the Bible and the Creeds sufficient? It is certainly possible to exaggerate the importance of theology, but it does perform a necessary function. Wrong theology can do churches a great deal of harm, but its dangers cannot be avoided simply by ignoring theology.

There are two reasons for this, and I mention the more positive of them first. It is of the nature of the Christian faith that it impels men forward to theological activity. The very use of the phrase "the Word of God" to describe God's revelation implies this. Words convey meaning in the most precise and responsible way known to man. We cannot make the response of faith to the Word of God without trying to articulate it in similar meaningful terms. Our ability to do this will depend on our gifts and calling, but for the man who is called to sustained intellectual activity, his faith is not properly appropriated—it fails to register as true in his experience—unless he makes an effort to reach such understanding. Anselm of Canterbury gave currency in the twelfth century to two phrases which express the essence of theological activity: *credo ut intelligam*, I believe in order that I may understand; and *fides quaerens intellectum*, faith in search of understanding. These phrases do not mean, as pious Christians and unsympathetic outsiders both sometimes take them to mean, that the Christian reaches faith entirely irrationally and then looks around for reasons which will justify him in holding to it. If this were true, theology would become, in F. H. Bradley's famous phrase about philosophy, a matter of finding bad reasons for what we believe by instinct. Anselm is speaking on another level than this. Faith does invade men at the deepest level of their being, but part of its nature is that it brings an intellectual illumination with it, which impels men to define what has happened to them and relate it as rationally and coherently as possible to the rest of their experience.

This search for understanding has been present in the Christian community from the beginning. A fully articulated theological system is not to be found in the New Testament, but the Gospels and the Epistles are moving rapidly toward it as their writers find themselves driven more and more to account for the significance of what has met them in Jesus Christ. And it is worthy of note that practically every creative age in the history of the Church has seen a renewal of theological vitality. This is not to say that the relation between faith and theology is simple and direct. Ages when system-building is at its most active often seem to be those which follow rather than coincide with ages of renewal and reformation. And the emergence of theology depends on other things as well as faith—the appearance of gifted individuals, educational opportunities, and the stimulus of intellectual challenge, for instance. But, broadly speaking, it can be said that theological illumination is one of the great gifts which faith brings to men. Paul and John, Irenaeus and Athanasius, Augustine, Anselm, Thomas Aquinas, Luther, Calvin, and the theologians of the nineteenth and twentieth centuries provide invaluable help in discerning God's will for us today. We need to do more than simply reproduce their work in our own situation, but in these days, when the sense of living tradition is often so weak, it should be emphasized that the Christian theologian has more affinity with, and can learn more from, these men of faith than from the fashionable exponents of "the human predicament" in his own time.

This should be borne in mind when we consider the status of the Creeds and Confessions of Christendom. In some of the more liberal Protestant seminaries, an attitude of what might be called resentment toward these has become typical. They are rarely mentioned without the adjective "outworn" or "restrictive." Such an attitude breaks the commandment to honor one's father and mother. The ecumenical creeds—the Apostles', the Nicene, the *Quicunque Vult*, together with the Chalcedonian Definition—were largely based on earlier statements of faith which had their roots in Scripture and in the Church's liturgies. They represent the considered judgment of the Church, at that time formally undivided, that the essential Christian faith possesses certain definite characteristics which must be preserved if it is not to disappear. No one can accept them without question, but no one can maintain the continuity of the community of faith who does not recognize an obligation to *listen* to what they have to say, with the recognition that our fathers believed that special illumination was given to them in a time of crisis to see that, when the issues are posed in a particular way, faith must mean this rather than that. The same is true, with a lesser degree of intensity, of the Confessions which were formulated by particular churches chiefly at the time of the Reformation. Most churches rightly insist on a considerable measure of liberty of interpretation of their own Confessions on the part of those who are required to give formal assent to them, but this must not be used as an excuse for simply ignoring them. The richness of the theological heritage of the whole Church is diminished if those who belong to churches with Confessions do not recognize a responsibility to interpret them as positively as possible within the setting of the ecumenical situation.

The negative justification for the study of systematic theology is hardly less important. It is not the Christian faith alone which impels men towards theology. The devil also is a theologian. The whole history of religion is full of attempts to define God in other terms than that of his Word, Jesus Christ. It is important also to realize that these attempts take place within as well as outside the Church, that the Church has to deal not only with unbelief and idolatry but also with heresy. The latter is often more insidious and harder to detect than the former. "A man's foes shall be those of his own household." The nearer they are to him, the deadlier they are likely to be. The most deadly are those who are nearest of all to him, those who lurk within his own mind. The theologian's greatest enemy is pride, and he will always be on his guard against the danger of falsely externalizing his opponents. As soon as he begins to think of himself as the automatic champion of the truth, he has become a theological Pharisee and can no longer act as the servant of the Church's service. The critical task of theology is primarily a self-critical one, in relation both to the theologian as an individual and to the Church which he serves.

Failure to see this has been perhaps the greatest source of weakness to theology in the past. One indication of this has been the tendency to exaggerate the distinction between dogmatics and apologetics to which some reference has already been made. People have supposed that dogmatics is concerned with the central doctrines of the Christian faith on their own terms, which is true enough; but also in such a way that their self-evident truth is taken for granted. Objections to their truth are to be dealt with under the separate heading of apologetics, "Christianity defensively stated." It is in this subject that men sally forth, from the prepared position whose boundaries are defined by dogmatics, into enemy territory to deal with such matters as the evidences for the existence of God, the historicity of the Gospels, the nature of miracle and prophecy, the problem of evil, the relation between religion and scientific truth, or whatever seems to be the uppermost objection to Christian faith at a particular time.

There are several reasons why this is an unsatisfactory way of dividing up the subject matter of theology. The chief is that it does not do justice to the nature of the encounter between faith and unbelief. No major Christian doctrine can honestly be expounded without reference to the possibility of its not being true. What reality can be given to discussion of the Trinity, for instance, if all the time we are not facing the question of whether the Father is truly known through the Son in the Spirit? Or how can we elucidate the atoning work of Christ unless we are asking whether he really did die for our sins and rise for our justification? Once men arrive at faith, they do not then take it for granted. To do so would make faith to be a form of worldly security rather than the venture of commitment which it is, a venture which always leads us into fresh places where we meet fresh challenges from experiences which appear to contradict it.

Another objection to this distinction is that it encourages an exaggerated notion of the novelty and profundity of modern objections to the Christian faith. Lying behind this is the misleading popular notion that most of our Christian forefathers did not have to struggle through doubt and difficulty as we do, but were blessed with a mysterious gift called "simple faith." It is true that each age is unique in important respects and that modern conventions of thought and behavior do not predispose people to believe, but the threat of unbelief always exists and faith seeking understanding always has to do so by overcoming its apparent contradiction. Anyone who reads the Bible with the pious cobwebs blown away will know that it expresses the battle between faith and unbelief with a concreteness and intensity which we can rarely rival today. If we want to know the worst that can be said against the Christian God, it is not to Marx or Nietzsche or Bertrand Russell or Sartre that we turn but to Jesus Christ upon the cross.

The reason for this is that it is God's self-revelation itself which most clearly sets forth the issues between God and man. It is his failure to make adequate allowance for this that is the chief weakness of the "apologetic theology" of Paul Tillich, which has great influence in the U.S.A. Difficulties in the way of faith loom largest when we are grappling with the reality of faith. Theology has an apologetic interest, but it is not something additional to its "kerygmatic" interest; it is inherent in the effort of its own exponents to make the kerygma intelligible to themselves.

The criterion by which the reliability of any theology must be judged is that of its faithfulness to the Word of God. That Word is Jesus Christ, as testified to by prophets and apostles in Scripture and as known in the Spirit in the Christian community. It is a living Word, which speaks to men afresh in their own situation, although always coherently with what God has said in the past. It is this living nature of the Word in the Spirit which must always keep the theological enterprise open. There are some theological issues which may be held as relatively settled, such as the nature and limits of the canon of Scripture or the broad outlines of the doctrine of the Trinity or the considerations which must be borne in mind in any effort to state the doctrine of the person of Christ. But as we have seen, even these cannot be treated as completely sacrosanct, while over large areas new issues arise and old ones have to be restated. The theological task can never be thought of as the recapitulation of past dogma, although in some churches it is often treated as such. To suppose that it can is not only to deny the freedom of the human spirit, it is also much more significantly to deny the freedom of God in his revelation. Because his Word is living and because his people are pilgrims on this earth, the Word always has more light and truth to break forth from it. Yet it is always from the Word, and not from the spirit of the age or the general religious consciousness that the light breaks forth, however much we may be stimulated by these to seek it. The theologian must always look forward, but even at his most venturesome he will realize that it is not along a private road of his own but one on which God wants all his people to walk that he must travel.

III

What are the subjects normally studied in the central discipline of systematic theology which is now sometimes called dogmatics? As might be expected, they vary with the particular outlook and situation of particular individuals and schools. Yet there is a good deal of common ground.

It is, for example, a familiar practice to present a systematic theological statement in the form of a commentary on the Apostles' Creed. Karl Barth's *Credo* and *Dogmatics in Outline* are cases in point, although his large *Church Dogmatics* follows a different scheme. The original edition of Calvin's *Institutes* is a classic example of a major work of theology in this form, although it deals as well with some matters not directly mentioned in the Creed. Other theologians work out their systems under the headings of the different persons of the Trinity. Tillich does this in his *Systematic Theology*, in his very characteristic way. Others are expositions of Church Confessions. Barth's Gifford Lectures on *The Knowledge of God and the Service of God* expound the

Scots Confession of 1560. The *Summa Theologica* of St. Thomas Aquinas follows its own order.

A good example of the typical main themes of classical theology is provided by the chapter headings of the compendium of Protestant Scholastic theology compiled by Heinrich Heppe from Reformed theologians of the sixteenth and seventeenth centuries. These are: natural and revealed theology; Holy Scripture; the existence, notion, and attributes of God; the Trinity; the decrees of God's predestination; creation, angels—good and bad, man, providence, the covenant of works and its violation; sin, the covenant of grace; the Mediator of the covenant, Christ and his work and person; his state of exanimation and exaltation; the calling, justification, sanctification, perseverance, and assurance of the saints; the sacraments and the Church.

This is mentioned not as a model upon which to base theological work at present but as a point of reference from the past. It has the merit of reminding us, by its comprehensiveness, of the dangers of impressionism in this field. Indeed, if it is to be criticized, it is because it is not systematic enough for the needs which should be met in our present situation. It reminds us, for example, that traditional theology does not say as much as we appear to need to say today about the doctrine of the Church and its ministry, about the state and the secular order, about marriage and the family, and about the calling of the Christian in the life of the world. Yet this traditional list of themes underlines the fact that certain matters must be dealt with if theology is to be truly systematic, and that they must be dealt with in relation with each other, in a sequence which reflects the movement of revelation and of man's response to it.

Most modern theologians would probably want to include most of the subjects dealt with in traditional theology, although with differences of emphasis and with some additions. They would maintain that to be systematic, theology must include a statement of the nature of theological method, of the doctrine of the Trinity, of God and his attributes or perfections; of creation; of Jesus Christ, his person and work, and related to him, of Christian anthropology in terms of man, sin, and grace; of the Spirit and the Church. Beyond this, there might be several variations of approach. Borderline disputes inevitably arise between various theological disciplines, as they do between theology and other disciplines. Where the doctrine of providence comes might be a matter of debate. Some might say that it should be considered in relation to creation, others in relation to the Spirit. And in these days there are many theologians who would consider it more appropriate to treat eschatology in relation to Christology rather than as the last chapter of their system.

Two of the most contentious points in modern theology are those which deal with the position of natural theology and of ethics, respectively. Some would argue with Karl Barth that to show an interest in natural theology is not to take seriously what is involved in God's initiative in self-revelation. Others would argue, along with traditional Catholicism, that natural theology has its proper place as part of the prolegomena to theology as well as providing a basis on which rational discussion is possible between believers and unbelievers. The question of theological ethics is not so passionately debated. Karl Barth claims that ethics should be thought of as part of dogmatics, under the heading of the Command of God. It is true that this is how ethical prescriptions arise in the Bible, and it is also true from the Christian point of view that ethical judgments must be closely related to basic theological insights. Barth himself shows how much value there is in this in the later volumes of his *Church Dogmatics*. Yet he also indicates some of the danger of this procedure. He is sometimes tempted to draw more out of the biblical material than it really offers, while he cannot be as precise as he should be in dealing with many complex issues, especially those where the Bible offers very little direct guidance. Christian ethics should probably be related to dogmatics rather in the same way as preaching is. Ethical questions must be seen in the light of God's truth as revealed in the Word, but a great deal of attention has obviously to be paid to the particular situation in which they arise, and no one situation is exactly like another.

This does not mean, however, that the direct contribution of the Bible, and of Christian tradition, to ethical understanding is insignificant. Along with a readiness to face new issues for which these can give little obvious help—such as those of Christian obedience in the tangles of modern financial arrangements or scientific research—we need also to become aware of the resources available from the Christian past to help us in dealing with many of the perplexities of the present. Along the whole range of theological work, we still suffer a good deal from the false individualism and the impressionism which have been discussed earlier. No one can presume to comprehend the whole counsel of God. The characteristic way in which God's truth comes home to a man is as a personal insight in a particular situation. But every theologian must see that it is not a private insight and that it needs to be related to the Church's general understanding of God and his ways.

This implies several things for the work of theology in the future. First, theologians must see their work as much more of a co-operative enterprise than it often has been in the period of rivalry between different schools and confessions from which we are just emerging. The joint theological activity promoted by the ecumenical movement in the last generation has been of great service in this respect. Secondly, theologians must work together to ensure that all parts of the theological enterprise are as adequately dealt with as possible, so that the Church's ministry may be the more effectively served. We have seen that the doctrines of the Trinity and of Christology have received a great deal of attention in the course of the history of theology but that others have been badly neglected. The doctrine of the Church is being intensively studied today. The doctrines of the Spirit, of creation, and of providence, to name only three, continue to receive insufficient attention.

In order to do this the theologian needs, thirdly, what H. R. Niebuhr has called "the gift of the Catholic vision." He must have a synoptic view of Christian truth which enables him to see how his special interests are related to the rest and which enables him, as T. F. Torrance puts it, "to think through every doctrine into every other doctrine." This vision is one of the greatest gifts which theological education should provide, and those concerned with theological education must always carefully consider how they can best put their charges in the way of it. That provincialism and sectarianism should be associated in many people's minds with theology is a sad commentary on the failure of theological education to do its job. What the theologian needs to see in these days more than ever is that he will fail to avoid these dangers if he has a purely seminarist approach to his task. Theology is often most true to itself when it holds active conversation with other disciplines. The theologian of all men must realize that he cannot protect the integrity of the faith by burying the talent of God's truth in the ground. He must be prepared to put it out to usury in the commerce of the world, especially in the greatly enlarged world of today. This means running risks—but, again, the theologian of all men should know that it is only as we lose our lives that we shall find them.

7. Theology and Ethics

James M. Gustafson

What then . . . is an "ethic" which by definition makes a theme of the ethical? And what is an ethicist? We can begin more easily by saying what, in any case, an ethic and an ethicist cannot be. An ethic cannot be a book in which there is set out how everything in the world actually ought to be but unfortunately is not, and an ethicist cannot be a man who always knows better than others what is to be done and how it is to be done. An ethic cannot be a work of reference for moral action which is guaranteed to be unexceptionable, and the ethicist cannot be the competent critic and judge of every human activity. An ethic cannot be a retort in which ethical or Christian human beings are produced, and the ethicist cannot be the embodiment or ideal type of a life which is, on principle, moral.

Dietrich Bonhoeffer[1]

This quotation from Bonhoeffer might very well be abrasive to some of the most cherished expectations that men have from the study of Christian ethics. When students read a book or article on Christian ethics, they often would like to have spelled out for them how everything in the world ought to be. Unfortunately the world is in strife between groups and nations; men ought to be at peace with one another in Christian love. Unfortunately the motives one has are often compromised by the situation in which he must act; men ought to be able to live with a purity of intention regardless of the consequences. Or when one reads a book

---

[1] *Ethics*, N. H. Smith, trans. (New York: The Macmillan Co., 1955), p. 236; German edition: *Ethik* . . ., E. Bethge, ed. (München: C. Kaiser, 1949).

on Christian ethics, he expects to find a great deal of moral wisdom, for it is assumed that the writer of such a book ought to know better than others what to do and how to do it. The ethicist, readers expect, should be able to define the goals toward which men ought to be working, and he should be able to guide their use of proper means to achieve them. Or the book on Christian ethics ought to be a guidebook to Christian conduct, some might say. The reader faces a particular temptation, obligation, or opportunity; an ethics book ought to tell him the proper rules by which to act. It ought to say whether premarital sexual intercourse is right or wrong, whether resort to coercive power in international relations is right or wrong. And the writer of such a book ought to be able to survey the human scene and say the appropriately moral things about gambling, war, affluent society, and family life. Or one might read an ethics book in order to nourish his moral life; it ought to have the effect of cultivating his own moral wisdom. And one might hope that the author of such a book would be an exemplary man—he ought in his action to demonstrate the Christian moral life.

Fond hopes that the study of Christian ethics will lead to the resolution of all the serious moral questions that face human beings are bound to meet disappointment, and for some very good reasons. Dietrich Bonhoeffer's circumscription of an ethic and an ethicist would not be seriously challenged by most men working in the field of Christian ethics today. Many of the crucial issues over which there are differences of judgment, however, lie within the boundaries he suggests. If an ethic cannot "set out how everything ought to be but unfortunately is not," does this imply that it cannot suggest how *some* things ought to be? If "an ethicist cannot be a man who always knows better than others what is to be done and how it is to be done," does this imply that he cannot be one who *sometimes* knows better than some others do what ought to be done and how it ought to be done? If an ethics book cannot be an unexceptionable guide to moral action, does this imply that it cannot *give any direction* to human conduct? If "the ethicist cannot be the competent critic and judge of every human activity," does this imply that his learning may not make him *more competent than some others* are to judge *some* human activity? If the study of ethics does not create Christian moral men, does this imply that it is *absolutely divorced* from the actual moral existence of the Christian community?

BIFOCAL CHARACTER OF THE STUDY OF CHRISTIAN ETHICS

On the one hand Bonhoeffer is saying in effect, "Do not expect the study of Christian ethics to be *immediately* applicable to all moral problems." On the other hand, what many persons expect from the study of Christian ethics is moral wisdom, moral counsel, moral rules which will resolve the tensions they feel in their personal moral responsibilities, or in the issues of the world. A distinction between *ethics* and *morals* is useful to set in order two tasks that are involved in Christian ethics. *Ethics* is often used to refer to a task of careful reflection several steps removed from the actual conduct of men. It is a theoretical task: reflection on the ways in which moral action occurs, the assumptions and presuppositions of moral life. *Morals* is often used to refer to the actual conduct of men. It is a practical task: giving direction to human behavior in the light of what one believes to be right, or good. At the level of *morals* one is asking, "What ought I to do in this place of responsibility?" "Is what I am interested in *really* good?" At the level of *ethics* one is asking, "What fundamental principles are involved in determining an answer to the moral questions?" "What is the nature of obligation?" "What is the nature of the good?"[2]

In the study of Christian ethics, these two sides are always present: the clarification of the fundamental principles of the Christian life, and the interpretation of how the Christian community needs to make moral judgments and to act in the light of its faith and its religious convictions. For example, in one of the greatest American books in Christian ethics, Reinhold Niebuhr's *Nature and Destiny of Man*,[3] the student is given an interpretation of human nature, defined in relation to historical and philosophical

[2] For an unusually clarifying essay on this matter, see H. D. Aiken, *Reason and Conduct* (New York: Alfred A. Knopf, 1962) pp. 65–87. Aiken distinguishes four levels of moral discourse: the expressive ("That's good!"), the moral (approximately as above), the ethical (approximately as above), and the post-ethical ("Why should I be moral?").

[3] Two vols. (New York: Charles Scribner's Sons, 1941 and 1943).

alternatives, in relation to Scripture and human experience. This is *theological ethics*. He is also given direction as to how one thinks about the moral world in the light of these theological ethical convictions. This is *Christian morals*. The meaning of being a sinner, being under God's grace, and being under the absolute law of love is not given to exhibit Reinhold Niebuhr's ethical brilliance; it is given so that men may more adequately fulfill their moral obligations to God and to the finite world of men. In Roman Catholic papal encyclicals on ethics,[4] one finds a brief exposition of the fundamental convictions of that Church pertaining to man's moral nature, the natural law, and the effects of redeeming grace—ethics. But these are given for the purpose of guiding men in their responses to issues of economic justice, of political policy, and of marriage and family relationships—*morals*. Or in Karl Barth's writings on ethics in his *Church Dogmatics*, the basic theological ethical principles derived and expounded in terms of his Christology in Volume II, Part 2 are supplemented in Volume III, Part 4 by extensive discussions of what it means to have faith in this Christ in marriage, in relation to the preservation of life (war, abortion, capital punishment, etc.), and in other areas.[5] Some writers choose to work primarily at the basic principles, and to some earnest moral men often appear abstract and impractical. Among American writers, H. Richard Niebuhr in both *Christ and Culture* and *The Responsible Self* works primarily in the *ethics* side of the discipline.[6] Other writers are concerned to inform the moral action of the Christian community with a sense of urgency and relevance, writing tracts for the times from Christian viewpoints. To some students of theological ethics, such writings often appear to be milk rather than good red meat.

The double-sided enterprise goes on in the classroom as well. There are teachers of ethics who lead their students into the refinements and intricacies of the problem of law and gospel, or

[4] See, for example, E. Gilson, ed., *The Church Speaks to the Modern World: The Social Teachings of Leo XIII* (New York: Doubleday Image Books, 1954), and T. P. McLaughlin, ed., *The Church and the Reconstruction of the Modern World* (New York: Doubleday Image Books, 1957).

[5] G. W. Bromiley and T. F. Torrance, eds., Vol. II, Part 2 and Vol. III, Part 4 (New York: Charles Scribner's Sons, 1957 and 1961).

[6] New York: Harper & Brothers, 1951; New York: Harper & Row, 1963.

into the exegetical and theological foundations of the idea of the state, without ever addressing a problem of human conduct or indicating that moral judgments in politics require many other considerations besides Romans 13:1–7. They feel vindicated by being "theological," or by a sense of dealing with what is "really basic." There are also teachers of Christian ethics who are so concerned to be relevant that their lectures become extended social commentary, or more sociological and political than theological in the fundamental thought patterns that direct them. Neither emphasis is without its virtues, and neither without its vices. The main virtue of the first is that it clarifies the foundations in the Christian message for understanding the relation of God to the world and man in theological ethical terms; its most common vice is that it often assumes that the resolution of an exegetical or theological problem is the resolution of a moral problem—that to find a correct theological doctrine of the state is a more important contribution to the Christian community than to clarify choices between parties and candidates in an election by a discussion of the moral issues involved. The virtue of the second, more practical view, is its effort to be informed by what is actually going on in the world, and to promote the activity of the Christian community in the particular moral issues and judgments that time-bound men face. Its most common vice, however, is oversimplified thinking about the relation of theological and ethical principles to empirical data and present struggles of men.

The distinction between *ethics* and *morals* is shared by theologians with philosophers and with writers from other religions. There are philosophers who seek to avoid any realm of practical life in their discourse. R. M. Hare, for example, in *The Language of Morals*, conceives of ethics as "the logical study of the language of morals."[7] Language, not human action, is the first point of reference for analysis; and certainly Hare does not seek to prescribe human behavior. But even with his special abstract interest, the actual morals of the philosopher are not hidden. Among other examples that Hare uses in working out his abstract problems is the importance of taking a bath! Other philosophers have moved between "ethics" and "morals" more freely. Bertrand Russell and

[7] Oxford: Clarendon Press, 1952, p. v.

John Dewey, both talented in abstract discourse, have written
tracts informed by their basic reflections on many moral topics
that face men. The general field of ethics, Christian or non-Christian, seems to demand a double-sided approach—reflection on basic
patterns and principles, and reflection on what men ought to do.

THREE CENTERS OF ATTENTION IN ETHICAL THOUGHT

The theoretical and practical concerns of ethics become inter-
woven at various points; or to put the issue in Henry David
Aiken's terms, men move between the levels of moral discourse.
The question "Why be moral?" might be answered in such a way
that a response to the question "What ought I to do?" is entailed.
The major portion of this essay will delineate three substantive
concerns of ethical reflection that are held in common by Christian ethics and other ethics. With each, however, the distinctive
approach of Christian ethics is differentiated. The three substantive concerns are with the location and nature of the good, or
value; the nature of man as a moral agent in the world; and the
criteria of judgment needed for the determination of conduct.

Location and Nature of the Good

Jesus said, "Why do you call me good? No one is good but God
alone" (Luke 18:19). Aristotle asks, "What then is the good of
each? Surely that for whose sake everything else is done. . . . Now
such thing happiness, above all else, is held to be."[8] "And God
saw everything that he had made, and behold, it was very good."
(Gen. 1:31). For R. B. Perry, "The highest good is doubly ideal.
It is the ideal object of an ideal will. It is an ideal object in the
sense that it is constructed out of the objects of the original interest which compose the integral will. . . ."[9]

These four selections all use the word *good*. It obviously has
different references; Jesus was speaking about men, and then about
God; the author of Genesis was speaking about the goodness of
created beings; Aristotle wrote about happiness as the end, the

[8] *Nichomachean Ethics*, W. D. Ross, trans., Bk. 1, chap. 7, in R. McKeon,
ed., *The Basic Works of Aristotle* (New York: Random House, 1941),
p. 941.
[9] *General Theory of Value* (New York: Longmans, Green & Co., 1926),
p. 687.

ultimate goal and purpose, of men; Perry is involved in definitions of *ideal objects* and *ideal wills*. For Kant, the issue of goodness was located in the human will. And more references could be given. The student of ethics is compelled to assert that in one way or another every writer in the field gives some location or locations of the good and engages in some discussion of its nature. For some philosophers it is defined in very inclusive terms—being itself is good. For others, there are objective values, or essences of various forms of the good that exist as things in themselves. For G. E. Moore, the good is simple and indefinable, like the *yellow*. For hedonists, the good is pleasure; for some rigorists the human good is obedience. For H. R. Niebuhr, things are of value in relation to God and to each other. The location of the good is thus sometimes defined to be within the self—a satisfaction of some desire or interest; sometimes as objective—something real existing out there; and sometimes in relational terms. Its nature is sometimes understood as indefinable, sometimes in terms of utility, sometimes in terms of desire, sometimes in terms of *being*.

Christian ethical reflection also interprets what the nature of the good is and where it is located. Theologians turn their attention to this problem not in a speculative frame of mind, but in an effort to understand what the fundamental presuppositions of the Christian life are. Even in this search for clarification of assumptions they are not engaged in something unique; most philosophers in their definitions of goodness begin with the fact that it exists and men experience it, therefore one is provoked to reflect upon it. But when the theologian turns his attention to this problem he begins with certain convictions of the Christian community. These convictions are not merely propositions taken from Scripture and treated like the premises of arguments; they are the convictions that inform his life of faith—indeed, they are the convictions of his faith. The nature and location of the ultimate good are delineated in religious, theological terms. The understanding of the manifold forms of goodness in creation and human experience is explicated in terms of the relation of these things to the goodness of God. Others may answer the question, "Why be moral?" in terms of "It is natural to be moral, i.e., to seek one's own happiness." The Christian answers it differently. He is moral

because God is good, and because God has called him to responsibility for the goodness of the world in which man lives. He is
moral out of gratitude to the goodness of God, made known in
creation, made known in the preservation and governing of the
world, made known in the face of Jesus Christ. God is good; God
has created all things and seen that they are good. The theological
side of Christian ethics is directed toward the interpretation and
specification of the Being and Goodness of God. In relation to
him, and to his goodness, all created forms of life have their appropriate value. In relation to him, man is obliged to seek the good
of others, to concern himself with the care and well-being of men
and nature.

Theologians interpret the nature and source of the good differently. For the Catholic tradition, which thinks in terms of natural law, God has created men with an inclination toward the
good, and an inclination away from evil. Thus there is a goodness
in nature which seeks to realize itself; it can be known, and this
knowledge used to direct conduct. To be created by God is good;
to *be* good is to act in accordance with one's true nature given in
God's creation. For Lutheran interpretations, God's goodness is
made known to men in his law and in his gospel. In his law it acts
to keep order in the works of men and the world of nature, it
gives a structure to human society so that men can live together.
In his gospel, God's goodness (specified in terms of righteousness)
is given for the justification of men, for the forgiveness of their
sins, and for them to share in human existence. For some contemporary theologians—for example, Karl Barth and Dietrich Bonhoeffer—the center of goodness, indeed *the Reality*, is Jesus Christ.
They remind us of the assertions in Colossians and Ephesians that
all things are created in and through him; that he has overcome
the principalities and the powers. Jesus Christ is the Reality—of
the good, and all of life is to be lived in such a way that it attests
to him. In "liberal" Protestant ethics, the reflections on the nature
of the good have been somewhat different. God is love; love is
good; the Christian life seeks to realize love in every possible situation. Jesus, both in his life and his teachings, expressed the centrality of love as the good, and thus in direction from him, and

in imitation of him, men are to be inwardly loving in their intentions and motives, and to be outwardly loving to establish those relations among men that most closely approximate love.

For most Christian writers, human goodness is always and only a secondary good. It is a created good—only God is good in an ultimate sense; and it is a corrupted goodness, for men have not lived in accord with the goodness of God. Christians understand the possibility and the actuality of goodness in the world as dependent upon the prior goodness of God. Men are righteous (a word which requires much more specification than can be given here) only by virtue of God's righteousness. Goodness in creation is in every moment dependent upon God's goodness. Or, if the Christian life is defined in being directed toward an end, toward a goal, it is a goal determined by a vision of God's goodness. Or, "We love, *because he first loved us*" (I John 4:19).

The more theoretical reflection about God, his nature and his activity, is carried on through study of the Scriptures and the theological tradition. The Bible makes the message of God's goodness known to men; it is in the Bible that a people (both the people of Israel and the Christian community) has recorded its action in the light of God's goodness; its understanding of what is required of man in the knowledge of God. Within Scripture there is the movement back and forth between theology, "ethics," and "morals," between convictions about the nature and activity of God and the nature and activity of man in relation to God. So also in Christian ethical reflection there is movement back and forth between an understanding of God as the one who alone is good, but created all things good, preserves all things, and acts to redeem all things on the one hand, and the interpretation of human life and its current responsibilities in the light of these basic convictions on the other.

Christians' *attitudes and basic dispositions* toward the world are governed by their acknowledgment of God as the good: they are his servants; they are dependent upon him; they tend and care for a world which is not theirs but his; they are responsible to him. The *actions* of the community are directed by the *knowledge* of God's goodness: its members seek to preserve the good that God has created; they seek to act in such fashion that love and order are enhanced in the human community; they seek to act in such fashion that good is redeemed out of evil in the world.

Philosophers and other men have convictions about the good in the light of which they act, and counsel the actions of others. Christians are not unique by virtue of having such convictions; they are distinguished by the convictions that they have. Their interpretation of what is worthy of men's interest and pursuit, of men's care and energy, is governed in large part by their religious convictions. These convictions are specified and expounded in the Bible and in the tradition of the Church. God is good; created beings are good by virtue of God's goodness; men ought to seek the good in accordance with God's own good activity and in accordance with man's knowledge of God's goodness. This power and goodness of God is made known in Jesus Christ. Knowledge of goodness is given in knowledge of Jesus Christ and in the interpretation of life in relation to him.

Nature of Man

In Genesis 1:27, the famous biblical assertion about man is made: "So God created man in his own image, in the image of God he created him. . . ." Immanuel Kant wrote concerning the principle of reason in man:

Thus nothing remained but that perhaps an incontrovertible, objective principle of causality could be found which excluded every sensuous condition from its determination, i.e., a principle in which reason does not call upon anything else as the determining ground of the causality but rather by that principle itself contains it, thus being, as pure reason, practical of itself. This principle, however, needs no search and no invention, having long been in the reason of all men and embodied in their being. It is the principle of morality.[10]

St. Paul wrote, ". . . for I have already charged that all men, both Jews and Greeks, are under the power of sin, as it is written: 'None is righteous, no, not one; no one understands, no one seeks

[10] "Critique of Practical Reason," in Immanuel Kant, *Critique of Practical Reason and Other Writings in Moral Philosophy*, L. W. Beck, trans. and ed. (Chicago: University of Chicago Press, 1949), p. 210.

for God. All have turned aside, together they have gone wrong; no one does good, not even one' " (Rom. 3:9–12). He also wrote, "Therefore, if any one is in Christ, he is a new creation; the old has passed away, behold, the new has come" (II Cor. 5:17). Erich Fromm has written, "If he faces the truth without panic he will recognize that there is no meaning to life except the meaning man gives his life by the unfolding of his powers, by living productively...."[11]

Discussions of ethics always include the delineation of some view of man. Indeed, the understanding of the nature of man is one of the keystones to every ethical system. For some interpreters, man is fundamentally a rational being, capable of knowing what the good is, and capable of directing his conduct according to that proper knowledge (Kant). For others man is governed more by his self-interest than by his benevolence for others. Some picture man as a creature with conscience, capable of bringing self-love and love of others into harmony with each other (Butler). For Berdyaev, the essence of human nature is a radical freedom, so that man in effect has the capacity to create himself and his world. But those who believe that men are determined by the mores of their communities (Durkheim) or by some law of nature which requires that each creature struggle for himself, would radically disagree.

One finds a variety of portraits of man in the literature of Christian ethics, as well. For Roman Catholics, the problem of morality lies as much in knowledge of the good as it does in the will to do the good; in fact, man's will is governable by his intellect. In the Protestant tradition the human will is seen to be the locus of much of the moral problem; men are curved in upon themselves as an expression of their sin (Luther). For some Christians, man is viewed primarily under the aspect of sin: to be sure, he is justified by God's grace, but for purposes of morality it is best to remember first that he remains sinner (R. Niebuhr in some places). For other theologians, man is viewed primarily under the aspect of grace: to be sure, he remains a sinner, but the primary fact of his existence is his justification and sanctification by God, and a view of his moral existence begins at this point (Barth, F. D. Maurice).

[11] *Man for Himself* (New York: Rinehart & Co., 1947), p. 45.

Christians and non-Christians alike have their theories about human nature, and these theories are important aspects of their views of moral activity. Philosophers may see man in relation to his community, or in relation to his libido, or in relation to some definition of a law of nature. Theologians see man in relation to God; the basic perspective in which he is understood is that given in the Bible and Christian tradition. When Christians engage in ethical reflection, then, they have a distinctive point of reference for their interpretation of man as the moral agent. Theological understanding of man is sometimes reduced to propositions about human nature on the basis of some of the first theological premises, but more frequently it has existential qualities to it. The intention is not to make universally applicable statements about men, so much as it is to understand the existence of human beings, made for each other, in their relationship to God. Christian interpretations are interpretations in faith; they are informed by the life of the community of men who acknowledge God as Lord, and they are informed by the knowledge of God who has brought mankind into existence.

In Christian ethical reflection, the interpretation of man's moral existence is centered in large measure on his relationship to God. He is a creature: thus he is not able to claim for himself final authority in anything that he does. He is always one who is under authority; he sees himself to be under the sovereign action of God. He is dependent; nothing is his by his own right, he is "more acted upon than acting," in the words of Luther. He is limited; God has limited him by his creaturehood and continues to limit him by the particular circle of life into which he is born and lives. He is sustained; God's own governing power sustains him, and he is sustained by others whom God has created for him—his family, his government, his church. He is restrained; God restrains him through the restraint of others who act upon him. But in all the aspects of his creaturehood he is created in the image of God: he can participate creatively in the activity of history; he can act for others as God has acted for him in Jesus Christ; he can have purposes for his existence as God has purposes for the whole of creation.

Man, in Christian ethical reflection, is understood to be under obligation to God, to be called to a life of obedient service to God. He is also understood to be part of a rebellious humanity, a disobedient humanity, which seeks to overcome the limits of its creaturehood and claim for itself the right to determine history. The interpretation of what man ought to be and to do is made in relation to what God wills man to be and to do. God has disclosed his activity in the history of the children of Israel; he continues to be the Lord who calls men to obedience to him within the events of their history and culture, their family and economy. Thus in man's moral reflection he is obligated to seek to discern what God is calling him to be and to do in his duties and opportunities in life. But he thinks and acts in repentance, for he knows that he is a creature whose ways are not God's ways, and that he has estranged himself from God in unfaithfulness and disobedience to him.

But man is not only created and ruled by the Lord God; God is also man's Redeemer. This also informs man's existence. He is called into his moral activity by God, who has acted for the redemption of the world in Jesus Christ, and who continues to act redemptively in the world. The Christian image of man is constituted in part by the knowledge that God is good—that he has revealed himself in Jesus Christ as the Redeemer of all things as well as the Creator. Thus there is a newness of life; there is ultimate assurance of the triumph of righteousness over the powers of sin, death, and evil; there is a love that overcomes the world. There is freedom, not only by man's natural capacity to initiate action, but freedom from self-justification; freedom to love, freedom to take risks. Theologians differ in their interpretation of the significance of man under the aspect of God's redemption. For some, the primary weight rests on the fact that man is free from bondage to sin because God has acted to forgive him; this is one of the stresses of the Reformation. For some, God's grace is infused into the mind and the will of man through participation in the sacraments, and thus his capacity to act is enhanced; this is a stress in traditional Roman Catholicism. For John Wesley and others, God's gift of grace in conversion really restores man's nature, so that he can overcome his sins and live a morally new life. For such a person as F. D. Maurice, whose theme was "Christ is the head of every man," it meant living in the assurance that love is more real than sin, that life is more real than death, that goodness is more real than evil.

The Christian reflects upon the significance of man's life for other men in human community. Theologians in the biblical tradition have always stressed the social character of man's existence. Men are called to sustain each other, to know each other, to restrain each other, to live for each other. God has so created life; God's love so impels men to live together. Thus the natural communities in which men live are understood in the light of their function for men under the divine activity and order. And particularly, theologians view men as called to be in the community which acknowledges God to be the Lord: the community of the Church.

Convictions about man are obviously not unique to Christian moralists; they are a main ingredient in every moral view. But the Christian interpretation is differentiated by a particular point of reference: man is understood in relation to God—Father, Son, and Holy Spirit. This understanding affects men's disposition toward the world—it is God's, and only in a secondary sense their own; it is to be ordered through human action in accord with what God wills and what God is seeking to do. Man's view of himself is that of a servant of God, one who is under obligation to God. It also affects the ways in which men think about their purposes and actions in the world. Men are to be related to one another in a manner fitting God's creation and redemption; they are to fulfill the purposes and duties which they discern to be true for humanity under God's disclosure of himself. The mirror in which they understand themselves, singly and together, is Jesus Christ, the revelation of God.

Criteria of Moral Action

Just as writers of books of ethics all have something to say about the nature of the good and the nature of man, so also they reflect upon the criteria of moral judgment. Kant's propositions which state the categorical imperatives are well known. For example, he states it in the following way at one point: "Act only according to that maxim by which you can at the same time will

that it should become a universal law."[12] The "double love commandment" from the sayings of Jesus is even better known: "The
first is . . . 'you shall love the Lord your God with all your heart,
and with all your soul, and with all your mind, and with all your
strength.' The second is this, 'You shall love your neighbor as
yourself' " (Mark 12:30–31). In the Decalogue, we are given a
whole set of criteria for conduct: "Thou shalt not steal, Thou
shalt not kill," etc. Stephen Toulmin defines the function of
ethics in the following manner: "We can provisionally define it
as being 'to correlate our feelings and behaviour in such a way
as to make the fulfillment of everyone's aims and desires as far
as possible compatible.' "[13]

Each of these selections suggests certain rather specific considerations or criteria that men ought to have in view as they determine their course of action. One ought not to do anything that
he would not wish everyone else to do; one ought to love the
neighbor; one ought to strive toward a harmony of self-realization
of various persons. There are others that are readily recalled from
the literature of ethics: seek the greatest good for the greatest
number, "Do unto others as you would have others do unto you,"
etc. Criteria are sometimes stated as the goals to be sought in action; sometimes they are stated as laws or governing rules. In the
biblical literature, "Seek ye first the Kingdom of God," is a reli-
gious-ethical statement that defines a goal to be sought; "Thou
shalt not commit adultery" is the statement of a governing rule.
Traditional terms of differentiation between these two basic
postures in relation to the moral life are *teleological ethics* and
deontological ethics. There are writers in both Christian and non-
Christian ethics who seek to hew rather closely to one general
pattern or the other, but most writers move freely between them.
St. Paul, for example, in a remarkable passage of moral counsel
in the framework of the Christian gospel (I Cor. 10:24–11:1)
apparently sees no serious tension between statements of both
types. He admonishes Christians, "Let no one seek his own good,
but the good of his neighbor,"—a goal-directed statement; but he

[12] "Foundations of Morals," in Kant, *op. cit.*, p. 80.
[13] *Examination of the Place of Reason in Ethics* (Cambridge, Eng.: The
University Press, 1950 and 1960 [paperback]), p. 137.

also asserts, "Be imitators of me, as I am of Christ,"—a statement of a pattern to which the Christian life is to be conformed. Perhaps it is fortunate that St. Paul was not tutored in the fine distinctions that professors of ethics have learned to make!

The ends that men believe ought to guide conduct are related to their views of the good and of the nature of man. If pleasure is the chief good, and if man is a rational animal capable of directing his action toward such an end, obviously the criterion of action could be stated in terms of an end: "Direct your action toward the maximization of your pleasure." Or it could be stated in terms of a moral law: "So act in every situation that your pleasure is enhanced." Christians view the criteria of action, however, not with reference to man alone, but with reference to what God enables and requires men to do. Their interpretation of moral responsibility is set within the framework of God's disclosure to man that he is his Creator, his Ruler and Judge, and his Redeemer. It is also set within an understanding of man as a being called to loving obedience by God, who enables and requires man to live responsibly. Perhaps the most important differentiation of Christian reflection about moral conduct, however, is that it places responsibility within man's relationship to God. For Christian morality, the ultimate loyalty is not to the criteria set by any human community; the court of judgment is not a system of ends or laws designed by moral philosophers. Christians *live in a sense of personal responsibility to a living God* in their actions. Thus the ultimate criteria of moral action are never derived from a book of rules, as if such were the final authority. They are never derived from a set of humanly defined goals. The Christian seeks in his moral judgments to be obedient to the living God, who is seeking to address man in each particular responsibility, and whose activity is reflected in each event. Thus the various relative criteria that Christians use are more like lights to aid them in walking in the way that God is leading, than ends to be achieved by calculated means, or laws to be obeyed at all cost.

St. Paul told the Corinthians, "All things are lawful, but not all things are helpful." The life of the Christian community is not finally judged by the legality of its behavior—with reference to moral as well as ritual laws defined by men. Rather, moral judgment requires a discernment of what things are helpful and what things are not helpful. In response to what God enables and requires, how do we discern what things "build up"? How do we discern what manner of life is worthy of the gospel of Christ? (Cf. Phil. 1:27 ff.) The Christian is not without guidance. Indeed, he finds his own moral judgments and actions directed by much that is in Scripture, as well as by the counsels of the Church in the tradition and the present.

St. Paul did not hesitate to suggest that Christians imitate him, as he imitated Christ. The Gospel narratives abound in the call to discipleship; to follow Jesus Christ. The persistence of this theme is by no means accidental in the history of the criteria for Christian action. Dietrich Bonhoeffer has written the most powerful tract in our time on this theme. In *The Cost of Discipleship* he quietly affirms that Jesus Christ calls men to perfect obedience, and to suffering.[14] The words of Jesus and the life that he lived both bring to view the cost of living out a responsible moral existence in discipleship. John Calvin is a part of a long tradition of Christian writers who interpret discipleship in the language of self-denial and cross-bearing, echoing again the call of Jesus to deny ourselves, take up our crosses, and follow him. This imperative mood is heard together with the indicative in discerning our moral responsibility in the light of Jesus Christ. God's deeds for man in him permit us to seek the good of the neighbor; to identify ourselves with the suffering, the oppressed, and the outcast. But we are also required to follow him—to have his mind. In Barth's language, "permission" and "command" are not antithetical to each other; rather they are two sides of the same thing.

The teachings of Jesus stand as our judge in our particular moral obligations, and they give direction to our consideration of the responsibilities we have in the tangled, complicated spheres of our lives. We cannot literally apply them and expect to resolve the complex political, economic, and personal issues that confront us. But we would hardly be true to our heritage in the Christian community if we thought about these complicated issues without hearing the counsel of the words of Jesus—without viewing these issues in the light of the One whose name designates our very lives.

[14] R. H. Fuller, trans. (2d rev. ed., New York: The Macmillan Co., 1960).

Scripture contributes from many of its passages to our consideration of what we are to be and to do in moral life. The Old
Testament gives many accounts of the life of a people who interpreted their own participation in history under the sovereignty
of God. From their action, and their understanding of their action, we can better see our way on the path of obedience. St. Paul
borrows freely from the Stoic wisdom of his day in filling out
the meaning of not being conformed to this world, but being
renewed in our minds by Jesus Christ. The Christian community
is not bound to a single definition of a categorical imperative, or
even to a single moral proposition drawn from Scripture. It is
not definable exclusively as "the people who follow the law of
love." In living obedience to a living God, it seeks to discern and
to act in responsibility in the light of God's revelation in Scripture, with its richness in variety as well as its singleness of purpose.

But Christian *morality* is never derived from Scripture alone,
nor is it explicable out of dogmatic propositions alone. To be
responsible to God requires that one have knowledge of the
world in which he is called to live. Thus there is a pressure toward knowing as accurately as possible the human conditions in
which Christian obedience is exercised. In political judgments,
wisdom and knowledge in the political arena are brought to bear
in the determination of conduct. In international relations, knowledge of alliances and balances of power, of the technical ways
of maintaining peace, of ideologies and aspirations of men are all
points of consideration in the determination of judgment and
action. Knowledge of the effects upon the family of an indus-
trialized, bureaucratized society are important in discerning the
particular moral responsibilities of Christians in that area. Further,
the Christian community does not simply intuit what the right
moral action is by having the Bible in one hand and the newspaper
in the other. A procedure of critical reflection within the community, and within each Christian man, is necessary. Perhaps
there is here and there an artist, or a virtuoso of Christian morality, who seems naturally to do the right and the good—the *saint*.
In the main, however, the ethicist has a function in the community to guide its reflection and aid in its consideration of what is
required.

The criteria of Christian conduct are not necessarily exclusive of the criteria defined by other communities or other moralists. Many particular considerations are shared between Western humanists and Christians, between political philosophers and theologians. But not every assertion of every moralist can be absorbed into the criterion of Jesus Christ. The criteria of racist morality, whether defined by Nazi Aryan moralists or by Southern White Citizens Councils, are clearly antagonistic to the principal considerations given in the Christian gospel. The criteria of a secularist's struggle for economic justice, however, are more congenial. Christian morality is distinguished not by each particular detail but by the ultimate loyalty, and therefore the ultimate criterion, under which it brings all relative criteria. Christians have to use reason in their judgments and actions as much as other men do; they reflect upon them in such a way as to seek to discern the mind of Christ, the will of God. But Jesus Christ is not just a criterion of judgment; he is the living Lord of the community. Thus moral reflection never has the absolute importance it might have for some philosophers: Jesus Christ may enable and require actions that are imprudent according to canons of rational morality. The presence of the Spirit in the Church might prompt an obedient action which is not defensible by even the best rational reflection of the wisest and most learned theologians of the Church.

THE RELIGIOUS, EXISTENTIAL CHARACTER OF CHRISTIAN LIFE

Just as philosophers reflect "ethically" on basic principles, and "morally" on conduct, so do the theologians. But the fundamental understanding of the nature of moral life is to be radically distinguished between them. The Christian life is a life of faith (both loyalty and confidence, in the terms of H. R. Niebuhr[15]) in a living God. The moral life of the Christian community is deeply conditioned by the fact that it lives in faith in God, the Father of our Lord Jesus Christ. It trusts in him—he stands over all human communities, codes of morals, and ethical thought as the object of ultimate loyalty. It lives in responsibility to him, and views all the historical particular responsibilities in the light

[15] See *Radical Monotheism and Western Culture* (New York: Harper & Brothers, 1960), pp. 16–23.

of obligation to God. It hopes in him—moral evil and defeat never lead it to despair. The life of morality is an expression of the life of worship and devotion, just as it is of the life of theological reflection, for the consciousness of God is sustained by "religious" activities. The moral action of the community is thus understood in personal terms, as well as in institutional and rational terms. Each man is personally responsible to God for the conduct of his life. The community bears a sense of personal obligation to walk in the way that God leads. There is no easy separation between the life of faith and the life of morality; thus the nourishment of the more distinctively religious relationship also affects the more distinctively moral relationships. And man's moral actions are performed with a sense of *personal* responsibility for other men and for the world of nature and social institutions. The activity of men wherever they live and work is understood to be activity in response to God's sovereign lordship.

This existential character of the Christian life makes rationally closed and consistent "systems" of theological ethics dubious. Men have written "systems" of Christian ethics, and undoubtedly will continue to do so. There will continue to be those who believe that "love" is the single foundation upon which Christian ethics is built, to the neglect of faith and hope. There will be those who build their views around a vision of God and interpret the history of the field in the same manner, as did Bishop Kirk.[16] There will be others who stress the idea of Christian perfection, interpreting the Christian life on the basis of the efficacy of conversion to transform moral character. Others will find the keystone in man as sinner, and from this point interpret the morality of men in the world. Some will fix upon the sovereignty of God, and seek to view in all events the presence of the divine Lord. Others will fix the study of ethics upon a doctrine of natural law.

While the drive toward coherence in the interpretation of Christian ethics is good and necessary as a part of the pedagogical and academic work, it can readily be distorted into a pattern that has falsely designated the fixed points. If love becomes the fixed point, one needs to remember H. Richard Niebuhr's warning that

[16] K. E. Kirk, *The Vision of God* (London and New York: Longmans Green & Co., 1947).

to say "God is love" is not to say "Love is God."[17] If a doctrine of man the sinner becomes too fixed as the major premise of Christian ethics, the efficacy of God's redeeming work might be underestimated. If the teaching of Jesus, or the example of Jesus, is the center, a Tolstoyan interpretation may occur in which Christian ethics becomes merely a statement of the law of life to be set along side of other such statements. Every effort to make a closed system of Christian ethics stumbles finally on the richness and openness of the Christian life.

Theologically conceived, Christian ethics has a fixed point of reference—it is God's nature and his action, revealed in Jesus Christ, in Scripture. But there are no single and simple propositions that exhaust this center. There are many indicators of it, in the story of the people of Israel and the experience of the Church. There is a unique revelation of it in Jesus Christ. But the one who is revealed continues to rule and to redeem, and thus he can call men to new and surprising forms of obedience, as well as to the relatively customary actions that fulfill his purposes. The Christian life is lived in obedient response to the living God. Much can be known about his nature and activity, about what he enables and requires men to be and to do. But the human response *is not to propositions or knowledge about God*; it is the living God, active in creation, in the Son Jesus Christ, and in the Holy Spirit in the Church, to whom the world and the Church in the world are called to obedience. This is response not to a single portrait of Jesus Christ, etched by the imagination; rather to the living Son of the Father, who is risen Lord, teacher, example, redeemer, and sanctifier. It is response not to a moral consensus drawn out of Scripture or tradition, but to the promptings of the Holy Spirit as men deliberate together to discern the mind of Christ in their moral responsibilities. An understanding of moral life as being related to the living God sits loose to the saddle of all closed rational systems of ethics—Christian or philosophical.

Circumscribed systems tend to close off the richness and openness of events in the world to which we are called to live in responsibility. No ethic, Christian or non-Christian, can prescribe

[17] See *Christ and Culture* (New York: Harper & Brothers, 1951), p. 17.

on the basis of some fixed touchstone what one's response to particular persons or events ought to be. There are some limitations that might be set: for example, surely a relationship of love rules out sadistic cruelty as a moral virtue in the family. But the response of love is conditioned by the particularities of the child and the parent, the particularities of the events of this day rather than yesterday. Similarly in other spheres of man's moral existence, there is an openness which calls for readiness to hear what God is requiring of men in the new time and place. A system of Christian ethics that seeks to determine too precisely the proper form of the state from the Book of Romans or the Book of Revelation will stumble on changing historical events. "Authority," for example, is something different in a Western democratic state of the twentieth century from what it was in Europe during the period when kings claimed divine right. It is different in eastern Europe from what it is in the new nations of Mali and Indonesia. A rigid prescription of the form of the state on the basis of some prior fixed ethical statements is futile; thinking about the nature of the state in relation to the heritage of ethical reflection *and* the historical events in which states are acting and taking shape is fruitful. Moral action takes place in a continuing field and time span of activity, it initiates changes and directs events that are already occurring. Thus Christian morality must keep in view the openness of the historical and natural world in which men are called to responsibility.

The study of ethics, then, in its utility for morality, lies in the understanding, clarification, direction, setting of limits, and illumination of the way in which responsible men participate in human life. But the study of ethics can never replace the personal responsibility to act—in relation to the action of God and to the actions of other men.

8. Theology and Philosophy

J. Heywood Thomas

Many will feel that the best answer to the question "What is Philosophy?" (and similarly the question "What is Theology?") is the answer which some Oxford philosopher is said once to have given—"What those books are about." However, the terms are not only names of disciplines pursued in universities and concerning which books are written, but they are also problematic concepts. Today the question of the relation of philosophy to theology has a more than merely theoretical importance. For it is not too much to say that the inadequacy of logical positivism as a philosophy was revealed by its inability to give theology any place in its universe. In his well-known Eddington Memorial Lecture Prof. R. B. Braithwaite pointed out how the verification principle gave way to the use principle, because if we accepted the former then such statements as moral and theological statements were "nonsense."[1] For many people one of the sources of their original interest in philosophy was their anxiety to "discover whether philosophy could provide any defence for anything that could be called religious belief however vague."[2] Anyone who has looked to philosophy for some kind of substitute for religion will have reached the same conclusion as Russell did, rejecting in turn free will, immortality, and God. Perhaps this misuse of philosophy is

[1] R. B. Braithwaite, *An Empiricist's View of Religious Belief* (Cambridge, Eng.: The University Press, 1956).
[2] Bertrand Russell, *My Philosophical Development* (New York: Simon & Schuster, 1959).

something that belongs only to the past (though it could be argued that the radical empiricist tradition in philosophy is not without its pseudoreligious claims), and there can certainly be no doubt that some fifty years ago philosophy and theology were almost identical studies. It will be useful to begin with a survey of this change in our intellectual situation despite the fact that one cannot give any full account of it.[3]

The relations of philosophy and theology in this century can be described by a musical metaphor as a movement from romantic harmony through discord to an essentially modern harmony. In the early years of the century the dominant philosophy was absolute idealism—"Hegelianism modified by Anglo-Saxon caution"—and it was still in the ascendant. As Paton graphically puts it, "to say that it was already on the wane would be . . . to judge by hindsight rather than to express the feeling of the time."[4] Philosophy as thus understood had little trouble in finding room for theology, for in their different ways the philosopher and the theologian were doing the same thing. Almost any philosophical or theological work of this period would reveal this, but Edward Caird's *The Evolution of Religion* is an excellent illustration. For Caird everything is capable of rational explanation, and the ultimate principle of explanation must be spiritual, namely God. So philosophy and theology come to the same conclusion.[5] But already in the twenties philosophy was being changed, and the work of Russell, Moore, and Wittgenstein was exerting influence.

[3] A full account can be obtained by consulting the following sources: H. J. Paton, "Fifty Years of Philosophy," *Contemporary British Philosophy*, H. D. Lewis, ed., Third Series (New York: The Macmillan Co., 1956), pp. 335–54; and Paton, *The Modern Predicament* (New York: The Macmillan Co., 1955), pp. 19–58; R. G. Collingwood, *An Autobiography* (New York: Penguin Books, Pelican ed., 1944); Leonard Hodgson, *For Faith and Freedom* (New York: Charles Scribner's Sons, 1956), Vol. I; Frederick Ferré, *Language, Logic and God* (New York and London: Harper & Row, 1961), pp. 1–66; H. D. Lewis, "Survey of Recent Work in the Philosophy of Religion," *PQ* (April and June, 1957) and "Recent Empiricism and Religion," *PH* (July, 1957); I. T. Ramsey, "Empiricism and Religion," *CS* (June, 1956).

[4] Paton, "Fifty Years of Philosophy," p. 341.

[5] Edward Caird, *The Evolution of Religion* (New York: Macmillan & Co., 1893), Vol. I, pp. 4–68.

Even so, the revolution in philosophy had yet to be accomplished. To quote Paton again,

> All of this was taken calmly by Oxford in its stride. The man who succeeded in fluttering the dovecots for the first time was A. J. Ayer in his *Language, Truth and Logic*, and this was not published till as late as 1936. Perhaps the flutter was only a mild one, but I should hesitate to repeat in print some of the things said about him at the time. Whoever may have failed in the art of communication, he certainly did not. He exposed the nature of Logical Positivism, if I may so express myself, in all its naked horror, and he did so with a plausibility worthy of John Stuart Mill at his best.[6]

By 1937, he continues, "the Cam was flowing into the Isis, and it seemed to me that a fresh era had begun."[7] In this fresh era how did philosophy relate itself to theology? For the logical positivist theological assertions, like moral assertions, were nonsense. Neither type of assertion stated any verifiable facts and so neither could have any meaning. If they referred to empirical situations at all, the only content of meaning they had over and above this reference was "emotional," so that they expressed my emotions or attitudes.[8] However, logical positivism was not the only modern manifestation of the English empiricist tradition, and from Moore on the one hand and Wittgenstein on the other, there developed in English philosophy the kind of movement which has since dominated the English scene and has been variously named logical analysis, linguistic philosophy, or linguistic analysis. The important difference from the point of view of theology was that, unlike the logical positivist, the linguistic philosopher did not judge statements according to the dichotomy: either they are statements verifiable by sense experience or they are meaningless. The linguistic philosopher asked what the function of theological statements was or what jobs they did. This did not mean that we were now back where we began; on the contrary, it made the

---

[6] Paton, "Fifty Years of Philosophy," p. 346.

[7] *Ibid.*, pp. 349–50.

[8] See A. J. Ayer, *Language, Truth and Logic* (New York: Dover Publications, 1946), pp. 118 ff.

difference between philosophy and theology all the clearer. Nor
again did it mean that theology could expect philosophy to reinforce its claims, since the philosopher could very well decide that
the function of theological statements was that of entertaining us
or comforting us with fictional stories. But it did mean that a
fresh era had begun in philosophical theology, and that there was
a possibility of some sort of co-operation between philosophy and
theology. For just as philosophy distinguished itself from science,
recognizing that questions of fact about the universe were matters for scientific investigation and that the relation of philosophy
to science was that of elucidating the logic of scientific language,
so in relation to theology, philosophy has come to see its task as
that of describing the logic of theological language. So the phase
of discord has been replaced by that of "modern" harmony.

The philosopher of religion nowadays recognizes, then, that his
task is primarily a critical rather than a creative one. He is not
concerned to act the play but to criticize the performance that
he sees before him. The old method of philosophizing about
theology was not so modest. It set out to furnish proofs—that is,
to prove theological conclusions from nontheological premises.
There are two reasons why this is no longer the way we set about
philosophy of religion, both of which could be expressed by saying that the old method presupposed a view of philosophy which
has now become old-fashioned. Since some people do not take
any kind of fashion seriously, it will be as well to make the two
points in a more direct fashion. The first is that, as I have mentioned above, we now regard philosophy as essentially a subject
which has no direct relation with things, so that the language of
philosophy is second-order rather than first-order. This means
that, just as the material world is not the direct concern of the
philosopher ("Do I see two lamps or one?" can be either a matter
of investigation [science] or a matter of reflection [philosophy]),
so God is not the philosopher's direct concern. Perhaps both the
philosopher and the theologian now see that theology does not
result from metaphysical inquiry but from the direct relations of
the religious man with God. Thus in recent years the theologian
has often insisted that theological thinking is an ecclesiastical un-
dertaking, thinking done in and for the community brought into

being by the revelation of God. There may have been some philosophers who have lost faith in theology because they looked to philosophy to provide them with some independent way of attaining religious truths, but philosophy is not another way of learning what revelation teaches us. Its business is to deal with what we may broadly class as logical questions in regard to religious beliefs, and in this sense of the word we can discern a widening of the scope of logic to include the study of forms of language. So philosophy is spoken of as a linguistic study—this is where it begins, because concepts cannot be studied, described, or criticized except with reference to the concrete situation in which they are tested. To call philosophy a linguistic study can be very misleading, but it is less misleading to start from such a description than to begin, as some theologians do, by describing philosophy as a study of reality. The philosopher of religion studies religious language with a view to placing it on the map of language. His first task is then that of describing as carefully and exhaustively as he can the various forms of religious discourse so as to bring out their likeness to, and their difference from, other forms of discourse.

As I have already said, this understanding of the task of philosophizing about theology is less ambitious than the old method, which was an endeavor to prove the truth of theology. This meant that theological conclusions were proved from nontheological premises; for without such a reference to an independent source there would be no proof. The abandonment of this method is due to our realization that in philosophy we do not prove anything. This was put trenchantly by Waismann in his paper "How I See Philosophy": "No philosopher has ever proved anything. The whole claim is spurious. What I have to say is simply this. Philosophic arguments are not deductive; therefore they are not rigorous; and therefore they don't prove anything. Yet they have force."[9] As Waismann went on to say, the difference between logic and philosophy was that philosophy did less and more than logic. It did less than logic because it never establishes anything conclusively; and more, in that, if successful, it effects a change in

[9] F. Waismann, "How I See Philosophy," *Contemporary British Philosophy*, *op. cit.*, p. 471.

our whole mental outlook. To call philosophical arguments proofs would be to confuse them with formally valid ones. Such a confusion might lead us to attempt to apply to the former the criteria for evaluating the latter, and this could only result in the rejection of all possible philosophical arguments as invalid. This would surely be to miss the point of philosophical arguments. Or again this confusion of philosophical arguments with logical ones might lead someone to "tidy up" philosophy and present it as a "respectable" study by attempting to force philosophical arguments into the deductive mold, in this way making philosophy a formal science. In this case philosophy would have won respectability at the cost of becoming an irrelevant game. It is worth stressing that there is one respect in which philosophical arguments are like logical ones: despite the fact that they are not rigorous they have force. They are not compelling, but they do have a bearing on conviction. But in saying this we must be clear that the way in which they bear on conviction is often like the way in which poetry bears on our convictions. The philosopher is a strange animal—often he seems to be something like a scientist, often like a logician, and often like a poet. It is where analysis grows into proof and proof becomes a matter of vision that philosophy appears. One other point must be mentioned about the old notion of the task of philosophy of religion. By seeking to prove the theological position from nontheological premises it denies that there is ultimately any difference between theological and nontheological language. This is quite contrary to the view that is implied by the use principle that every area of language has its own logic, and that the justification of any proposition has to be done from within its own area. This is the kind of antireductionist attitude that has characterized not only moral philosophy (e.g., formulations of the naturalistic fallacy) but even more obviously epistemological theories of perception (the rejection of phenomenalism).

Once again, then, we are brought back to the point that the philosophical theologian (or philosopher of religion) will concern himself with the examination of the many and varied forms of religious discourse. The first thing that this involves is the classification of the different types of language and meaning that appear in religion. Thus within Christianity the language of liturgical prayer is not the same as the language of the Creeds; nor again is the language of the Creeds the same as the language of the pulpit. Those parts of the Gospels which seem to have no other function than that of telling a story are to be distinguished from those parts which express the author's faith in Christ. There are thus both descriptive and nondescriptive forms of discourse in the Gospels. Again, the descriptive statements are not homogeneous, because there are historically descriptive statements and nonhistorical descriptions. In the Fourth Gospel there is a fusion of the languages of poetry, of mysticism, of metaphysics, and of history. The philosopher of religion will be concerned to show the logic of such biblical language. In doing this he resists the temptation to proceed as the philosopher usually does, by taking specimen sentences from the language that he investigates, isolating them, and then offering an analysis of them. Otherwise, like so much recent philosophy of religion, we shall be concerned with such bizarre samples of religious language as "God exists." If we are appealing to ordinary language in our examination of theology, the ordinary language to which we must appeal is biblical language. In philosophizing about theology we are dealing with language about the self-revealing God, and this means that we are dealing with the belief that God has spoken. In so far as the Bible expresses this conviction, and is for all Christians in some sense an authority, it is to the language of the Bible that we should turn to find the typical use of talk about God and Christ. One reason why analytic philosophers have concerned themselves only with the general question of the meaningfulness and character of religious language is that this fundamental notion of revelation in theology brings us into collision with the radical empiricism which has been the attitude characteristic of analytic philosophy. It cannot be anything to do with the fact that such philosophy is analytic, for theology is also in many ways a matter of analysis. The cause lies rather in the belief that revelation cannot be called knowledge. It is argued that if anything can be said, then it can be said clearly, and whatever cannot be said clearly cannot be meaningful. So philosophy is described as the dissolution of problems engendered by unclear language and the solution of problems which can be clearly stated. But, as Marcel has said, a problem is not the same thing as a mystery.[10] A problem is something which can be solved and which ceases to be a mystery for me when I have solved it. Mystery is something fundamentally different. It remains mysterious even when understood, because understanding here is understanding of what is beyond our comprehension. It is the linguistic philosopher's faith that there is no unfathomable mystery that has led him to turn his back on the language of faith as revealed in the Bible.

The philosopher of religion then need not fear the linguistic or analytic method as such, though he must beware lest he make the same disastrous assumptions as so many practitioners of the technique and so land himself in a divided universe. But if he has walked carefully and has proceeded to the examination of the language of faith in its natural habitat is all well? Not necessarily, for he may find that the painstaking description of the various forms of religious language leaves him with the further task of deciding whether these statements are true or false. In describing the various forms of Christian language, for instance, we must distinguish between those sentences which are statements of fact and those which are not assertions at all. There are so many examples of the latter in Christian language that we must distinguish several subspecies of them, and this is why it is pointless to characterize religious language as emotive language. There are exclamations, petitions, thanksgiving, and vows to be found in the broad class of liturgical language, and the Bible is also rich in examples of precepts, exhortations, promises, and aspirations. But ultimately the interest of these forms of language derives from the meaningfulness and truth of the assertions in religious language. Many important things can be said about religion which are interesting even if religion is not true; but in the end we take religion seriously because we are convinced of its truth. Religion is very much a matter of belief, and the religious man is not content with meaningful statements but only with what is true. In various ways the question of truth poses a task that the modern philosopher

[10] G. Marcel, *Being and Having*, Katharine Farrer, trans. (Boston: Beacon Press, 1951), pp. 100–101, 117. Cf. also his *Philosophy of Existence*, Manya Harari, trans. (New York: Philosophical Library, 1949), p. 91.

of religion tends to avoid. I shall mention two, one of which had, and still has, a great attraction for theologians and another which has been the practice of philosophers who have been impressed by a certain resemblance between religion and morality and theologians who have tried to "flee the evidential."

It will be said that the analysis of religious language should be done with reference to those specific experiences which we call religious. Thus all our statements are expressions of our experience. This kind of theory can take two forms. It can either identify religious belief with religious experience or say religious belief is based on religious experience.[11] In either case the main weakness of this kind of view is that it does not make clear what is meant by "religious experience." The expression may mean certain types of emotional or historical experiences which bring home to a person the realization of God's presence and activity in the world.[12] If this is what is meant, then we must explain how we are able to use the concept "God" with regard to these situations. How did we obtain this concept in the first place? It is often said by religious people that only the eye of faith discerns the handiwork of God, that the course of history has often a mysterious clue to God's gracious purposes which only faith can perceive. What this means is that only the person who begins with the idea of God can say anything about the work of God in the world. So we are driven to say that we derive the very idea of God from religious experience. This position will often depend on a rigorous distinction between the relatively uncertain propositional knowledge of God which theology contains and the certain knowledge which comes in the direct experience of God.[13] Whereas when we are convinced that we are in touch with reality we have certain knowledge, the attempt to express this in theoretical terms involves us in increasing uncertainty. Theological formulations are inadequate, we are told. But, even though it is true to say that knowledge is always knowledge of the real world, it does not follow that such knowledge by acquaintance is unre-

[11] Cf. John Baillie, *The Sense of the Presence of God* (New York: Charles Scribner's Sons, 1962), pp. 64 ff.
[12] Cf. John Baillie, *Our Knowledge of God* (New York: Charles Scribner's Sons, 1939), pp. 132, 143.
[13] Cf. Baillie, *Sense of the Presence of God*, pp. 9–10.

lated to knowledge of propositions. And to say that we have experiences of a certain kind is not to say anything which necessarily implies that these are religious, unless what we mean by "religion" is experiences of this kind—in which case there is no relation between them and God. Experiences do not carry labels, as we saw earlier; and furthermore, they need independent justification. As Hobbes said, when a man tells me that God has spoken to him in a dream, this ". . . is no more than to say he dreamed that God spake to him."[14]

The other way of avoiding questions concerning the truth of religious statements is to analyze faith as self-commitment to a person. Thus it is often said that religious belief is belief in a Person and not a belief that certain things are the case. This is indeed true, and it is necessary to see how all religious belief is a matter of commitment—of truth for me, as Kierkegaard put it. But this distinction does not imply that statements of my belief in someone do not involve me in statements of belief that such and such is the case. Clearly, for example, I cannot believe in my doctor unless I also believe that he does exist. More important, it is some belief about what he is that justifies my belief in him. If this were not the case there would be no way of distinguishing between my belief in my doctor and my irrational trust in the charlatan who practices "medicine" in the market place. Now the point is not that there is no commitment involved in my belief in my doctor but rather that commitment is made to him rather than to the other person because of what he is and what he has done. To move to a religious example, I believe in Jesus Christ as Lord and God and so I do not believe in the Buddha. What does this mean? It means that I regard what Jesus said and did and what he was as at once affirmation and justification of the claim that he is Lord and God. We are once more involved in talking of revelation, for my statement "Jesus Christ is Lord and God" is born of the revelation in him. When Peter said in Caesarea Philippi, "Thou art the Christ," he was told by Jesus that flesh and blood had not revealed this to him but the Father. Peter knew what he had said, and he had said it because it was true; and, had he been asked

14 Thomas Hobbes, *Leviathan*, chap. 32. (New York: E. P. Dutton & Co. [1914]), p. 200.

why he had said it, he could have produced some evidence for saying that it was the case.

The status of such evidence is what the philosopher of religion must discover. Here the challenge of empiricist philosophy is felt very keenly. For the empiricist philosopher will ask whether the denial of certain historical facts which are said to be part of the story of revelation will falsify the assertions of faith. This general problem of the evidence for theological assertions becomes two problems at least. There is the problem of history with relation to belief in Jesus Christ and also the problem of factual evidence with relation to belief in God. In these and all other problems of philosophy of religion the borderline character of the study is very clearly revealed. Standing on the borderline between theology and philosophy the philosopher of religion is open to the pressures that come upon him from both sides. We have already seen how philosophical pressures lead him into certain problems concerning the use of language, but we shall also see that he does not escape the pressures which come from the side of theology. Sometimes indeed these pressures and criticisms overlap with those that issue from philosophy.

Let us first take the matter of the relevance of historical evidence to the doctrine of Christ. Ever since Kierkegaard theologians have been concerned to draw a distinction between statements of fact and statements of faith.[15] For these theologians the assertion that Jesus was the Christ has to do with the response of faith and not with historical fact. We can learn much from history but "about Christ . . . nothing can be known, He can only be believed."[16] This is the theme on which so many theologians have written their respective variations. Now the opposition to this kind of view from within theology is concerned to point out that ultimately such a view does not do justice either to the statement that Jesus is the Christ or to the Christian faith as a whole.

[15] See his *Training in Christianity*, Walter Lowrie, trans. (New York: Oxford University Press, 1941), p. 28; *Philosophical Fragments*, D. F. Swenson, trans. (Princeton, N. J.: Princeton University Press, 1936), pp. 20 ff., 86.; and *Concluding Unscientific Postscript*, D. F. Swenson, trans. (Princeton, N.J.: Princeton University Press for the American Scandinavian Foundation, 1963), *passim*.

[16] *Training in Christianity*, ibid., p. 28.

It will be said that when we confess Jesus to be the Christ we mean that he really did live and that his life had certain characteristics. The conservative critics of the so-called existentialist theologians realized that matters of historical fact such as the reality of Jesus' existence, the kind of life he lived and the way he died, and what happened the first Easter morning are very relevant to the doctrine of Christ, and that they must take the uncomfortable consequences of the historical character of their faith. Again they would say that the events justified the Christian's faith, and that this does not justify itself in a vacuum, as it were. All these are issues which the philosopher will approach, and find himself hovering between clear epistemological positions as he asks whether it would make any difference to Christian faith if all the events related in the gospel story were shown to be false. For what is at stake here is the notion of truth, and the kind of position we take depends on whether we regard faith in terms of the correspondence theory of truth. That is to say, the fundamental division in theology between those who regard historical scepticism as irrelevant to faith and those who wish to base faith in history is paralleled by the division in philosophy between realist and idealist positions. Thus the philosopher of religion finds theological and philosophical pressures coinciding. The application of philosophical analysis to the interpretation of the theological debate will help both the philosopher of religion and the theologian, for the former will be helped to see the logical structure of the doctrinal statement, while the latter will be helped to see that the deficiencies of the "existentialist" position derive from confusions about the ideas of truth. It is thus clear that the opposition of belief to knowledge and of faith's certainty to historical probability is born of confusion about the use of "know" and "probability." To say that historical statements are probable is not to say that they show deficiency which is not to be found in statements of faith. The fact that we can call historical statements probable to distinguish them from logical or mathematical statements, and statements of faith certain so as to distinguish them from mere opinions, does not mean that historical statements and statements of faith can be opposed to one another.

Let us take the second problem, which in some discussions may lie behind the first. For the theologian may say that statements about God are not statements of fact. If he says this he will find himself criticized by his own colleagues, who will be quick to point out that God's existence is the most important fact, that God is the *ens realissimum*. There are then certain beliefs which seem to be about matters of fact and which are fundamental to Christianity; for statements about God are referred to the world in which we live. Thus the theologian will say that God loves us and that nothing is irrelevant to this statement. Not a sparrow falls without the heavenly Father knowing it. But the theologian will go on to say that "God loves us" is not an empirical statement which is verified by some state of affairs such as the prospering of the godly. But if no situation verifies this belief, then no situation falsifies it either. The theologian will here be tempted either to make his beliefs a matter of how we look at the world or to present his subjectivism in a more sophisticated fashion by talking of them as symbolical statements.[17] But the theologian will also insist that, though there is a sense in which God is not known by evidence, there is also a sense in which we have abundant evidence of what God is like and what he does. Once again the issues between the theologians are seen to be issues which find their parallels in philosophy; for the issue of truth as correspondence is clearly the same kind of problem as we have here. Neither the theologian nor the philosopher of religion can hope to make any headway until the nature of these problems is made clear.

There are two aspects of the problem of God. Since all theological statements are, by definition, about God, then despite the fact that the term "God" does not perhaps appear in them, God is really the subject of all theological statements. However, as we have seen, God is described as a transcendent being. The word "God" seems then to name an individual, and if this is so then its meaning can only be given by indicating the individual. A name has no content of meaning; it serves only to denote the individual named. But clearly in the case of God this is impossible; we cannot point at God. This raises the problem of showing

[17] Cf. Paul Tillich, *Systematic Theology* (Chicago: University of Chicago Press, 1951–63), Vols. I and II, *passim*.

the rules for using the word "God." There is the other problem: that any statement about God refers also to life, that no statement is theological which does not logically involve the speaker. The statement "God made the world" does not simply state a fact but also involves me, when I utter such a statement, in certain beliefs about the attitudes which are proper for me. But not only this—the justification of such attitudes is to be found in the fact that the original statement describes. That is to say, the statements that I make about God relate him to the world, and this presents a different problem from the first. Whether or not we say that the term "God" is really a proper name and not a predicative expression, there is no doubt that the religious man thinks of God as a real being somehow personal in character—hence the popularity of such old definitions of religion as personal communion with a transcendent Person. The problem of God's existence, however, is simpler than the problem of characterizing God. Is there any sense in which the existence of God can be proved? There are traditional arguments which, ever since Kant's detailed criticism in *The Critique of Pure Reason*, have been dismissed as evidently invalid; and very often where the arguments of St. Thomas Aquinas are accepted they are put in a form somewhat different from that in which they are given by the Angelic Doctor. But does St. Thomas' proof (*demonstratio quia*) have the kind of rigor of which I spoke earlier? Is it not rather true, as Kierkegaard said of the whole business of proof, that the conclusion emerges by a leap?[18] In which case, to talk of proving God may be said to confuse the kind of decision that is involved in religious belief with totally different matters. The traditional proofs, however, articulate an ontological insight which is at the root of such decision.

The task of characterizing God raises, we said, a much more complicated problem. If the predicates used of God are true, then there must be some empirical anchorage for such descriptions. But it is clear that the empirical anchorage for such descriptions

---

[18] *Philosophical Fragments*, p. 34. For a discussion of what St. Thomas means by proof, see E. A. Sillem, *Ways of Thinking about God* (New York and London: Sheed & Ward, 1962) and Victor White, *God the Unknown* (New York: Harper & Brothers, 1956).

does not offer a straightforward test of these descriptions. In a word, we have the old problem of analogy. According to the classical doctrine of analogy no statement concerning God, with the exception of negative statements, is literally true. Yet these statements do not reveal an ambiguous use of their terms, and so we say that we predicate these concepts of God analogically. All statements concerning God must make use of language which in the first instance is used to describe the world, and so all descriptions of God are analogical. If we use such analogical language successfully of God, this means that we are able to indicate quite clearly that the language is no longer to be understood in its primary sense. That is to say, the way of analogy presupposes the way of negation, and so religious language always moves back and forth between affirmation and negation. And here we see, not only how every concept which we may want to use to describe God has to be balanced by another concept which has a different, perhaps even a contrasting, emphasis, but also the way in which theology is very much like metaphysics, which also has its paradoxes and negative concepts. It is easy to see from the history of theology how it has absorbed into itself from time to time certain metaphysical notions such as the absolute, being, and nonbeing. This kind of borrowing, however, is always done to further a theological purpose. The fascinating plundering of metaphysical treasures has tended to make theologians blind to the very different purpose to which these concepts were then put. Ever since Tertullian the Christian Church has not lacked theologians who will say either that we must have a synthesis of philosophy and theology or that we should separate the two rigidly, showing that Athens has nothing in common with Jerusalem.

I spoke earlier of the difficulty of balancing the various analogical predicates used of God, and we saw how the philosopher's interests overlapped here with those of the theologian. What the latter is concerned with dogmatically the former deals with neutrally, for he is not directly concerned with theological data. Consideration of two related subjects will again bring out this overlap: the doctrine of creation and the problem of evil. We are often told by the theologian that the confession that Jesus is the Christ is central to the biblical conception of creation. The

New Testament claims that the man Jesus was the divine "Word" by whose power the world was created. The individual Christian and the Christian Church were both then regarded as a new creation.[19] Here is perhaps the beginning of the identification of the purpose of Creation with the redemption of man. This reading of the doctrine of creation will lead the theologian to interpret the Incarnation as some kind of invasion of the world. Bultmann's insistence that the New Testament reports the story of the Incarnation after the pattern of redemption mythologies could be described as an attempt to open our eyes to the dangers involved in an uncritical acceptance of the old idea that the purpose of Creation was the redemption of man. It may be argued that Bultmann himself puts forward an impossibly anthropocentric view of Christianity, but this need not concern us now. My point is rather that when he tells us that modern man finds that these old myths conflict with his scientific world view, one such conflict is that between regarding the world as simply the stage on which the drama of redemption is played and the interpretation offered by an evolutionary theory. To regard the Incarnation in this way is to think of the Word as if he had no relation to the world, whereas what we have in the Incarnation is surely a Word spoken in the context of the concrete. "True theology begins where Christ himself began, in the womb of the Virgin—that is to say, in the concreteness in which the Word of God has come to us."[20] It was said by some critics that Barth's theology tended to make so radical a separation between God and the world that it made the Incarnation a logical impossibility. Be that as it may, when the philosopher points out that some views of the Incarnation involve this devaluation of Creation, the theologian recognizes that this is in fact a devastating criticism of such views of both the Incarnation and Creation. The work of Teilhard de Chardin which has —understandably—been so severely criticized by some English

[19] Cf. N. A. Dahl, "Christ, Creation and the Church," in *The Background of the New Testament and Its Eschatology*, W. D. Davies and D. Daube, eds. (Cambridge, Eng.: The University Press, 1964) and W. A. Whitehouse, "Christology and Creation," *Essays in Christology for Karl Barth*, T. H. L. Parker, ed. (London: Lutterworth Press, 1956).

[20] T. F. Torrance, *Karl Barth: An Introduction to His Early Theology, 1910–1931* (London: SCM Press, 1962), p. 170.

readers may yet prove to be a most beneficial influence in theology. For the great merit of his work is that he has tried to see the Incarnation and the Creation together, to understand the history of the universe as intrinsically, and not simply extrinsically, related to the appearance of Christ in the fullness of time, deliberately reviving the image of the cosmic Christ. In so far as theology has often failed to realize that any attempt to present our doctrine of Christ's person and work must take note of the way we understand the world in which we live, theology has been—to echo Bultmann—mythological.

Myth appears too in the problem of evil, but it is a different kind of myth that we find in theologians' attempts to solve the problem. Though it was a romantic poet and not a romantic theologian who said he believed this world to be "a vale of soul-making,"[21] this has in fact become something of a stock answer to the problem.[22] I am not at the moment interested in denying this but rather only in showing how easily this kind of statement can be misconstrued. The great value of the statement is that it reveals what is so often forgotten about the problem of evil, namely, that it is in the first place a practical problem. When the religious man meets evil, the problem it raises is solved in behavior. Is he to lose his faith in God, to fall down under temptation, or is he to withstand temptation and "trust in God and do the right"? Newman spoke of the religious man's intellectual difficulties as "nothing but temptations."[23] How important a concept temptation is in the religious life can be seen from such instances as the story of Job, where for all his perplexity and his questioning Job is portrayed as the man who will not "curse God and die," so that his faith in God is ultimately justified. This is the kind of thing that makes us answer the problem of evil by saying that the world is a vale of soul-making. But have we stopped to consider what kind of souls this world will then make? And this

[21] John Keats, letter to George and Georgiana Keats, in *Letters*, H. E. Rollins, ed. (Cambridge, Mass.: Harvard University Press, 1958), Vol. II, p. 102.
[22] Cf. F. R. Tennant, *Philosophical Theology* (Cambridge, Eng.: The University Press, 1928–30), Vol. II, chap. 7.
[23] Letter to John Allen, *Letters and Diaries*, Vol. XI (London and New York: Thomas Nelson & Sons, 1961), p. 86.

really becomes two very different questions—the one concerning the facts and the other concerning the pattern of the moral behavior in question.

Let us concentrate on the moral behavior. When the widow in Richard Llewellyn's *How Green Was My Valley* hears of her husband's death she cries out against heaven and vows that she will never again worship in the Valley's Bethel. What is this kind of behavior? Whatever it is, it is not weak. It is rather the rejection as weakness of the kind of behavior we have been commending. So we must realize that we are concerned with the commending of certain ways of behaving, and here this can lead us into difficulties. In a well-known phrase Nietzsche branded Christianity as slave morality. Adequate or not as a characterization of the whole scheme of Christian morality, is not this an apt comment on what we have been saying is the Christian way of answering suffering? Take again Dylan Thomas' poem on the death of his father: "Do not go gentle into that good night."

> Do not go gentle into that good night,
> Old age should burn and rave at close of day;
> Rage, rage against the dying of the light.
>
> . . . .
>
> And you, my father, there on the sad height,
> Curse, bless, me now with your fierce tears, I pray.
> Do not go gentle into that good night.
> Rage, rage against the dying of the light.[24]

There are few better examples than Thomas' poetry of that positive kind of acceptance of suffering which is a victory over suffering. I repeat that my point is not that this is the wrong answer to the problem of evil, but rather that it is true only if it does justice to the complexity of what it is to resist temptation, a mode of behavior which is often closer to rage than it is to going gentle into that good night.

In conclusion let us go back to a point that I made earlier. Theology, I have said, was quite unlike science, inasmuch as it was not a matter of putting God as we put nature to the test—of

[24] Dylan Thomas, *Collected Poems* (New York: New Directions, 1957), p. 128.

putting the right questions so as to drag out the right answers.
We cannot put God to the test. And if we assume that there is
only one road to knowledge, and that is the way of questioning,
this is to rule out revelation from the beginning. Revelation means
that God has spoken, has "answered" before the "question" was
ever put. It is God who acted first—this is love, not that we loved
him but that he loved us *first*. As Christian theology is par excellence a theology of revelation, where even the very idea of
revelation is primarily a matter of naming a certain event,[25] the
proper method of theology is to analyze what has been disclosed.[26]
This reinforces my earlier description of the present relations of
theology and philosophy as essentially modern harmony. Christian theology cannot be opposed to analytic philosophy, simply
because it is analytic, since it is itself an analytic study. But to
proceed on the assumption that, because the datum of theology
is revelation, we possess revealed truth is the kind of abuse of
revelation which the theologian no less than the philosopher must
criticize. Tillich has spoken of the death of symbols.[27] The fact
that some symbols which a generation ago were living expressions
of lively experiences are now mere antiques cluttering up our
religious language should make us realize that there are revelations
to be seen anew. T. S. Eliot has spoken of the poet as the brave
explorer of the lands beyond the reach of the common imagination. All art has this transcendent character, and in our day the
theologian does well to turn more and more to the artistic imagination in his willingness to receive revelation. Not metaphysics
wrapped up in a neat package but the subtle process of philosophical analysis is the true handmaid of theology.

[25] Cf. Karl Barth, *Against the Stream* (New York: Philosophical Library,
1954), pp. 211, 215.
[26] Cf. Torrance's description of the radical change in Barth's theological
method in his recent study of Barth's early theology, *op. cit.*, pp. 180 ff.
[27] *Op. cit.*, Vol. I, p. 240.

9. Theology and the Natural Sciences

W. A. Whitehouse

Theology has its own subject matter. The tasks imposed by that subject matter are many and various. To each of them there is an appropriate disciplined approach. These tasks all arise from the fact that men make acknowledgments, in speech and in conduct, of the "God" to whom they aspire in religion and to whom they are related in "faith." To criticize these acknowledgments and to help with their revision or reconstruction is the general task assigned to theology. In discharging it, theologians have always been influenced, and rightly so, by the prevailing cultural context. The present context is one where people are liable to feel uncertain in professing any belief which is not supported by those expert in scientific knowledge and speculation. Direct support from these experts is not to be expected in matters of religion or theology, but there will be uneasiness if their own expertise contributes to religious scepticism or to contempt for theology as an ill-based and misguided pursuit.

During the last four hundred years, scientists have produced physical, chemical, geological, and biological accounts of our world's structure and of the functioning of all its components; accounts which do not easily harmonize with accepted versions of religion, more particularly of Christianity. A harmony of cosmological and theological outlook was a feature of Christendom in earlier days. It was the product of intense intellectual and cultural struggles, and it was never securely established so as to be immune from criticism. There is nothing strange about the fact that the struggles have been revived, in new forms and changed circumstances, and good theologians have always tried to do more about it than merely to defend inherited resources, accepting such modifications as are forced upon them. But theologians no longer dictate the terms of the struggle. In the present cultural climate it is the scientists who have come to rank as authoritative guides to human needs and possibilities. The irrelevance of God, except as a therapeutic idea of debatable value, and the reduction of religion to a psychosocial phenomenon infested with immaturity—these are working convictions for a large proportion of mankind. The concerns of theology have come to seem peripheral; and many able persons are quietly suspicious, or openly disparaging, about its credentials as an intellectual discipline.

The scientists themselves have not, as a rule, actively promoted this change in human self-awareness, though they have generally acquiesced in its growth. The evangelizing voices have been in apostolic succession from Marx and from Comte, names which remind us that the extension of scientific claims from the physical to the sociological fields has been of crucial importance in shaping the present cultural situation. In 1844 Marx wrote that "natural science will in turn incorporate the science of man, just as the science of man will in turn incorporate natural science"; and Communist culture is the apotheosis of this conviction. Social science, Comte declared, would complete "the upward flight of our contemplations of reality" and impress upon those contemplations the systematic character they previously lacked "by providing them with the sole universal link of which they admit." Theology and metaphysics, former pretenders to the role of universal integrators, "will have for our successors only an historical interest."[1] The relation between theology and the physical sciences is therefore a limited theme within a wider concern. Yet it is a matter about which no theological worker can afford to be ill-informed.

[1] These citations are borrowed from W. G. Runciman, *Social Science and Political Theory* (Cambridge, Eng.: The University Press, 1963), p. 4. For Comte's view of "social physics" as the legitimate heir which will displace theology and metaphysics, cf. also *The Fundamental Principles of the Positive Philosophy*, I. 31–33.

I

First let us consider how best to envisage the interaction of these intellectual enterprises. Their independence is now generally appreciated, and a metaphor frequently used is that of "territories," with frontiers, frontier engagements, and diplomatic relationships. It is a metaphor to be used with caution, for important common ground may be obscured by attempts to map out the provinces of science and of theology so that the two kinds of enterprise may enjoy peaceful coexistence. Each enterprise takes off from the ground of common experience, all aspects of which are within its scope. Both enterprises direct our attention toward the same structure of actualities and possibilities, which, in the opinion of both scientist and theologian, is not ours to create in some arbitrary fashion, but rather is to be sought and recognized for what it is. For science, it is true, the primary target is the physical universe; or, more precisely, those relations in it which, when intellectually grasped, bring its structure and functioning within man's theoretical and practical range. But this target is pursued within boundary conditions: man in his personal subjectivity and corporate historicity, on the one hand; and on the other, the mystery which envelops the ground of being and of reason. The development of scientific thought casts incidental light upon these boundary conditions, and attention may be explicitly directed toward them at crises in the struggle for scientific advance. For Christian theology, the chief topics are God and man; but the physical world is not outside its purview, first because it is in this world that man is constituted and set to function, and secondly because the God to whom men aspire in Christian faith is acknowledged to be the ground, and in some sense the explanation,[2] of the world.

Retaining the "territories" metaphor, but only in so far as it draws attention to distinguishable enterprises, we can begin to explore frontier relationships by asking next whether the state

[2] Cf. G. F. Woods, *Theological Explanation* (Welwyn, Eng.: J. Nisbet, 1958), or H. H. Farmer, *The World and God* (New York and London: Harper & Brothers, 1935).

of affairs suggests conflict or truce or synthesis. It is conflict, or the threat of conflict, which generally draws attention to frontiers, and in this case there has been plenty to observe. In recent years the course of traditional conflicts has been plotted by cool historical study, and the real issues have been eased and time-conditioned misconceptions undermined. It is, however, unrealistic to suppose that no occasion for conflict remains. Dr. J. S. Habgood's recent essay entitled "The Uneasy Truce Between Science and Theology" ought to disturb the equanimity of those who "assure us that there are now no grounds for conflict between the two disciplines, and that they should never have been fighting in the first place."[3] In any case, a truce—even one based on the genuine eradication of latent conflict—can be sterile and thus uninteresting. Interest shifts quickly from prospect of conflict to prospect of fruitful synthesis. But in this respect, exhortation and pious hope far exceed achievement. Some essays in integration are, of course, available. Scientific humanists, Sir Julian Huxley for instance, make proposals which take up religion into an integrated pattern of explanation with cosmic scope, but how the discipline of theology should be practiced (if at all) in this context is difficult to envisage. Teilhard de Chardin's synthesis, with firm if limited roots in science and in Christian theology, is of disputed worth. A. N. Whitehead's contribution to metaphysical construction, though temporarily eclipsed, is still in the air. The notorious gulf which at present separates the world of science not only from the world of religion but from the worlds of politics, poetry, and day-to-day living, is a standing challenge to bridge-builders. Yet synthesis may be much too strong a word for depicting what one may reasonably hope to see along the frontier of science and theology. The felt need, as expressed by many acute and sensitive persons, is not for a synthesis, but for a theology standing in its own right but expressed with greater openness toward the physical sciences.

[3] In *Soundings*, A. R. Vidler, ed. (Cambridge, Eng.: The University Press, 1962), p. 23. This essay contains detailed allusions to exploitations of the "territories" metaphor. Cf. also M. B. Hesse, *Science and the Human Imagination* (New York: Philosophical Library, 1955), p. 155.

Christians often say that they welcome every improvement in men's understanding of the physical universe, and argue indeed that the framework of distinctively Christian convictions provided an unusually congenial and liberating context in which empirically based sciences were able to develop.[4] Let us, then, take an optimistic view of the frontier situation and consider the case of a man who is reasonably at home on both sides of the frontier and who would claim, if asked, that he is living a reasonably integrated life. He knows where his integrity is exposed to strain, and is aware that mental indolence may be concealing from him the desperateness of his plight; but he would regard it as wild exaggeration to say that he is a commuter, engaged in schizophrenic shuttling between two cultures. Such men exist, in larger numbers than we are led to suppose by some who write on this topic.

Such a man will not be tied by his Christian faith either to biblical patterns of cosmology or to traditional ways of affirming human dignity. Human living, he might say, is properly viewed as a biological phenomenon: a response, generated from inherited and acquired resources, to an environment which is being lucidly and comprehensively mapped by the sciences. Human functioning, as every human agent knows, has its "inner aspect," and it is from one feature of that inner aspect—conceptual thinking— that these sciences, and theology, have alike emerged. They are among the great constructs of spoken discourse in which men engage in order to express and improve the human condition, and also to raise it to ever higher stages of conscious self-direction. Conceptual thinking gives to men a grip, both upon inner condition and upon outward environment; a grip in virtue of which they enjoy significant independence both of internal basic drives and of external stimuli. It has turned human speech into a means of communication impressively rich in nuance and amenable to the communicator's control. Further, the interplay of human lives, entrenching upon one another and upon the common en-

---

[4] This latter thesis is especially associated with the name of Michael Foster, allusions to whose work will be found in most of the books written on this subject since 1939. Cf. Hesse, *ibid.*, pp. 43–45.

vironment, has produced organized social settings, which in turn have become subject matter for legal, historical, and sociological thinking. Again, no human community has failed to develop activities (games, visual arts, music) and types of discourse (metaphysics, ethics, literature) which express views and aspirations about how personal richness of life is best attained. To suppose that this mystery of human life has no more ultimate ground than a "system of nature" is implausible—if by a "system of nature" is meant a cosmic phenomenon capable of over-all description in physico-chemical terms supplemented as appropriate by biological or historico-sociological terms. Human experience is, of course, rooted in such a "world." But from the earliest days of myth-making it has been a major matter of human concern to scrutinize the fabric of experience for intimations of "otherworldly" Deity. This religious quest has led in some cases (though not all) to a conviction that man, and the natural world in which his life is rooted, are also rooted in God. From experience of living by Christian faith it is evident that this age-old concern is not misguided; that its theistic conclusion is not misconceived; and that the concern is being sustained, appropriately and fruitfully, in the discipline of Christian theology.

The claims made in the last sentence of the paragraph above provoke questions and comments, in minds broadly described as secularist, which no Christian can afford to disregard. To the dogmatic secularist, "religion (and morality) are nothing more than illusions to which men have had recourse to sustain and inspire them in the unceasing struggle for power." Other persons, less dogmatic, see no ground on which to proceed beyond some kind of agnosticism. Human science, they say, now so describes the character and constitution of the world, and man's life within it, as to obstruct all ways through the world to the God toward whom men have aspired in Christian religion, and whom they have tried to talk about in Christian theology. Whether or not a student of theology chooses to join in the public argument about what is at stake, he will to some extent have to argue with himself. From time to time he needs a revised view of what there is to argue about and what should be done to help matters forward.

What follows in the remainder of this essay is necessarily selective but may provide useful clues about where to turn for more adequate briefing.

II

Science, it has been said, is "one of the greatest spiritual adventures that man has yet known." For many of us there is an initial problem about how to look at the territory of the physical sciences and appreciate what goes on there. Unless those who work on the theological territory have actually done some scientific research, their view must be that of interested spectators who can never know the ground in the same way as do the men who do scientific work. They must learn what to look for and must listen patiently to warnings about inadequate appreciation. The façade of "results," theoretical and practical, presented to the spectator by physical science has long since transcended the grasp of any single mind, and what the layman must try to appreciate is the solid core of achievement behind that façade. This comes into view, but only haphazardly, through the work of popularizers; for better appreciation it is useful to consult the historians and philosophers of science. Practicing scientists are apt to make disparaging remarks about the familiarity with their territory which is open to laymen through these channels. These remarks are justified when the layman proceeds to operate with a neat abstract story about the "essence" of scientific achievement, a story so framed as to contain the scientific enterprise within a net of generalities any one of which may be falsified by what is in fact happening in some laboratory or other. Warned, but not frightened off, by such remarks, let us observe what we can.

The most obvious, but crucial, aspect of the achievement is that through scientific research men have acquired fuller, more penetrating, and better-organized awareness of the physical constitution—and the operations—in virtue of which things are as they are. Science has improved our stock of explanations. The improvement is evident in both theoretical and practical respects. New accounts of the world's more interesting features have established themselves because they have greater *clarity* and are filled out with explanations of greater *cogency* than those hitherto available. No one claims for them the virtues either of finality or of completeness, but this makes them more, and not less, attractive. This theoretical achievement goes hand in hand with the development of new techniques for the more masterful manipulation of physical possibilities. These innovations, like the theoretical ones, are liable to be superseded by others which are still more promising. In both cases, however, many of the innovations look like permanent additions to the stock of human wisdom.

At this point voices are raised to warn us of impending danger. The innovations have already had a disruptive effect upon human awareness and upon the fabric of social life. Further disruptive effects, indeed the absolute disruption of human life, loom before us as lurid possibilities. Clarity in an account, or cogency in an explanation, are relative to a particular epoch and depend on presuppositions which have gained currency in that epoch; just as on the practical side it can be argued that masterful manipulation is not a self-authenticating achievement, nor indeed a matter for rejoicing unless the purposes of such manipulation can be established and imposed with adequate wisdom. Scientists themselves, like the observers who try to get the feel of their achievements from outside, have realized that their enterprise must be maintained within a humanist framework if it is to be kept from becoming demonic. The Christian-classical humanist framework has, however, been undermined in ways which should be in the forefront of a theologian's mind when he considers what his contribution might be to this situation. "The greatest spiritual adventure that man has yet known," has had its repercussions upon his capacity to contribute.

The culture of Christian Europe, itself the womb of modern science, was one where considerable religious capital was vested, so to speak, in prescientific accounts of the world and in age-old acknowledgments of limits to human competence. With the success of theoretical and practical innovations, much of the invested capital lost its market value. Verbal currency deriving from the earlier situation has nevertheless remained in circulation, its cash value becoming more problematic with every fresh chal-

lenge from critical philosophers alert to science. An elementary
example is the notion of influence from heaven upon mundane
affairs. Each month, as the moon comes to the full, the tides of
the sea rise higher and weak-witted men have fits of madness and
a monthly cycle is evident in the physiology of women; and all
this suggests a mysterious correspondence between happenings
in the heavens and happenings on earth and in human beings.[5]
Stimulated by Galileo's demythologized concept of motion, scientists made the distinctions which led to clearer knowledge about
which objects in the heavens act directly upon which terrestrial
beings—by what means and with what effects. Or again, consider
one aspect of the struggle to rationalize chemistry. Men of the
eighteenth century who were learning to view the world with
Newtonian eyes looked at the fascinating spectacle of what
Newtonian matter could do by way of displaying energies and
undergoing transformations. The great abstractions of Sir Isaac's
physical theory afforded no explanation of this spectacle, but by
sustained effort and struggle men extricated their thoughts about
it from the traditional but confused idea of a world charged
with "spirit." Once energies were distinguished (kinetic, thermal,
electrical) and the transformations were plotted by means of a
new theory of "elements," this "spirit" notion—which, like the
"influence from heaven" notion, had hitherto linked physical and
religious thinking—was stripped in physical usage of all the overtones which established the link, and indeed lost its scientific
usefulness altogether. The use of these notions in religious discourse was not discredited, but henceforth that use had no rapport with the fuller and more penetrating awareness of the world
to which men had attained. The Christian-classical humanist
framework into which these notions entered became less obviously applicable to men's real situation.

Another factor in the process which has undermined that
framework has been graphically depicted by C. C. Gillispie's
thesis that aspects and areas of natural occurrence have been
steadily swept within the realm of "objectivity," a realm whose

[5] The example has been borrowed from Stephen Toulmin and June
Goodfield, *The Fabric of the Heavens* (New York: Harper & Row, 1962),
p. 18. This is Vol. I of *The Ancestry of Science*.

advancing "edge" covers more and more of the world's interesting features.[6] Once inside the realm, these features are displayed in the light of an inherent autonomy which calls for no explanatory factors beyond those brought into the scientific account. They do not have to be rooted in "God"; and where previously they seemed to have an intimate connection with man's deepest interests, their "objective" presentation leaves man "alienated" in his subjectivity from his objectified environment. Pious men failed at first to discern the full implications. With Newton, and with "natural theologians," they believed it possible to "argue the existence of God from what science had discovered, and his government from what it had not." New territory embraced by science could still be deemed eloquent of creation, though not of personal Providence. The resistance put up in the nineteenth century to geological and biological theories based on the principle of uniformity is, from this point of view, instructive and illuminating;[7] but these disciplines, too, have established their right to clarify natural processes in terms of autonomies, and to dispense with any room for appeal to cosmic personality as a necessary explanatory factor present in some form or other in the mysterious background.

A third factor, more difficult to assimilate than the other two, has come into play within scientific experience and has made people talk in recent years about a final break with Christian-classical presuppositions about the quest for truth. The quest for truth matters because truth is all that men may safely trust. The criteria by which to distinguish truth from falsity have been differently conceived at different epochs; scientific enterprise has lent weight to criteria of an empiricist flavor and discredited any that savor of authoritarianism or traditionalism. But until very recent times these disputes about criteria have not affected a persistent conviction that truth is "known reality," a fusion of intellect and being in a reliable mind. The quest for truth has been broadly seen as the approximation of theory (and of practice in the wake of theory) to predetermined reality, whose

[6] Cf. C. C. Gillispie, *The Edge of Objectivity* (Princeton, N.J.: Princeton University Press, 1960), chap. VI.
[7] Cf. R. Hookyaas, *Natural Law and Divine Miracle* (Leiden: 1959).

"principles" are displayed in any achievement fit to rank as truth. Scientists work with theoretical constructs, but these are no longer deemed to serve as ever closer approximations to true statements about what the world is like, or ought to be like, in some absolute sense. They are "tentative formulae for doing things." The quest for truth has become an experimental and creative pursuit in a sense not hitherto conveyed by those adjectives. Truth is what emerges in the act of testing theory against experience. It is marked essentially by *novelty*. It may not be regarded as there to be merely uncovered—there "in principle," waiting as in a womb to be delivered by the midwifery of thought. It requires for its *creation* our manipulation of the world. It has been suggested that the hard core of what emerges can be expressed wholly in the negative form of limitations—statements of what we cannot do. If this is so, no question arises about why it merits trust. But in fact the products of scientific enterprise are aggressively positive, and some answer must be given to the question of whether or not they merit trust. No clear answer is forthcoming except by means of the positivist criterion that they merit trust when "the good of persons" is manifestly being promoted—which is the line taken by "scientific humanism." Scientists are content to work with a "modest positivistic epistemology," with implications for the human situation not yet fully explored. Further exploration[8] may help to clarify for the next generation a new humanist framework which will be open toward the territory of theology—as so-called scientific humanism is not, since an appeal to "the good of persons" does not call for theological clarification when it can be amply clarified by other disciplines.

Scientists are vividly aware that many factors constitutive of physical and biological reality are not yet within the net of scientific explanation. What is not known to the confederacy of science looms larger in the good scientist's mind than what

[8] An important pioneer work in this field is M. Polanyi, *Personal Knowledge* (Chicago: University of Chicago Press, 1958). Consult also the article "Contemporary Science and Human Life," by Erik Ingelstam, *ER*, Vol. IX, No. 4 (July, 1957), esp. pp. 370 ff.

is known. But, *qua* scientist, his aim is to extend the net in appropriate ways and to preserve *scientific* agnosticism about matters which must in principle elude the net. Theology, and theological anthropology, may win his confidence, but they will do so on grounds other than those he can call scientific. It is not within the scope of this essay to explore this possibility. The point to be made here is that if these disciplines are to commend themselves and their results to scientific workers and those impressed by scientific achievements, then those who practice or rely on them must be keenly aware of what the confederacy of science has done about its own special topic, man's knowledge of the physical universe. In very many respects the universe has become much clearer than it was. If, in other respects, it has become more bewildering, this is not a source for antiscientific propaganda or for smooth talk about the limitations of science. The new clarifications have met with resistance, frequently inspired by religious preoccupations. But what has been undermined through this resistance is the worth of the religious preoccupations and not the scientific innovations. The most embarrassing feature of the current situation is that explanations which now yield clarity have no links with religious belief, as had older explanations in terms of "purposes" or in terms of "second causes," themselves the effects of a "First Cause" to which men may make their way by "reason."[9] Man has been deprived of the "cosmos" which, on Christian-classical presuppositions, gave meaning to his life and cogency to his religion. Christian men in particular have been forced to acknowledge that the world of nature and the world of events do not keep within the framework provided by the Bible. Physical and biological reality no longer bear obvious witness to the Bible's theme of God's historical purposes with men. The physical universe has therefore become, once again, a competing authority, threatening to supersede all other alleged authorities in matters of ultimate

[9] The detailed analysis upon which this observation rests may be studied in the book to which this essay is heavily indebted, John Dillenberger, *Protestant Thought and Natural Science* (Garden City, N.Y.: Doubleday & Co., 1960).

human concern. Joseph Campbell puts the point clearly in his reference to

that most important mythological tradition of the modern world, which can be said to have had its origin with the Greeks, to have come of age in the Renaissance, and to be flourishing today in continuous, healthy growth, in the works of those artists, poets, and philosophers of the West for whom the wonder of the world itself—as it is now being analyzed by science—is the ultimate revelation.[10]

III

Tension between scientific awareness and religious convictions imposes strains which vary from person to person. Historical study of older conflicts has eased unnecessary sources of strain and shown how much adjustment has been possible when misconceptions were cured. In the minds of people who do not think much about these matters there is a formidable legacy from earlier days of conflict, and a good deal of patient education is necessary to remove it as occasions arise. Christians equipped to lend a hand with this service, and with the more constructive tasks of relating their religious convictions to scientific culture, must take their bearings from an up-to-date diagnosis of the points of strain and from the most sensitive prescriptions for dealing with them.[11] In this essay there is room for only a quick preliminary glance at the situation as currently understood, relating it so far as possible to earlier preoccupations.

How, first of all, do we best envisage the competing authorities between which tensions arise? Is it still a matter of Darwin versus the Bible, or of a self-sustaining material and evolutionary universe versus the Bible's God? It is better to say that two personal

[10] Joseph Campbell, *The Masks of God*, Vol. I (New York: Viking Press, 1959), p. 7.

[11] Among the books to be recommended are two of particular merit, one by a scientist and the other by a theologian: Harold K. Schilling, *Science and Religion: An Interpretation of Two Communities* (New York: Charles Scribner's Sons, 1962) and E. L. Mascall, *Christian Theology and Natural Science* (London: Longmans, Green & Co., 1956). There is a full and helpful bibliography in Dillenberger, *op. cit.*—itself a book of quite outstanding merit but distinguishable from the two selected for mention by its historical rather than systematic approach.

commitments may or may not come into competition within the same human individual: commitment to the authority of God expressed in the gospel of Jesus Christ and communicated through the Bible, and commitment to the authority of the scientific enterprise and its fruits. In general these can be viewed as complementary and not as competing authorities, but difficulties can and do arise, sometimes through discordance but more seriously nowadays through lack of any co-ordination.[12] The question is whether a Christian man can commit himself to the "great spiritual adventure" of science without straying into un-Christian religion or "post-Christian" mythology. Doubts about this possibility cast a blight upon upper-class English education during the nineteenth century, for after the publication of the *Origin of Species*, science, in the eyes of clerical headmasters, became tainted with irreligion. The effects of the blight are still evident here and there in England a century later. The doubts themselves are given a further lease of life with every new disclosure of how socially dangerous science can be, though they are easily smothered by each fresh reminder that it is the key to economic and political well-being in the modern world.

To the Christian scholar and gentleman nurtured on classical literature and philosophy, commitment to science appeared to mean commitment to dogmatic "materialism" and to evolutionary "naturalism," neither of which was compatible with commitment to Christian faith. What has happened on the battlefields where these war cries once rang out so clearly? The issues at stake have become uncomfortably subtle and elusive.

The reality whose structure is disclosed by physics, chemistry, geology, and the life-sciences is not well represented by the model of a material mechanism functioning as a closed system, whose "laws" men may hope to trace, only to discover in the end that they themselves are wholly absorbed in the machine. This crude materialistic image of how man must come to terms with ultimate questions under the authority of science continues to haunt human minds, in spite of steady resistance from all points of the philosophical compass—including Marxism. Its menace lies in the

[12] I have discussed the latter point more fully in *Order, Goodness, Glory* (London and New York: Oxford University Press, 1960), pp. 11 f.

suggestion that everything associated with *mind* or *spirit* is, in the last analysis, reducible to properties of "mindless nonspiritual matter." "Personal" being, whether human or divine, could then, as such, have no ultimate place in reality. This metaphysical assumption is a specter firmly disowned by scientists. The representation of so-called "mindless nonspiritual matter" has become problematic in ways which necessarily divest science of metaphysical assumptions, whether these be detrimental or favorable to humanity and to theology. The detail of this development is not easily expounded, though physicists have done their best to explain to a lay audience the source and nature of the problems. The root of their difficulty in explaining the issues is, perhaps, the essentially negative character of their story. They are faced with insurmountable obstacles if they regard the happenings which are their object of study as activities or qualities of a basic material substance, whatever character they choose to ascribe to it. The *systems* ("entities" is too loaded a word) which they study in particular *states* by means of *observables* ("qualities" again is too loaded a term) are capable of mathematical representation, but cannot, without confusions and contradictions, be represented by symbols taken from the world of everyday perception, such as *position, velocity, identity, causality*—the basic concepts with which science formerly hoped to give a consistent picture of the universe in "material" terms.[13] How to formulate a *positive* concept of reality which accomodates these negative facts without strain, is still an open problem and a fascinating challenge to new exploits in "natural philosophy." To the religious person it is a relief to be told that we must all abandon the idea of an "outside" world, closed in itself, to which manhood must be subordinated. If, however, he wants to go on making the important religious declaration that God, by creation, has given to men a world in which to live, it has become very difficult to see what this declaration is *about*. The way is wide open for reducing the great issues of human living to matter-of-fact problems, soluble by man's technical know-how. Salvation, if any,

[13] Cf. *ER*, *op. cit.*, for articles by H. H. Wolf and Erik Ingelstam alluding more fully to this topic. There is a brief bibliographical note on p. 371.

can only be seriously sought from man himself, with no reference to hypothetical external factors such as God, angels, and demons, or metaphysical powers of any kind.

At this point attention shifts naturally to the impact of science on philosophy, for it is through that discipline that much of the impact is mediated to theology. The presence in this volume of a separate essay on theology and philosophy must serve as some excuse for what would otherwise be an inexcusable omission from this present survey of the ground jointly occupied by scientists and theologians. There are, however, two aspects of what is happening in this field which, even so, are worth mentioning here. First, there is a new self-consciousness about the nature and use of language. The language of science is conventional language whose use, and therefore meaning, is essentially operational. The language of theology is symbolical, and over much of the field it is used analogically. Do theologians understand what they are doing with language to the extent that scientists do? Are they able to cope with problems raised about the adequacy of religious symbolism?

The second matter has to do with method. If we accept Karl Popper's "hypothetical-deductive" account of scientific method, the scientists takes a problem which may be suggested by some human need or by some scientific or prescientific belief which calls for re-examination. This directs his attention to selected data for which he seeks an explanation. Its formal structure is "causal," but causal in a strict conventional sense. Explanations consist of statements that "x determines y" in accordance with some universal or particular law; with specified initial conditions and with an assumption of validity for the appropriate law, predictions can be made; and these must be tested experimentally, so that a selection can be made from among possible explanations, some of which will be falsified by the experimental testing. By this method, no explanation is *confirmed* in any absolute sense; but some survive for subsequent ordeal-by-experiment. Experimentation runs right through the fabric of this method, from the original choice of problem, through the invention of concepts for specifying initial conditions, on through the postulating of laws, to the final ordeal of practical testing. This modest epistemology has won the confidence of scientists and makes them radically suspicious of the seemingly more arrogant procedures associated with the other disciplines. They cannot, in principle, regard their own structures of explanation as either complete or unrevisable. But they cannot see how theological explanations can, with any seemliness, be added to their own achievements to produce enlarged and integrated vision. In the light of their difficulty, has the theologian thought out what it is that he has to offer, and by what method he has managed to establish it?

From these abstract, but none the less pressing, areas of concern, let us turn to the second of the traditional battlefields. Does commitment to scientific investigation mean that one is committed to an evolutionary view of nature which is incompatible with Christian faith? To an evolutionary thesis which is fundamental for biological theory—yes; to a position incompatible with Christian faith and theology—not necessarily! It was Augustine, chiefly, who gave to the Western Church a connected conception of nature. He presented it as the work of one true and gracious God and therefore, in the positive aspects of its existence, wholly good. The natural creation lies between God and the human soul and is a vehicle of God's communication with men. In classical thought it could scarcely be viewed as the instrument of a rational and sovereign Creator unless unchanging forms and principles were built into its structure and were manifest to the rational human mind. Augustine, his predecessors, and his medieval successors saw themselves chiefly as participants in the drama of redemption, and were liable to regard the physical universe and their participation in its processes as substratum, or even shadow, rather than as substantial constituent in their own lives. What they had to say about the physical world was limited to a few themes, obviously chosen under the influence of the struggles with other faiths which Augustine in particular had sampled. The world, they affirmed, has been created, and well created; it has been corrupted, but nevertheless preserved; it is administered with providential wisdom, both through regular government and through miraculous interventions; it is destined to be brought through judgment to renewal in glory. These themes were developed in climates of thought where it was inconceivable that evolutionary characteristics might go deep into the structure of the world. As a result, Christian tradition provided no resources for meeting and coming to terms with a scientific thesis of evolution, which offended the religious sense of propriety in many respects hardly worth reiterating here.

The evolutionary thesis has been accepted in Christian theology, and indeed has been used, somewhat loosely and romantically, to portray an "ascent toward consciousness" which fits well with theological themes about man's unique place in the universe, redemption through love, and eschatological unification. But all is not well as between Christian theology and developmental biology; and it is no accident that younger scholars of ability, from many different cultural and ecclesiastical backgrounds, are hard at work at the present time sorting out the issues at stake in this particular field.

At the same time the biologists are racing ahead with exciting new work, and the theologian cannot be at all sure that he is keeping up with them at the points which may concern him most.[14] Here is a tentative list: There is the question about continuity between living and lifeless "matter." The controversy inside biology between mechanism and vitalism is being steadily transcended by new developments in biophysics and biochemistry. There is the question about the techniques of evolution, and the epoch-making step toward an answer in the theory of genetic codes. At the other end of the biological scale there is the question about continuity and discontinuity as between human and other animal behavior, and the new biological meanings for terms like *mind* or *spirit* as applied to men. There is a marked tendency among biologists to conduct excursions into the field of ethics, with "survival value" as a principal criterion for judgment, so that *good* is liable to mean "successful," and *evil* is deprived of its more militant and malignant connotations. There is a potent and more precise meaning for that emotive word "progress," to denote increasing all-round biological efficiency, expressed through greater independence of an environment and increased control of it. These theoretical innovations go hand in hand with de-

[14] Cf. W. H. Thorpe, *Biology and the Nature of Man* (London and New York: Oxford University Press, 1962).

velopments of technical power, not only over plant and animal life, but (through biochemistry in conjunction with medicine) over the life of men in its most intimate personal depths as well as (through psychology) in its social manifestations. What has the gospel to do with all this, or this with the gospel? Of the tensions which arise from these points of strain, no end is in sight. Theology, indeed, has hardly begun to recast its anthropological thinking so as to reckon with them.

If "materialism" was a threat to the basic religious convictions enshrined in all "natural theology," Darwinism was an even graver threat for it menaced the heart of the Christian gospel—the drama of creation and redemption. At both points of erstwhile strain, much has happened to alleviate the stresses originally felt. The embarrassments for Christian theology have altered, but they have not diminshed in intensity.

In the Copernican world the Christian estimate of man made good sense. But what weight can be attached to it in face of the immensities of space and time revealed by modern knowledge? What importance can be assigned to man if humanity itself is no more than an infinitesmal grain of sand in an immeasurable sandy waste? What answer is there to the accumulating evidence of the complete dependence of the most intimate psychological processes upon physical events? What if everything the theologian talks about is simply the effect of the reflection of conditions of the brain?[15]

To this *cri de coeur* about man's feeling of insignificance we must add the other chief source of embarrassment: that the world as known to the scientists, the world which they are teaching us all to know and live in as *one* world, is a world which does not express the reality of God in any recognizable way. The hiddenness of God in his world is an accepted theological postulate which is now being grasped more radically, but in itself it is not a sufficient remedy for the difficulties with which faith has to wrestle when commitment to the Christian gospel is taken, as it

[15] J. H. Oldham, "Karl Heim on Faith and Science," in *TH*, Vol. LVI, No. 397 (July, 1953), p. 243.

should be taken, to include commitment to the enterprise of science and its fruits.

IV

Nothing in this essay should lead the reader to assume that the writer himself is discouraged by his own theological responsibilities, or that anyone else should be discouraged by theirs. On the contrary: there is work to be done; there are resources for doing it; and there is promise of joy in the effort. In the "Notes on New Directions" toward the end of his historical survey, John Dillenberger surveys the prospects with skill and judgment, and the reader should consult his pages for advice with which I wholeheartedly concur.[16] It is difficult to forecast how future work will develop. Anything said about it must have the character of pious hopes and personal intentions and should therefore be said very briefly.

In the first place, it seems that nothing in the climate of scientific culture has a rightful claim to deflect Christian theology from fundamental fidelity to its own proper object, Jesus Christ and his Lordship. There is always more to be learnt about the practical meaning of this fidelity; and the Church's practice of theology, within this faith and as its proper discipline, has often been marred by blindness and folly. But the terms of the job have always been reasonably clear, and there is no case for a radical departure from them in order to produce some revolutionary New Theology. That the work is associated with a community of faith is no ground for disparaging it. Scientific work also, it has been pointed out, has its community aspect.[17]

The task which confronts theology, vis-à-vis the impact of physical sciences, is to help all men to see their world, and to see the work of scientists within it, "under God." What is to be done about this?

First, we might learn to speak more clearly about what the religious man (and the theologian) looks for, but does not expect the scientist to talk about *as part of his science.* It is something

---

[16] Dillenberger, *op. cit.*, pp. 255–92.
[17] Schilling, *op cit.*

"caught in the structure of physical events"; something which, when discerned, evokes worship and trust. *Consciousness, culture, personality, values, history*, are all realities alleged to be of this non-natural kind—using the scientists' version of "natural"; but the allegation is precarious, and in any case it is not as feasible as was once hoped to build upon an awareness of these things and reach assurance about a God who evokes worship and trust. The theological affirmation should be made by pointing to the possibility—in Christian belief, the actuality—to which the word *grace* refers. Personal grace; which gives, initially, with perfect freedom; bears with corruption; rescues and regenerates in a way which brings true authority to bear upon human life and admits man as a partner with Deity by participation in the mystery of reason, healed and renewed: *this* is the actuality in which all events, all phenomena, all experiences, are embraced and by which they are permeated. The physical world is not a plain expression of such grace. And it is reasonable to hold, as Christians do, that the "order of grace" is, by God's sovereign and gracious will, dependent upon his incarnate Word and disclosed to men in Jesus and through him.

If this be clearly understood, those who believe it might find it possible to construct a "theology of nature"—*not* a "natural theology"—by looking at physical reality in the hope of recognizing hints or echoes of grace in its ambiguities, and providing an orderly report which all men could at least listen to, and perhaps find helpful, in the present stage of scientific and technological culture. At the same time, those who believe the news of grace (and their theologians) might look more closely at the communal human enterprise which is science. In developing science, *man* is expressing himself and asserting his humanity in a fashion which is creating *history*. A parallel observation holds for what he is doing in the community of Christian religion; and there it is firmly believed that history is the context in which grace appears most plainly and where its triumphs are to be looked for. Despite the tensions which occur, and will occur, between these two expressions of communal human vitality, there is a possibility of consistent mutual service, of intrinsic value to both, if each community will converse with the other about the things which bear on the *quality* of human history. It has been traditionally expected of theologians that they should have some competence in philosophy. What matters today, perhaps, is a greater competence in the fields of ethics, politics, and sociology, to be acquired, not in theological isolation, nor in a specialized school of "social studies," but precisely in conversation with partners coming from the community of science—the conversation to be assisted, of course, by helpful experts from the particular fields where scientists and theologians meet and converse. There is no assurance that mistrust will be dispelled, or that we shall come to see more clearly how faith and science interact to the glory of God and the blessing of man. But as conversation develops, in these or other fields of common human interest, there is reasonable hope that we may come to see both the achievements of the physical sciences and the resources of the Christian gospel in richer terms and deeper perspectives than any which have yet appeared.

10. Theology and Social Science

Gibson Winter

Theological ethics encounters new problems with the emergence of a technological society. Man has ethical responsibility for an abundance of human life and resources but meets this task with an inherited ethic of scarcity. World-destructive threats shatter national and cultural boundaries, yet Christian social ethics have viewed war in a context of limited conflict. Theological formulation itself is subject to questioning, since it is still absorbing the shocks of historical criticism. Thus, theological ethics finds itself alienated from contemporary culture, and this alienation is symptomatic of a deep estrangement between Christian thought and the surrounding world.

Christian ethics has two referents: a universal message and the contemporary situation, and a dialogue between these poles is necessary to disclose their meaning for history. Theological ethics needs a partner for such a dialogue; this partner is ready at hand in the social sciences. Theological ethics is concerned with the pattern and direction of development of society; social science is likewise concerned with these structures or forms of social development. There are, of course, obstacles to dialogue within both disciplines, since dialogue can lead to mutual criticism and correction. There is precedent for such a dialogue, since both disciplines do in fact borrow from one another; however, this borrowing tends to be surreptitious; now the problem is to make the borrowing public and give an accounting of its rationale.

The proper focus for such a dialogue is the common subject

matter: both disciplines inquire into the forms which shape and sustain human life, both inquire systematically into man's nature and fulfillment. Without the correction of empirical investigation, theological ethics falls into formalism. Social science, on the other hand, dissipates its energies all too easily in sheer empiricism, missing the important questions about man's freedom and destiny to which such a science could make an important contribution. There are, of course, deeper problems in such a dialogue: the perspectives which have dominated these two disciplines obstruct real dialogue; in fact, creative dialogue will only become possible as these dominant perspectives are challenged.

THE PROBLEM OF DIALOGUE

The dialogue between theological ethics and social science opens as a debate, for the two disciplines take sharply divergent perspectives on man and the patterns of his life. Although both are concerned with man, theological ethics investigates those patterns which guide man's action to its fulfillment in an ultimate and universal sense, whereas the social sciences inquire into the effective structures which shape man's action.[1] The common ground between the disciplines is the patterning of action. However, if one assumes that the effective structures are the only possible and true structures, then social science is the only science of man's action in society. Theological ethics would be little more than a sign of maladjustment. If one assumes that the effective structures are utterly distorted by human sin, then social science discovers nothing normative about the patterns of action in which man may find fulfillment; social science becomes a vain attempt to discern order within human disorder. These are the dominant perspectives: naturalistic social science, which reduces theology to an adjustive psychological mechanism; and organicist theological ethics, which relegates social science to the task of recording man's aberrations in its own idolatrous perspective.

[1] The author is indebted to Alvin Pitcher for this way of formulating the task of theological social ethics; throughout this chapter theological ethics is used in the same sense as theological social ethics—see Alvin Pitcher, "Theological Ethics in Paul Tillich and Emil Brunner: A Study in the Nature of Protestant Theological Ethics" (unpublished Ph.D. dissertation, University of Chicago, 1955).

Naturalistic social science emerged in the eighteenth and nineteenth centuries in the atmosphere of a victorious natural science
—Christian dogma had lost credibility; social disorder had come
with the industrial revolution; Western society faced the task
of reorganizing its existence on a new foundation. The obvious
model for such an enterprise was physics. Social science undertook the Gargantuan task of giving moral direction to the industrial societies of the West.

There were, of course, several varieties of naturalism in this
social scientific development, since the understanding of nature
was changing from a mechanistic notion of elements in orderly
motion to an evolutionary conception of social forms undergoing
change in an interdependent process.[2] However, naturalistic social
science in general reduces experience to forces underlying and
shaping experience—whether these be neural charges, libidinal
energies, economic interests, or inputs and outputs of pleasurable
and painful sensation.[3] In order to know, one traces qualitative
processes of experience back to the simpler, quantitative inter-
actions on which they are founded. Thus, man and society are
conceived of in terms of external, causal processes, whether these
be external to human will because they propel the will from
instinctual levels or because they operate on man from his en-
vironing conditions. Since these are the causes of action, an
inquiry into the effective structures of human action must pre-
occupy itself with calculating these forces and estimating the
directions in which their energy is shaping the process. Since the
extreme naturalistic position presupposes a deterministic world,
an adequate social science would one day be able to trace all the
major forces shaping society, defining their directions mathe-
matically.[4]

[2] This process has been traced by R. G. Collingwood, *The Idea of Nature*
(New York: Oxford University Press, Galaxy Book, 1960), esp. the Introduction.

[3] I am particularly indebted to the discussion of these problems by Richard
McKeon, although the formulation in this chapter is entirely my respon-
sibility; see especially Richard McKeon, "Philosophy and Method," *JP*,
Vol. XLVIII, No. 22 (October, 1951).

[4] A sophisticated statement of this position was given in a faculty seminar
at the University of Chicago by A. R. Radcliffe-Brown. See his *A Natural
Science of Society* (Glencoe, Ill.: Free Press, 1957).

Two qualifications of extreme naturalism have been stated within the social scientific tradition itself, though many social scientists simply disregard them in favor of a simple naturalism. First, a naturalistic science of external causality is not appropriate in the human sciences, since human action ultimately involves the transmutation of external forces to subjectively directed behaviors. No calculation of external forces can obviate the task of interpreting the transmutations which such forces undergo in the processes of human action. To understand action is to participate in the intentional structures which shape its continuity in the world. Pragmatic naturalism emerged from this particular criticism, since the meaning of the situation and the significance of action were interpreted from the perspective of the actor, and yet the fundamental forces directing the actor's interests were still defined on a naturalistic level.[5] This was an important modification in social scientific method, since it opened the door for significant dialogue with other disciplines concerned with man.

Secondly, naturalistic social science presupposes the possibility of objective knowledge of action by the observer; the implication of this view is that the observer is separate from the known. Natural science and social science have acknowledged the intervening role of the observer's perspective during recent decades, but many scientists refuse to acknowledge the significance of this mediating role of consciousness for the status of the sciences. Not only does man's perspective and concern shape his environment selectively and determine the possibilities of his experience, but his consciousness and world view also mediate the total process in which his existence is embedded.[6] There is, in this respect, no

[5] Max Weber developed this critique out of the tradition of historical and cultural sciences; see *The Methodology of the Social Sciences*, E. A. Shils and H. A. Finch trans. and ed. (Glencoe, Ill.: Free Press, 1949). Talcott Parsons clarified this shift to a subjective orientation of meaning in his *Structure of Social Action* (Glencoe, Ill.: Free Press, 1949), but he shifted back from the voluntarism discussed in this work toward a naturalistic base in subsequent works; see especially *Working Papers in the Theory of Action* (Glencoe, Ill.: Free Press, 1953) and *The Social System* (Glencoe, Ill.: Free Press, 1951).

[6] This subject has been widely discussed in phenomenology; see especially Alfred Schuetz, *Collected Papers*, Vols. I and II (The Hague: Martinus Nijhoff); see also the author's forthcoming volume on the problem of theological ethics and social science, in which the themes of this essay are sus-

absolute objectivity in natural science; there is no purely rational structuring of action, for men shape their course of action, even as the scientist shapes his own research, according to concerns, values, interests, and a cultural world view.

These subjective limitations of all science—the mediation of the structure of the objective world in a personal consciousness—set radical limits to neutrality and objectivity in empirical investigations of the patterns of human action. This limitation does not obviate the importance of reliable observations and systematic attempts to discern patterns in human action, but knowledge of the action of man in society is not neutral and objective, any more than the activity of the investigating scientist can be reduced to a set of external forces—he investigates from a perspective which selects. Human action is a manifestation of concern and values; social science manifests its own concerns and values in its process of inquiry. The presupposition of radical naturalism in social science is thus contradicted by the very project of social science itself. This insight reveals the continuum between science, ethics, and religion—these are all human projects, manifesting human values and concerns in relation to the world; these are different kinds of discourse reflecting human intentionalities. Therefore, the claim of one intentional structure, in this case that of natural science, to dictate the criteria of truth in all fields of discourse is an absurd dogmatism.[7]

What I have designated as the organicist perspective in theological ethics refers to an understanding of existence which presupposes a vision of the total structure of reality. This vision of totality provides a conceptual whole within which particular experiences and patterns can be understood and evaluated. The organicist perspective takes two principal lines of development in

tained but from a more fruitful philosophical perspective. One of the clearest statements is given within a different tradition by Dorothy M. Emmet, *The Nature of Metaphysical Thinking* (New York: The Macmillan Co., 1946), esp. chaps. 2 and 3.

[7] This position is not at all self-evident and would be opposed by many social scientists and commentators on social science who see its future in approximation to the exact sciences; for example, George A. Lundberg, *Can Science Save Us?* (London and New York: Longmans, Green & Co., 1947), pp. 35 f., and Barbara Wootton, *Testament for Social Science* (New York: W. W. Norton & Co., 1950), esp. chap. 2.

theological ethics. One tradition conceives the principle of being or totality as voluntaristic; the logos of being is not accessible to reason nor is it determinative for this ultimate will. The divine will transcends all structures of existence; it is known only in its disclosures in history; it is received in acknowledgment and obedience as conformity of the human will to the determinative will of the Creator and Redeemer. Law is the command of this will, but forms and structures are always relative to the ultimate will. For the other line of development, the logos of being gives structure to the universe—a logos which can be apprehended by reason, at least through special revelation. In this tradition, any discontinuity of reason and logos arises from the sinful clouding of man's rational vision.[8]

The organicist perspective within the theological traditions has denied man's access to the vision of totality, whether as will or logos. Man's rebellion or estrangement creates a discontinuity between human will and ultimate will, existence and essence; hence the discerning of forms to shape man's fulfillment depends upon a source of knowledge beyond man, even as human fulfillment in action depends upon a source of power outside of man. Christian traditions have stressed ultimate will or logos; these traditions also make more or less radical interpretations of sin. In every case, however, the organicist perspective anticipates relatively little help from empirical science in the ethical task, since man's discrete experiences need to be grasped in the context of ultimate and universal meaning before their ethical significance can be apprehended, and, in any case, these experiences are so warped by sinful rebellion and anxiety that they disclose little that is valid about man's essential nature or ultimate fulfillment. We shall see that qualifications have to be stated against this organicist position, but its divergence from the perspective of naturalistic social science is quite obvious. Naturalistic social science and organicist theological ethics do not make congenial

[8] There are, of course, alternative perspectives in theological ethics, but the organicist perspective interprets the views of the major dialectical theologians of this period. The position of H. Richard Niebuhr as a contextualist and of Henry Wieman as a process thinker represent important perspectives which do not fit this discussion. H. Richard Niebuhr's views approach more closely a viable position for dialogue with social science.

partners in the construction of a social ethic, since both tend to dogmatize from one or another frame of reference.

THE POSSIBILITY OF DIALOGUE

Despite the divergence of their perspectives, theological ethics and social science have a common concern with the patterns which shape human action. Their conflicts arise over the relativity of these patterns, how they are known, and their significance for the direction of social development. I have outlined the contrasting positions of empirical social science and theologically grounded ethics in their approaches to this problem of social patterning. We shall now consider the direction in which an authentic dialogue might develop; that is, the promise for dialogue as it arises from mutual criticism.

Complementarity

Social science offers no monolithic approach to the problem of patterns, but undermines traditional notions of the fixity of social forms. The dogmatic naturalist clings to the illusion of "natural laws" of human interaction, substituting formulae of human patterning for the intuitional forms of traditional theology. However, this dogmatic naturalism has yet to produce anything resembling a scientific law; the "laws of human action" are culturally relative and thus fail to support a notion of "universal laws." Agnostic naturalism sustains a notion of variability in social patterning over a very wide range. Certain universal foci of patterns are, to be sure, discernible—for example, institutionalization of relationships between man and woman, parents and children, neighbors, etc.[9] However, the meaning of such patterning is variable enough to raise questions as to whether one is discuss-

---

[9] This notion of patterning is developed in the volume, *Toward a General Theory of Action*, Talcott Parsons and E. A. Shils, eds. (Cambridge, Mass.: Harvard University Press, 1951). Clyde Kluckhohn's summary article on this problem of universal patterns indicates the wide range of variability around particular foci of patterning: "Universal Categories of Culture" in *Anthropology Today: Selections*, edited by Sol Tax from the International Symposium of Anthropology, New York, 1952 (Chicago: University of Chicago, Phoenix Books, 1962), pp. 304–320.

ing the same phenomenon in different cultures. Moreover, a strong case can be made for the hypothesis that social patterning develops in the course of human and cultural evolution, even though simplistic hypotheses of unilinear evolution have been discarded. Thus, economic forms and political patterning appear at certain stages of technical and social development. The political is an emergent phenomenon. One can detect enough variety between cultures and through time to discount the notion of fixed or absolute forms.

The relativity of social patterning is counterbalanced by the fact that every known society develops normative structures in order to guide and shape its co-operative and conflicting efforts. Societies are moral phenomena.[10] This fact makes possible a comparative study of normative social patterning; however, such comparative studies have to be pursued with extreme caution, since the meaning of particular patterns varies with the total configuration of the culture. Cultures are totalities with value structures; their processes and patterning are relative to that context. This awareness of variability of total meaning between cultures also enjoins caution in the evaluation of cultural developments from the very limited perspective of our own cultural situation. By the same token biblical ethics and doctrinal ethics, not to say philosophical ethics, encounter sharp opposition from a vigorous social science when they claim universal validity for social patterns which are embedded in some period in the biblical history or Western development. There are, to be sure, foci of problematic consideration around which some kind of patterning will emerge, but the meaning of that patterning and its validity are relative to the situation, the stage of cultural development, and the ultimate concerns which form the context of its emergence.

The dialectical theology which forms the principal school of organicist theology in our time, has also moved toward a recogni-

---

[10] This understanding of society was most incisively stated by Emile Durkheim at the early stage of sociological science; its significance as a cultural universal is also noted by Clyde Kluckhohn in his discussion of "Universal Categories of Culture," *op. cit.*

tion of variability in social patterning, since its principle has been voluntaristic and dynamic.[11] The more static formism of the Thomistic tradition attempts to grasp fixed structures for the patterning of human action, but even within Thomism there are signs of restlessness with the static character of the tradition.[12] However, the dialectical theology is rooted in the Protestant tradition, which invalidates any notion of eternal forms. Indeed, this Protestant principle of the relativity of all forms, as Paul Tillich has shown, has created serious problems for the Protestant attempt to guide the social development of the Western world in the crisis of the last centuries. One might argue, however, that this Protestant principle is precisely the point at which theological ethics and social science can meet and work in a complementary way toward a social ethic; the Protestant principle is consonant with the discovery of variability of patterning by social scientific study.[13]

Karl Barth's theology of freedom and humanity opened the way toward such a creative dialogue in the development of social ethics, but he has claimed more for his biblical ethic than is warranted, and hence closed the door to a constitutive role for social science. The *analogia relationis* upon which he founds his statements about the patterning of human action in society can never be more than suggestive of a direction of concern, since Barth's own position rejects any fixity of social forms.[14] Nevertheless, he

[11] The term dialectical theology was used with reference to this post-World War I theological development; the name seems more suitable than the later designation as neo-orthodoxy, which was rejected by most proponents of the new trend.

[12] By contrast, Dietrich von Hildebrand takes an extremely rigid position on such matters in his *Christian Ethics* (New York: David McKay Co., 1953), taking his point of departure from Pope Pius XII's warning against what might be called a contextualist approach.

[13] See "The Protestant Principle and the Proletarian Situation," in Paul Tillich, *The Protestant Era*, J. L. Adams, trans. (Chicago: University of Chicago Press, 1948), chap. XI.

[14] Karl Barth's fundamental position on ethics is stated in "The Gift of Freedom" in *The Humanity of God*, John N. Thomas and Thomas Wieser, trans. (Richmond, Va.: John Knox Press, 1960); the method of *analogia relationis* is expounded in *Church Dogmatics*, G. W. Bromiley and T. F. Torrance, eds., Vol. II, Part 1 (New York: Charles Scribner's Sons, 1957), pp. 225–54, but this is an epistemological principle which only leads to arbitrary interpretations in designating particular social patterns. For a dis-

makes statements about the subordination of the female to the male which depend upon the cultural context of the biblical world, even though they are stated as analogous to divine relationships such as that of Christ to the Church. The patterns of Israelite life were structured around the three basic forms of traditional society—husband and wife, parents and children, master and slave; these patterns of ethical order and religious symbolization are relative to that context. Barth's important contribution to theological ethics is his clear affirmation of the divine freedom and consequent human freedom in the biblical covenant; the Protestant principle of relativity of all forms including social patterns receives its charter in this covenant. Barth's injunctions against anthropology in the development of theological ethics are entirely unwarranted within his own perspective, for it is precisely man's freedom before God which burdens him with the responsibility to create those forms as God's partner through which life can be sustained and fulfilled. Ethics and theology can only be anthropology—otherwise they become idolatry. Any attempt to burden man with a new law of social forms derived from the paternalistic culture of the biblical period would be the worst kind of biblical positivism over against this charter of freedom; it would be utter idolatry.

Emil Brunner's notion of divine orders has a long and honored tradition in the field of theological ethics, especially within the Lutheran tradition; however, it represents an inadequate attempt to express the Protestant principle of the relativity of forms.[15] A voluntaristic understanding of God's nature and activity shatters

---

cussion of this latter point, see "The Social Philosophy of Karl Barth" by Will Herberg in *Community, State and Church, Three Essays by Karl Barth* (Garden City, N.Y.: Doubleday Anchor Book, 1960), esp. pp. 34 ff. If the analogies are used as suggestive, which would be the implication of the term *signposts* in "The Gift of Freedom," they become appropriate for the solution offered in the concluding section of this chapter. Karl Barth's fundamental position on theological ethics as divine command would give warrant for this interpretation; see *Church Dogmatics, op. cit.,* Vol. II, Part 2, pp. 535, 551.

[15] Emil Brunner, *The Divine Imperative,* Olive Wyon, trans. (New York: The Macmillan Co., 1937), esp. chap. XXVII; for a careful examination of this general problem, see Heinz Dietrich Wendland, *Die Kirche in der Modernen Gessellschaft* (Hamburg: Furche-Verlag, 1958), esp. pp. 29–35.

the notion of a natural law, but it opens the door to a genuine appreciation of traditional structures of society. This was the path which Luther took in his attempt to stabilize the social situation during the theological revolt against Rome; he replaced the natural law which the Church controlled with a political and social order which could support him on German soil. Emil Brunner develops this notion of orders of creation as a framework for the preservation of life in the societal spheres, while the rule of grace, love, and personal communion takes precedence in the community of faith and in the sphere of personal relationship.[16] The consequent dualism of internal and external relationships, a sphere of love and one of law, ends in a dialectic of personal relationships over against a conservative ascription of authority to inherited social patterns. The personal and loving relationships are intended to exercise a prophetic role in the societal spheres, since the preservation of a context for personal community is the task of the orders; however, the dynamic freedom of the Protestant principle is weakened by such an ethic, for social tradition and its inequities are supported as universal forms of divine intent.

Reinhold Niebuhr developed the dynamic character of the dialectical theology in social process much more fully than Barth or Brunner. He inherited a dualism of the ethic of love and the ethic of legal, societal patterns from the Lutheran tradition, but his reflections on the relationship of love to justice transmuted this tradition. Instead of a dualism of internal relationships of love and external relationships of justice, Niebuhr moved toward a prophetic ethic of absolute love as the transcendent norm by which all calculations of justice in the historical sphere are to be evaluated. Immanent social patterns become much more pragmatic under this transcendent critique, for the ideal of brotherhood cannot be actualized directly in history; it is approximated in terms of the two foci of equality and freedom.[17] The balance of interest with interest provides a counterpart in the sphere of

[16] Emil Brunner, *Justice and the Social Order*, Mary Hottinger, trans. (New York: Harper & Brothers, 1945), esp. chap. 15.
[17] Reinhold Niebuhr, *The Nature and Destiny of Man* (New York: Charles Scribner's Sons, 1943), esp. Vol. II, chap. IX.

social patterning to the ideal of equality of persons under the ideal of brotherhood. Organized political power preserves freedom of self-determination by limiting force and fraud, and yet it too is limited by democratic participation so that it does not become tyrannous; thus political organization provides a counterpart of the harmony of freedom to freedom in the brotherhood of love. The role of the Christian testimony is, then, one of active affirmation and prophetic critique from a transcendent perspective —the norm of love. Justice becomes a very pragmatic business of restraining excesses and approximating brotherhood in the rough-and-tumble of history.

Clearly there are serious problems in Niebuhr's ethic in terms of the abstract norm of love—problems of which he himself has been all too aware. Love ceases to be the formative power of history when it is conceived as an ideal. Nevertheless, the freedom of man's struggle for order is well founded in this ethic of pragmatic justice; the charter of freedom in the biblical understanding of God and man finds perceptive expression in Niebuhr's position. This perspective is often attacked as giving rise to an ethic of self-interest, but its true dynamic is the acknowledgment of man's historicity, the conviction of the relativity of all social patterning, and the profound sense of the love of God manifest in Jesus Christ as determinative for historical fulfillment.

Paul Tillich develops a theological ethic in which the dynamic of love plays a more creative historical role, thus overcoming the dangers of a static or ideal norm which has been so troubling in Reinhold Niebuhr's position. Tillich stresses the importance of social forms in a theological ethic, and yet he posits social forms or patterns which are evolving and changing in the process of historical life.[18] Tillich works from a vision of ontological structure or logos disclosed in Jesus as the Christ; in his ontological analysis, the elements of this structure provide the parameters within which life is preserved and saved under the conditions of

---

[18] The most succinct statement of Paul Tillich's ethical interpretation is to be found in "Ethics in a Changing World," chap. X of *The Protestant Era, op. cit.* An exposition of this ethic of love within the framework of the ontological elements is given in his *Love, Power and Justice, Ontological Analyses and Ethical Applications* (New York: Oxford University Press, 1954).

existence. We cannot treat such an ontological structure as more than an analogy of the life process inferred from experience and serving to reflect the logos structure encountered in Jesus as the Christ, and yet Tillich would claim more for the intuition of this structure than the position of analogy which I ascribe to it here. He acknowledges that the logos revealed in Jesus as the Christ unfolds in history, which is to say that these elements are themselves within the process of historical unfolding.[19]

Paul Tillich's position represents an attempt to hold together the voluntaristic and logos traditions in Western theology. Tillich rejects an ethic of static, eternal forms, so he can be grouped with Karl Barth and Reinhold Niebuhr against the later tendencies of Emil Brunner to assume a natural law position. On the other hand, Tillich rejects the radical voluntarism espoused by Barth in favor of essential structures through which love expresses itself in history. These essential structures or logoi are not ultimate and eternal forms, for they are transparent to a depth of being, a power of being disclosed through them. Nevertheless, they provide parameters within which life is preserved and saved. The task of theological ethics is to appraise the historical situation, its problems and claims, for the dynamic of love is creative of new possibilities and new forms. Paul Tillich thus joins Reinhold Niebuhr in attentiveness to the practical demands of the situation, but he directs attention to the ultimate concern and questions of ultimate meaning which are implicit in that situation, for love is not a transcendent norm for Tillich but the creative principle of the totality.

The difficult question with Tillich is whether the logos is itself in process under the dynamic of the ultimate principle of love. In this case, man is placed in freedom before the historical promise and task; his life becomes an opportunity to discern the

[19] This is a problem of the radicality of Paul Tillich's existential understanding; the disclosure of the logos as interpreted in "Ethics in a Changing World" and the notion of "History and the Christ" in *Systematic Theology* (Chicago: University of Chicago Press, 1957), Vol. I, pp. 99–101, would give warrant for the claim that this developmental understanding is implicit in Tillich's understanding of love as the principle of totality; for reference to the unchanging substance of the answer, cf. Vol. I, pp. 63 f.

possibility of love and to shape life in forms adequate to its expression. Such a position would be consistent with the Protestant principle, although it is much less structured than Tillich's own interpretation of logos. We can, therefore, stay closer to the true tension in the dialectical theology by affirming the dynamic, historical character of all social forms under the principle of love, while acknowledging the importance of essential structure through which life is preserved and saved in any historical period. Theological ethics then faces the double task of interpreting the meaning of love anew in its own time and investigating the structures of society which express or obstruct that meaning. The latter task is the work of social science, which becomes a full partner in the work of theological ethics. The relationship of social science and theological ethics is *complementary* in the investigation of social forms, since social science delineates effective structures, while theological ethics postulates a framework of ultimate meaning within which those structures can be evaluated.[20] Hence, the essential structures are disclosed within the effective structures, albeit in various degrees of distortion. The essential structures are historical creations. We are not dealing with two worlds—effective structures and ideal forms. We are facing the question of the proximate (sociological) and ultimate (theological) meanings of the patterns which shape human action and through which men project their faith and unbelief into history.

This complementary role of theological ethics and social science is proposed here as normative for the interpretation of

[20] Paul Tillich's method of correlation is a relationship of question and answer in the theological statement, where existence poses questions of ultimate meaning and thus provides the forms within which the Christian message is expressed as answer. Such a method of correlation involves a transmutation of the question, even as the formulation of the question involves a modification of the message, otherwise the question could not be answered. This dynamic understanding of the theological task has opened Paul Tillich to criticism, but it is essentially what is meant here by the complementary roles of social science and theological ethics in discerning the meaning in the effective structures of society and assessing the objective meanings disclosed in them according to the understanding of Jesus as the Christ. On the method of correlation, see Paul Tillich, *Systematic Theology, op. cit.*, Vol. I, pp. 30–31, 59–60.

social patterns. Karl Barth could endorse such a position, although he would allow a less constitutive role for social science in grasping essential structures; I would claim here that the idea of complementarity is more faithful to his evangelical theology of freedom than his notion of analogies of relationship. Reinhold Niebuhr's pragmatic ethic becomes much more dynamic when the principle of love is acknowledged as the source of life in all effective structures, even as love is the principle of life which is distorted in those structures. A critique of social forms is to be made, therefore, in terms of the meanings explored in social science, even as judgments about courses of action are made with reference to possible or effective structures. Reinhold Niebuhr has exercised both roles in his explorations of political issues. Emil Brunner's concern for order is also met without his structural treatment of love and justice. Finally, Paul Tillich's ontological analysis is given its warranted status as an analogy from experience, open to constant revision in the light of historical change, and yet pointing to the significance of forms in interpreting and expressing the reality of Jesus as the Christ.[21] All human action is understood as patterned, thus involving structures of intentionality and subject to evaluation in terms of the ultimate meaning of love. Theological ethics and social science meet in the exploration of these intentional structures of social process.

According to this interpretation, theological ethics asks in any historical period or particular culture about the intentional structures disclosed in the social patterning of that time or society. This is a task of reflection and consideration as well as empirical investigation; it is precisely the task of the human sciences. Hence, the role of social science is complementary to theological ethics in discerning social patterns, for social science considers the meanings implicit in patterns of social action, while theological ethics evaluates the ultimate referent of these meanings. Social science

---

[21] There is a tension in Paul Tillich's thought between his existential understanding and the status which he intends to give to his ontological analysis; this problem appears, for example, in the question as to whether the notion of "Being itself" is symbolic; there is no intention here to adjudicate in this debate, but only to indicate that the present analysis sides with the existential interpretation.

would rightly withhold judgments of the degree to which one or another ethical norm should be disclosed in a social pattern, at least so far as its empirical investigations are concerned. However, it would not be a human science if it refused to develop its empirical materials up to the point of discerning the intentional structures manifest in particular patterns of action.[22]

Unfortunately, much of the social scientific work in our period eschews investigation of structures of human intentionality; indeed, most of the studies now being done either consider the external conditions of human activity or infer certain subjective states from opinions and their correlates in social class or activity. Such studies provide the raw material of reflection on the structure of human intentionality in a particular culture or society. However, further reflection must take place before the work of theological ethics can be carried through to the stage of evaluation. Therefore, theological ethics has to work from its side with the raw materials produced by social science, preferably in collaboration with social scientists. If social scientists concern themselves with the human character of a human science, opening up the historical and intentional structures implicit in human action and social patterning, then the work of theological ethics becomes a dialogue of complementary concerns. If social science continues to mimic the exact sciences and attempts naturalistic reductions of the data, then theological ethics can only hope that the social scientists will publish as much of the raw data of their studies as possible, for the work of theological ethics will then involve an appropriation and deepening of the social scientific analysis.

In the sphere of social patterning, dialectical theology—at least in its most consistent internal expression and despite its actual aberrations—confirms the relativity of social patterning which has been so fully disclosed in social scientific study. In the character of this patterning, however, theological ethics points social scientific research to a much more profound assessment of the creative

---

[22] Peter Winch develops a thorough critique of the inadequacy of naturalistic reductions in the understanding of social action; cf. *The Idea of a Social Science* (New York: Humanities Press, 1958), esp. the discursive understanding of social relations, pp. 128 f.

and intentional character of this patterning, and consequently recalls it from its simple, naturalistic reductions to a creative task in discerning the direction of social formation and development. Thus, theological ethics turns to the social sciences to share in the task of illumining the patterns that are preserving life in order to discern those patterns through which life may be fulfilled.

Congruity

Even though this complementary role in discerning social patterns might be acknowledged by theological ethics, the universal principle of evaluation of effective structures remains a difficult point. How is one to evaluate such patterns? Naturalistic reductions obstruct serious attempts to fulfill the evaluative task of assessing the disclosure of love in the effective structures. The human sciences eliminate the human dimension by such reductions as Georges Gusdorf has noted; they impugn their own role by obliterating their true subject matter—the human in human science. This problem can be illuminated most aptly by recognizing that man's mode of being is historical; a science of man has to reckon with this historicity. In this context, the historical mode of being refers to man's capacity to transcend both his immediate situation and his past in terms of awareness of the future as that for which he is responsible in the present. Thus, man is the one who appropriates a past in the present as meaning for him; he is one who fashions a future in the present as his own project; he is one whose present is constituted by his grasp upon the future. Man's historicity and his reflection make it impossible to understand him as a simple product of the past or a simple resultant of external conditions. So far as social science can predict human action from external conditions and/or past sequences of events, it is dealing with broad uniformities of patterning; but it may not understand these processes and will not understand them apart from their meaning for man. These broad uniformities need to be understood in terms of their meaning for man and society, since they express man's projection of his future and are undergoing constant change and restructuring. The meanings disclosed in these uniformities are the real subject matter of the human sciences; hence, social science misses its target if it contents itself with recognizing the existence of certain uniformities in social patterning.

Pragmatic naturalism takes the intentional structures of action seriously; however, this theory of action has fastened itself to a naturalistic reduction which limits its serious consideration of intentionality. Max Weber had pointed to the crucial importance of understanding action in terms of the intentionality of the actors; Talcott Parsons followed this lead with considerable promise in his earlier studies. However, Parsons' theory of action has developed in recent years as an attempt to reduce all action to a set of functional alternatives on the assumption that a mechanistic balance of pleasure and pain is the key to understanding man. This functional understanding of action made it possible for Parsons to systematize alternatives and close off the meaning of the future as the field of man's creativity in social patterning.[23] We shall return to this problem of closure in another connection, but it is extremely important to recognize that social science obliterates its true subject matter—man and his intentionality—when it presumes to objectify the course of his action as a function of internal equilibrium. Such a functional understanding bears within it the implicit assumption that man's present can be understood on the basis of his past; that is, even his thrust to the future is an attempt to equilibrate a situation rather than create—to maintain past economies of pleasure. When a man's present action can be understood fully on the basis of his past, he is in a pathological state, for he can no longer appropriate his past in terms of a future but is dominated by his past. One is not astonished to discover, therefore, that the fundamental model for this functional theory has been the Freudian analysis of pathology; in action

---

[23] Talcott Parsons' transition to pragmatic naturalism occurred largely under the influence of Freudian theory on the action frame of reference. Note this transition in *Working Papers in Theory of Action, op. cit.,* esp. chap. 1; also Talcott Parsons and R. F. Bales, *Family, Socialization and Interaction Process* (Glencoe, Ill.: Free Press, 1955), esp. chaps. II–IV. Note this discussion of limitations in this Freudian model by Bruno Bettelheim in *The Informed Heart* (Glencoe, Ill.: Free Press, 1960), esp. chap. 1; the difficulty in Parsons' view is revealed by the importance of holding values constant.

theory, the pathological syndrome becomes the model for human action; obviously the model has utility for some low-level processes in social patterning but needs a more comprehensive framework to interpret it.

The historical character of man has important implications for the method of theological ethics, since it raises radical questions about the universality of ethical norms. The dialectical theology started with the Scriptural testimony as the material norm of theological reflection and consequently of theological ethics. However, the Bible no longer provided universal norms of conduct or objective facts on the basis of which an understanding of the norm of love could be established; historical criticism had undermined that possibility. The Bible is a record of interpreted events—events experienced as meanings and recognized as divine disclosures. Dialectical theology also rejected the liberal alternative of replacing objective literalism with a universal human nature by which our own subjective states would certify the truth in the biblical record. The task of selecting the crucial events and apprehending their meaning becomes, therefore, a creative work of faith—inseparable from the perspective of the period in which that task is undertaken; hence, biblical interpretation is to be understood as an appropriation of meaning which is relative to the consciousness of an historical period. Furthermore, the events are to be approached in terms of the intentional structures which gave them meaning in their own time. The historical Jesus is to be understood neither as a fact behind the witness of his followers nor as a universal representative of our subjective moral and spiritual inclinations. Hence, the historical concreteness of the selected events becomes a serious subject for inquiry, and the intentional structure of those events becomes the source of objective meanings.[24]

Exegesis is incomplete until the meaning of biblical events is translated into the universe of discourse of our world. Hence, theological ethics is not to be conceived as an attempt to elicit norms or social patterns from the biblical culture which can serve

[24] For a recent summary of this problem, see Amos N. Wilder, "The New Quest for the Historical Jesus," CC (January 7, 1963), pp. 245–48.

as criteria of evaluation for our own cultural patterns. I have already indicated that Karl Barth is inconsistent with his own theology of freedom in his attempt to do just this with analogies of relationship. Theological ethics has to translate meanings which are apprehended in biblical events into the idiom and social patterns of its own world. Theological ethics does not set itself to bring effective structures into line with ideal norms from biblical times. Theological ethics is a creative work of discerning the meanings within effective structures in the light of meanings disclosed in biblical events.

The difficult question for such an ethic is how it is to understand the *pattern* which it apprehends in the crucial events, for without such a pattern there is no possibility of evaluating the effective structures of our own time. The crucial event of love is disclosed in paradigmatic form, giving a gestalt or whole of meaning which cannot be isolated either from its context or from the ultimate meaning to which it points. Karl Mannheim referred to such events as *paradigmatic events*, which convey in the form of action those meanings which shape and direct life.[25] An historical understanding of man presses theological ethics to work with paradigmatic events in its task of evaluating and shaping the effective structures of society toward the preserving and saving of life. The crucial events are saving events because they are the paradigmatic disclosures of love as the power to sustain and fulfill existence; nevertheless, paradigmatic events have to be translated into contemporary patterns which embody their essential meaning. Theological ethics is not imitative but creative; it fulfills its creative and prophetic task by evaluation of effective structures in the light of paradigmatic events.

Historical reflection on the paradigmatic events takes into account the historical appropriations of the Christian Church; it continues the life of reflection and love through which the Church is present in the world; the changing appropriations of these events in the various contexts of Church and world encounter through the course of Christian history guide theological ethics

[25] Karl Mannheim, *Diagnosis of Our Time* (New York: Oxford University Press, 1944), pp. 127–33.

in its work of translation. Ernst Troeltsch undertook this task, but he attempted it on the basis of a subjective notion of universal humanity; in consequence, he juxtaposed ideal structures with effective structures without apprehending the relativity of the ideals.

Theological ethics and social science are correlated in this normative task of evaluating the effective structures in the light of the paradigmatic events. This is a correlation of changing forms and ultimate meanings; its norm is *congruity* of meaning between the intentional structures of contemporary existence and the paradigmatic events. The relative structures are, thus, the media of universal meanings; indeed, a fuller apprehension of the universal meanings in the paradigmatic events is inseparable from the realization and negation of these meanings in history. Ethical action and ethical reflection unfold the universal within the relativities of history.

Reciprocity

Complementarity of interpretation and congruity of meaning can only develop as theological ethics and social science become partners in dialogue. The difficulties of dialogue emerge, moreover, around the issue of validation of the meanings from which each discipline takes its departure. The claim to grasp ultimate truth is open to discussion in such a dialogue. The organicist claims a vision of the whole through which the meaning of the parts may be understood and the patterning of the parts may be evaluated. The meaning of human freedom and the course of history become accessible to theological interpretation if the theologian has such a grasp upon the totality.

We have seen in our analysis that the dialectical theology makes such a claim to totality in referring itself to the divine will. The historical perspective on man's consciousness refutes the claim of the dialectical theology to an ultimate vision in which the structure of totality is intuitively grasped. Consciousness is mediated in experience and in communal contexts which reflect the changing gestalts and perspectives of history. The paradigmatic events give gestalts of meaning as they are appropriated in faith, but those meanings are also constituted by the historical consciousness which apprehends them. To refer to God or the divine will or the ground of being or the source of being is to make reference to the presupposition of that gestalt of meaning, to affirm in faith the ultimacy of that event which impinges upon our existence, but such a reference is an analogy or symbol mediated in our own consciousness. There is no vision of totality here but rather a grasp of meaning and an affirmation of ultimate meaning disclosed in that historical event. The ultimacy disclosed in a paradigmatic event is not diminished by the relativity of our appropriation, but our appropriation is not to be confused with that ultimacy.

Theological ethics can only take the actual experience of man's historicity seriously by foregoing its own pretensions to a structural vision of the whole; by the same token, it contests any claim of social science to work from a grasp of totality. The organicist perspective is a denial of the historical character of consciousness; it has no more place in theology than it has in social science. The Protestant principle enjoins humility in reference to totality—a humility corroborated by social scientific inquiries into the changing character of claims to knowledge of the whole, changing moreover in terms of the historical interests and perspectives of the institutions which made such claims.

This humility enjoined upon theological ethics applies as well to social science, for naturalistic social science repeatedly attempts to establish a naturalistic or mechanistic whole within which it can analyze the functions of the constituent parts. This biological or physiological metaphor inevitably reinterprets human actions and events in terms of the maintenance of the equilibrium of whatever system is constructed by the social scientist. These models of social equilibrium have a certain utility in preliminary analysis; there is undoubtedly a tendency for men to perpetuate their past into the future, thus maintaining the patterns which they have inherited. This tendency to maintenance of patterns is particularly relevant on the lowest levels of human process; for example, patterns of bodily functioning and perceptual behavior are highly repetitive, whereas the more personal and expressive aspects of thought and communication assume a more creative character. Hence, the model of social equilibrium with its focus on maintenance of certain uniform patterns of interaction need not be discarded *in toto* as irrelevant. However, a preliminary hypothesis for research and exploration is quite different from a fundamental principle on the basis of which particular patterns of action in a society are to be evaluated; for example, the use of the model of social equilibrium to interpret religious activities may have some heuristic value in preliminary investigation but it reduces the intentional structure of man's wrestling with his ultimate concern to a matter of psychological or social equilibrium.

The social sciences have been plagued with these organicist models from their inception. Even pragmatic naturalism tends to close out the historicity of man's action and the human struggle with temporality, for pragmatic naturalism attempts to establish a bounded system of functional prerequisites within which it can make a functional analysis of man's behavior. This functional analysis diverts attention from the creative direction of man's work and social patterning, since it focuses upon the maintenance of the stability of the effective structures already developed in the past. Social scientific attempts to validate interpretation by a systematic definition of totality only place social science along with theological organicism in a sphere of speculation and analogy. Organicist social science commits the fallacy of postulating a social whole and then purporting to demonstrate the validity of that whole from the adequacy with which it accounts for the functioning of the parts—parts which are after all determined by the selective principle of the whole which has been postulated. This kind of circular demonstration of adequacy is not a procedure of demonstration, since the conclusion is already contained in the premise. Such demonstrations are always made ex post facto and thus give an appearance of scientific accuracy; they have never been used successfully for prediction. Social science rejects its authentic principle when it indulges in such tautologies; it refuses to reflect on actual experience, which is its only source of validation.

We need much more flexibility in the models that are used in social scientific inquiry. We need not discard all models of equilibrium, but they should not be confused with scientific demonstrations. They can be extremely useful in preliminary explorations of significant variables. We also need models which explore the role of problem-solving behavior and future-oriented action. We need above all to avoid the kind of pretension which led social science to claim a grasp of the totality of the social process, for the scientist who makes such a claim is himself a part of that historical process whose end he presumes to define. Theological ethics has an important critical role to play in its dialogue with social science—it can identify the pretensions to a divine reason which manifest themselves in social scientific inquiry. This unmasking of pretension entails, to be sure, a willingness on the part of theological ethics to face the critique of its own pretensions to ultimacy. This *reciprocity* in the discrimination of limits is the norm for dialogue between theological ethics and social science in dealing with principles and validation. Theological ethics at its best is a testimony to human freedom; it protests every attempt of social science to foreclose man's future. On the other hand, social science at its best is concerned with the changing meaning of patterns in human existence; indeed, it makes its best contribution to man's ethical aspirations by keeping him close to existence. Reciprocity between these disciplines serves then to sustain them on their authentic ground.

These possibilities in theological ethics and social science are largely contingent upon a development of serious dialogue around a common concern for man and the patterns which shape and guide his action. Social science is loathe to engage in such a dialogue, for it is busy with its great machine and grand theory—to use C. Wright Mills' caustic interpretation of its plight.[26] On the other hand, theological ethics has preoccupied itself with principle—searching Scripture, Church, and natural law for authority. In such a situation, theological faculties would do well to reconsider the course of their work in theological ethics and open the door to a dialogue with the social scientists.

The situation of estrangement between social science and theological ethics which I have outlined is characteristic of most aspects of the relationship of theology to the contemporary world. The dialogue of theological ethics with social science can thus provide a model for the opening of dialogue all along the line.

[26] C. Wright Mills, *The Sociological Imagination* (New York: Oxford University Press, 1959).

Such dialogue cannot be optional for the Church, since her being as the Church cannot be understood apart from her being for the world; she is thrust into such dialogue by her commission to be in the world as a testimony to the universal and ultimate meaning in which man's history finds fulfillment.

11. Theology and the Arts

Martin Jarrett-Kerr

I

Traditional works of divinity, even up to twenty years ago, do not include the subject of this essay, except occasionally as incidental illustration of some theological point already made, or as a piece of decoration, externally applied, to make the doctrinal edifice more attractive. Indeed, it is difficult to see where, in their layout, the present topic could have been situated. If, for instance, we look at a composite volume produced in Great Britain in 1939, and very expressive of the English theological climate of the twenties and thirties—*The Study of Theology* edited by K. E. Kirk—we find the following topics:

1. What Is Theology?
2. Comparative Religion
3. Philosophy of Religion
4. Psychology
5. Old Testament
6. New Testament
7. Symbolic Theology
8. History of Christian Doctrine
9. Ecclesiastical History
10. Moral Theology
11. Christian Worship and Liturgy[1]

[1] K. E. Kirk, ed., *The Study of Theology* (New York: Harper & Brothers, 1939).

If the theme "Theology and the Arts" had been thought relevant to this volume, where would it have come, and how would it have been related to the other topics? Perhaps it might have developed out of "Philosophy of Religion." For the heavenly trio, Truth, Goodness, and Beauty, were still appealed to in those days as "absolute values" which most people accepted and which were reckoned to speak of a Divinity behind them and guaranteeing their efficacy. To-day, as we shall see later, this would be doubly unacceptable; first, because "aesthetics" is at present regarded by most Anglo-Saxon philosophers as a changeling who has been dumped on them secretly and whom they are most anxious to get adopted elsewhere; and second, because most contemporary practitioners of "art" (writers and painters, etc.) find the word, and the concept, "beauty" either meaningless or distracting or both. Perhaps the essay might have been attached to "Psychology"? But again, creative artists would reject this subsumption. Or perhaps it would have come under the head, "Symbolic Theology," or perhaps "History of Christian Doctrine"? For the problem of the validity of "images," the wider aspects of the iconoclastic controversy, and the great and subtle theme of the mystical *via negationis*, or the "apophatic" knowledge of God—all these could be regarded as relevant to the place of the arts. But this is not in fact how these topics were treated in 1939. Under "Ecclesiastical History" a section might have been devoted to the changing patterns of Church art or Christian poetry; and under "Moral Theology" perhaps the visual arts might have seemed to provide test cases for the section "De Pudicitia," while literature might have been drawn on for examples of moral dilemmas. (Indeed, this way of treating the arts is a constant temptation to the theologian: by an instinctive reflex he finds himself asking, for instance, when studying literature, not "Is *Paradise Lost* a successful poem?" but "Ought we to sympathize with Satan?" or, instead of trying to judge "How is *Lady Chatterley's Lover* related to the rest of D. H. Lawrence's oeuvre?" he discusses "Are there extenuating circumstances which modify the guilt of Connie's adultery?" We shall, again, see later that this approach is almost wholly irrelevant.) And finally, though literature and the visual arts have historically been closely associated with "Christian Worship and Liturgy," the association is too marginal and utilitarian for the topic to be appropriately placed at that point.

II

The absence of this topic from works of divinity before about 1940 is a significant fact about those works. For the decision as to how "the arts" should be related to theology (or whether they need to be related at all) is itself basically a theological decision. Thus, in a Thomist system, poetic or visual beauty (*id quod visum placet*) is considered usually under the fifth of the *Quinque Viae*, the demonstration of the existence of God from the hierarchy of "values" in the created world. This is the conception which lies at the heart of a study such as M. Jacques Maritain's formidable and impressive (but, as we shall see, not unchallengeable) work, *Creative Intuition in Art and Poetry*.[2] It is implied in the late Eric Gill's work—both his sculpture and design, and his theoretical writings—in which a poem, a printing type, a teapot, and a string quartet are simply "things well made"; and the artist who makes them is reflecting the creativity of his Maker. On this view the atomic missile is also supremely well made and shapely: "nature," re-echoing the divine ordering, dictates that the shape which offers least wind resistance shall also be the most aesthetically pleasing. But one must then make—and it is implied that one can make—a sharp, formal distinction between a rocket *qua* aesthetic object and *qua* scientific or military apparatus. This view has its practical difficulties, and this is one of the main reasons why many theologians, even those otherwise sympathetic, find the scholastic approach unsatisfactory. But what is more to the point here: the same view as that of Maritain and Gill was also developed very effectively by the late Dr. Ananda K. Coomaraswamy (of the Boston Museum of Fine Arts); and he was not a Christian at all but, if the expression be allowed, a "Hindu Thomist." This suggests that the relationship between theology and the arts, on this view, is very remote; it is a relationship which is established by two or three connecting stages, any one of which may be successfully challenged by a nonbeliever.

At the other end of the scale we might plot a Kierkegaard or a

2 Bollingen Series XXXVI (New York: Pantheon Books, 1953).

Bultmann. (And Paul Tillich with some reservations belongs here too.) If, on the existentialist view, man's theological significance is largely to be deduced from, or detected in, his sense of "exile," of "dread," of "thrown-into-the-world-ness," of *Befindlichkeit*, then the arts will be related to theology in proportion to the clarity or vividness with which they reveal these qualities in man. Heidegger (who must be considered as a sort of a-theologian, perhaps, more than as a philosopher) has found a rich quarry for his work in the poetic aphorisms of the pre-Socratics and in the poetry of Hölderlin; and Bultmann has written perceptively on Sophocles. Indeed, it might even be said that where there is a "natural theology" the arts of man, though given a relative autonomy and a valid place in the hierarchy of being, are kept in their right place and prevented from achieving that privileged but dangerously isolated eminence which romanticism gives them; whereas theological existentialism may paradoxically, in denying the validity of the "orders of being," force the creative arts, as revelatory of man's *Existenz*, to bear more weight than they are really capable of doing.

III

But in speaking generically of the arts I have neglected a vital discrimination. For we can in fact construct a sliding scale which plots the relative nearness to man, or distance from him, of the different arts. At one end we have the "pure" arts: decoration, poetic essays in metrical form, music in which counterpoint is stressed almost at the expense of tone or melody, etc. At the other end we have the fully expressive warmth of the lyric or epic, the drama, the naturalistic novel, the portrait, the tone-poem in music. At the pure end specifically human considerations seem largely irrelevant. Indeed sometimes in so-called "abstract" or "constructivist" painting, in some forms of poetry, and in the contemporary "antinovel" there seems to be an almost desperate attempt to escape from the tangles of human existence into the restful world of pure form. The only difference between a stone smoothed by the tides and a sculpture of (say) Barbara Hepworth is that one has been worked by the natural forces of ocean and friction, the other by the deliberate operation of the sculptor. But once the thing is there its only relationship with man, its sole possibility of humanization, is to become the object of man's admiration: someone passing along the shore, or a spectator in the art gallery, observes "What a pleasing shape!"—and this could be said of either. The only human fact here is that such a remark could not be made by a passing chicken or a piece of seaweed. It is obvious that the relevance of art at this "pure" end of the scale to the study of theology is bound to be remote. And the real problem is that it is precisely this "pure" art which is claimed by many critics as the only authentic species. At the other, "impure" end (and we have to concede this to these critics), the artistic object may trespass so far out beyond the realm of the aesthetic as to be no longer art at all, but either "documentary" (in the naturalistic painting or novel) or sheerly orgiastic (in the emotive music or poem).

But what is interesting is that we can plot a somewhat similar graph in the relationship between the arts, as a part of human culture, and the "theologies." I have mentioned two extremes, the Thomist and the "theological-existentialist." But if we look more closely at the history of Christian thought we shall see that the line is not straight between these two extremes. One useful account of that history has been given us by the late Dr. H. Richard Niebuhr, in *Christ and Culture*,[3] though he offers us a rather different graph. He distinguishes five possible relationships between culture and Christian faith.

1. First there is sheer opposition between Christ and culture. This can be found, theoretically stated (though seldom, I suspect, consistently even believed, let alone applied) in some of the subapostolic Fathers; later by the Cathars or those of similar tendency; and later still by some on the extreme puritan wing of Protestantism or under the influence of Jansenism. On this view, the subject of the present essay would be meaningless: as meaningless as, say, an essay on "Cannibalism and the Theory of Prime Numbers."

2. At the opposite end of Dr. Niebuhr's scale, there is a fundamental agreement, even identity, between Christ and culture: Jesus is regarded as a "hero of human culture history." On this

[3] New York: Harper & Brothers, 1951.

view, the study of the arts would be simply a linear development of the study of religious inspiration. In between these two extremes there are three possible mediating positions.

3. On the third view Christ is the fulfillment of culture: and yet there is a discontinuity between the two—the discontinuity between grace and nature. Christ is the Christ of culture, but he is also the Christ "above culture." This Dr. Niebuhr reckons to be roughly the position of St. Thomas Aquinas.

4. There is a fourth view, according to which there is a continuous tension between Christ and culture. This view, then, agrees with (1) above that there is opposition; but adds that obedience to God leads to obedience to society, and therefore theological obedience has cultural implications. This would be roughly (substituting "the Prince" or "the State" for society) the position of Luther.

5. And finally there is the "conversionist" solution. It agrees with the preceding, (4), viz., that human nature as such is sinful, and therefore there must be a radical opposition between Christ and culture; but it goes on to say that Christ converts man in society and in culture—that, indeed, there is no man apart from culture and society. This is the position of St. Augustine and of John Calvin.

How would this scale be matched against the scale running between the "pure" and the "impure" arts? For, to take an example, a representative theologian of Niebuhr's No. 1 (i.e., one who holds that there is sheer opposition between theology and art) will surely say that the opposition is most serious where the art is least pure: art as "redemptive" or art as "therapy" is most likely to become a rival to theology; whereas the purest forms of art (decoration, or the fugue in music) is likely to be theologically least harmful. And this seems to be borne out by the fact that historically puritanism and iconoclasm have gone together—as can be seen most clearly in the Muslim prohibition of representational art. On the other hand, a representative of Niebuhr's No. 3 (i.e., one who holds that Christ is the fulfillment of culture) is likely to see the least discrepancy between "pure" and "impure" art: he will hold that basically any form of art is like any other form, in so far as it is simply a "well-made thing." Finally, a representative of Niebuhr's No. 2 (i.e., one who holds that there is a fundamental identity between Christ and culture) will be drawn to that idealist school of art analysis which maintains that the essence of art is in some very general concept, and the varying expressions of art, from the purest to the least pure—the most "programmatic"—are nothing but varying manifestations of the "self-unfolding of Spirit." This is confirmed by the similarity between Hegelian aesthetics and Hegelian theology.

It would be tedious and unsuitably technical to pursue these relations in more detail.[4] The main point is simply this: to speak of the relationship of theology to art is to picture in black and white what in fact needs a great number of colors. There is at least a double complexity in the relationship: from the theological side, because of the varieties of "theologies"; and from the aesthetic side because of the different ways of speaking about "art."

IV

I have suggested that there is an affinity between a "liberal" theology and an "idealist" aesthetics. If the affinity between these is not wholly imaginary, then the reaction against them will be seen to be parallel in the two spheres. Do we not feel that there are theological overtones to the following remark about poetry: "A reviewer last week spoke about poetry as the means by which the soul soars to higher regions, and as a means of expression by which it became merged into a higher kind of reality. Well, that is the kind of statement I utterly detest. I want to speak of verse in a plain way as I would of pigs—the only honest way."[5] Again, when in his Norton Lectures Mr. T. S. Eliot is discussing the difficulty of saying what a poem means, even to the poet who wrote it, he remarked half-jokingly that in face of all the varied interpretations the critics had given to his own poems, he had thought of adding as a prefix to any

[4] For those who find diagrams helpful, I have attempted to illustrate the complex interrelationships between "theologies" and "arts" in an Appendix. See below, pp. 221 ff.

[5] T. E. Hulme, "A Lecture in Modern Poetry," printed in Michael Roberts, T. E. Hulme (London: Faber & Faber, 1938), App. II.

second edition of *Ash Wednesday* the following lines from *Don Juan*:

> . . . .
> I don't pretend that I quite understand
> My own meaning when I would be *very* fine;
> But the fact is that I have nothing planned
> Except perhaps to be a moment merry.[6]

Now this seems a very long way from Shelley's notion of the poet as the unacknowledged legislator of the world. And it is also a long way from the even older notion of the poet as loudspeaker of the goddess' inspiration. The late Henri Brémond in an influential book, *Prière et Poésie*, devoted a whole chapter to "Aristote et la Poésie Dépoétisée," in which he attacked Aristotle's account of poetry.

There is no metaphysic, either right or wrong, in his *Poetics*. There is no other heresy than that of silence—the most dangerous of all—Aristotle's sin of omission, his disappearing trick. He has not written a single sentence from which one might convict him of setting aside the traditional view of the poet's inspiration and identifying poetic knowledge with rational. But then he has not written a sentence either—except to be sure that about catharsis—from which one might even suspect the contrary. To remain silent is to consent. Aristotle has kept his silence—silence for ever to be deplored—silence pregnant with catastrophe, pregnant, if I may so express myself, with Boileau.[7]

It is perhaps surprising to find somewhat the same view appearing, amid much else that is learned and perceptive, in the work of the Neo-Thomist Jacques Maritain.

. . . in creative intuition we have the primary rule to which, in the case of the fine arts, the whole fidelity, obedience, and heedfulness of the artist must be committed. . . . between this primary, primordial, primitive rule and all other rules of making,

---

[6] T. S. Eliot, *The Use of Poetry and the Use of Criticism* (New York: Barnes & Noble, 1955), pp. 30–31.
[7] Henri Brémond, *Prière et Poésie* (Paris: Bernard Grasset, 1927), chap. 2. Translation given in W. K. Wimsatt, Jr. and Cleanth Brooks, *Literary Criticism: A Short History* (New York: Alfred A. Knopf, 1957), p. 53.

however indispensable they may be, there exists an essential difference, so to speak infinite, as between heaven and earth. All other rules are of the earth, they deal with particular ways of operation in the making of the work. But this primary rule is a heavenly rule, because it deals with the very conception, in the bosom of the spirit, of the work to be engendered in beauty. If creative intuition is lacking, a work can be perfectly made, and it is nothing; the artist has nothing to say. If creative intuition is present, and passes, to some extent, into the work, the work exists and speaks to us, even if it is imperfectly made and proceeds from a man

c'ha l'habito de l'arte a man che trema,

—who has the habit of art and a hand which shakes.

At the summit of artistic activity, and for one who has long traveled along the road of the rules, finally there is no longer any road. For the sons of God are under no law. Just as finally the unique law of the perfect soul, according to the saying of St. Augustine (not literally of him, but it does not matter), is *"ama et fac quod vis"*—love and do what you want—so the unique rule of the perfect artist is finally: "Cling to your creative intuition, and do what you want."[8]

Now when this grandiose way of speaking of art is challenged today, as it widely is, it is challenged in the name of a humility and realism which has indirect, if not direct, theological significance. Who is puny man to think that he can so perfectly mirror the free creativity of God? Must we not comment with St. Anselm: *Nondum considerasti quanti ponderis sit peccatum?*

Of course, this reaction against idealistic aesthetics and against the romantic notions of inspiration and of the artist's magic role was not consciously a theological reaction. It is connected with the revolt against metaphysics and ethical intuitionism which started among the logical positivists and is still conducted, though in a modified form, by the linguistic analysts. Yet one cannot help feeling that in the puritan impetus of these movements there is something which cannot be wholly explained by the scientific

---

[8] Maritain, *op. cit.*, p. 60. Quoted in Wimsatt and Brooks, *ibid.*, pp. 110 f.

influence, and which stems partly from Christian theological
asceticism. At any rate, it seems incontrovertible that today the
zones of theology and of the arts, as also the zones of theology
and logic or epistemology, cannot be kept hermetically separated
from each other.

But it is time to be more specific.

It is a matter of historical fact that in ages of settled belief men
have tended to write well, and that in ages of declining belief
they have gone out of their way to discover some system of
belief, or some philosophy, which would provide them with a
framework and give unity and shape to their artistic experience.
. . . one of the difficulties about contemporary literature, one of
the things that often makes it look fragmentary and confused,
is precisely the fact that the writer is obliged to expend his energies in creating the conditions in which literature becomes
possible, instead of putting the whole of his talent into his
books.[9]

Therefore any study of literature (and this goes in varying degrees for all the arts) at any point in Western history will be
incomplete unless it includes some reference to the theology (or
substitutes for theology) of the time. Here are some examples
of the sort of studies that might be undertaken.

There are two striking studies in the early part of Erich Auerbach's *Mimesis*[10] which suggest the sort of thing that theologians
should take note of. One is a comparison between the narrative
styles of Homer and of the Old Testament, which brings out
their different attitudes to history and the importance of historical events. The other is a piece of "close verbal analysis" of
a key passage in St. Augustine's *Confessions* (Bk. VI, Sec. 13).
Auerbach is showing how Augustine's natural tendency to classi-
cize or "Ciceronianize" often clashed with his submission to the
biblical-Hebraic idiom, an idiom which had grown out of and
been shaped by the Hebrew-Christian experience. He takes as
his example the use of "parataxis" in "aperuit oculos, et percussus

[9] Martin Turnell, *Modern Literature and Christian Faith* (Westminster,
Md.: Newman Press, 1961), pp. 1–2.

[10] Willard Trask, trans. (Princeton, N.J.: Princeton University Press,
1953).

est." Alypius, in this passage, is at the gladiatorial show; as a Christian he should not be there, but he has compromised with his conscience by going, but resolving to keep his eyes shut. However, at the most exciting moment in the games the shouts of the spectators are so loud and compelling that he breaks his resolution. "He . . . opened his eyes, and was struck with a deeper wound in his soul than the other, whom he desired to see, was in his body . . ." (i.e., Alypius' moral fall was worse than the physical fall of the victim). *Aperuit . . . et*—classical Latin, points out Auerbach, would have used causal or temporal hypotaxis: "having opened his eyes, he was struck" (just as Greek would have used a genitive absolute). But in fact the idiom Augustine used is far more dramatic: just as in English it is more vivid to say, "He opened his eyes, and was struck . . ." (the light "and" makes for greater simultaneity) than to say, "Having opened his eyes, he was struck . . ." or "when he opened his eyes he was struck. . . ." And Auerbach's point is that Augustine slips into this unclassical construction because his knowledge of the Bible and of Christian experience had taught him something about events which classical Latin could not fully express.

In a very different field, that of visual art, Prof. Wladimir Weidlé published in 1950 a valuable (and almost forgotten) little study of the early Christian paintings of the catacombs, and shows the relevance of theology to their form, and to the very different form of classical Christian art from Constantine onward. The paintings he examines in some detail (with illustrations) are the wall paintings of the catacombs of Rome and elsewhere, and the reliefs decorating sarcophagi in Italy and southern Gaul: they all date from the third century A.D. (plus the last years of the second and first years of the fourth). What characterizes these paintings is that

the early Christian painter or sculptor made no attempt, even unconsciously, to let the form of his work answer in some degree to its specific religious and Christian content. As far as form goes, these works are no different from any technically comparable products of the pagan workshops of this period. . . . The form, in these carvings and paintings, simply carries their content, and makes no attempt to express or embody it. And this is the result, not of being afraid of art, or puritanically suspicious of "beauty," but of sheer indifference to art as such. The only interest art could retain for the early Christian was of the kind and degree of importance a modern believer may attach to the way that his Bible is printed or bound.[11]

This is, of course, in striking contrast to all great religious art, which has always insisted that "form shall be totally fused with its content." This early Christian art cannot even be called "symbolic"; we must use for it the word "signitive."

For a sign is distinct from a symbol in this, that its work is all done in passing its meaning on. It is not concerned with *expressing* that meaning, or with making the sign answer to the thing signified. . . . It makes no difference whether we write the figure three as 3 or as iii; all that matters is that we should not confuse it with the figure two. . . . [Thus, e.g.,] in the catacombs, the Good Shepherd was not an image of Christ at all, even in one special aspect, but simply a picture of a shepherd with a lamb on his shoulders; the shepherd is a sign—not so much even of Christ, as, let us say, of some thought about Christ. . . . from these conventionalised sketches all is eliminated but what is quite indispensable if the scene is to be recognised and its import understood.[12]

So that in fact this "is not an art at all. It is a language coined to convey thought within a religion." And yet these paintings have a charm of their own. Though all are concerned in various ways with death, they are all about initiation into life.

. . . there is nothing to compare with the impression that the catacomb paintings leave of a childlike joyfulness, light-heartedness, almost gaiety. This is not merely the result of the fact that it was not the convention of the ancient world to show death as a skeleton with a scythe. The truth is that for those whose bones were laid in these places there was no such thing as death.[13]

---

[11] Wladimir Weidlé, *The Baptism of Art* (London: Dacre Press, 1950), pp. 8–9.

[12] *Ibid.*, pp. 10–11.

[13] *Ibid.*, p. 34.

After the Edict of Milan, Constantine's recognition of Christianity, things changed altogether, and there ultimately emerged

that new, mediaeval, thoroughly religious and Christian art which gradually established itself, as well in the Eastern as in the Western empire. For this new art to emerge, bodily forms and animated figures had to become spiritual, a naturalistic art had to become transcendental: but such a regeneration could never be carried through within the limits of a normal development of taste and form. The roots of it lay not in art at all, but beyond art, in that one religion capable of the intensity of spiritual life to make art unnecessary, and so bring about, if not its death by direct means, at least its long mortification. This is what was accomplished in early Christianity, and what alone made possible the subsequent age-long flowering of Christian creative art. If art was to live and grow, it had to deny itself, and plunge, as though in the baptismal font, into the pure element of faith. . . . What was accomplished, in these years of self-denial and concentration on the thought of the baptismal mystery, was the veritable baptism of art.[14]

Here is clearly a theme for the theologian and art critic to work together upon, and one which cannot be understood by either side alone.

I doubt whether it is possible to appreciate fully the theology of the later Middle Ages without seeing how it works out in, e.g., the theme of Courtly Love, or how it expresses itself in (and even against the grain of) the imagination of a Chaucer. Therefore a work like Prof. C. S. Lewis' *Allegory of Love* provides an essential *theological* text for the period.[15]

Again, how can one see the movement from Aristotelian-Thomist to Baconian-naturalistic concepts more clearly presented than in the developing notions men had of the "great chain of being," and especially in the way this chain, from being pictured as ontological, or simultaneously existent at various levels, became "temporalized," or "emergent" through time? Thus the late Dr. A. O. Lovejoy's important book, *The Great*

[14] *Ibid.*, p. 35.
[15] New York: Oxford University Press, Galaxy Book, 1958.

Chain of Being, becomes an indispensable set-book for this topic.[16]

We are used to hearing of the "medieval synthesis"; and most of us who are not expert Latinists have to take this on trust. But there are those who would claim that the most lively and well-matched synthesis of Christian philosophy, poetry, prose, and religious imagination occurred in fact during the heyday of Anglicanism, in the seventeenth century; and perhaps only lasted at its most balanced and full for half a century. Some of the material for this judgment can be found in such works of popular exegesis as Basil Willey's *The Seventeenth Century Background*.[17] But the claim is most cogently and powerfully made by the late Dr. S. L. Bethell, and may be found worked out in some detail in his *The Cultural Revolution of the Seventeenth Century*.[18]

The Counter Reformation was enormously strengthened by the concurrent schools of mystical and ascetical theology. These had an influence far beyond their immediate and obvious realm. A relevant study of the way in which, e.g., the Ignatian Exercises influenced the imagery and the discipline of the imagination in the seventeenth-century poets (especially Donne and Crashaw) is to be found in the learned and sensitive book, *The Poetry of Meditation* by L. L. Martz.[19]

More subtly still: the scholastic *via analogiae* may be described as a very precise and logical extension of the instinctive human method of reaching the truth through the paradox, that is, through negation-plus-affirmation. Miss Rosamund Tuve's *Elizabethan and Metaphysical Imagery* has made clear that, whatever differences there may be between Elizabethans and Metaphysicals, they both had a common grounding in scholastic logic.[20] This does not mean merely that they were both trained in logic and used logical terms; but that both illustrated logic in their actual poems, and sometimes even used paralogisms, deliberately, to show the limitations of logic. This theme, or something like it, was taken up

[16] Cambridge, Mass.: Harvard University Press, 1936, reprinted 1957.
[17] New York: Columbia University Press, 1953.
[18] New York: Roy Publishers, 1951.
[19] New Haven: Yale University Press, 1954.
[20] Chicago: University of Chicago Press, 1947.

by the late Dr. S. L. Bethell in an article which would have been part of a projected book, but for his untimely death in 1955. The article was entitled "Gracian, Tesauro, and the Nature of Metaphysical Wit," and is an examination of two works on wit: Baltasar Gracian's *Agudeza y Arte de Ingenio* ("Conceit and the Art of Wit"), 1642; and Emanuele Tesauro's *Il Cannocchiale Aristotelico* (the Aristotelian Perspective-Glass), 1654.[21] These two seventeenth-century critics, one Spanish and the other Italian, would, Dr. Bethell claims, have had a similar background and a similar approach to poetry, to that of the English Metaphysicals. There is no space here, nor is this the place, for a full summary of Bethell's account. But what is immediately clear is the extent to which these writers' concept of "wit" is relevant to theology. Tesauro, for instance, says that wit is "a vestige of the Deity in the human mind." For "the angels themselves, Nature, the great God, in reasoning with men, have expressed with conceits, either verbal or symbolic, their most abstruse and important secrets." And this, says Bethell, which was recognized by these seventeenth-century "wit-writers," is the traditional mode of Christian poetry. He proceeds to analyze the famous hymn, the *Vexilla Regis* of Venantius Fortunatus, to show how the paradoxes are expressed:

> Arbor decora et fulgida
> Ornata Regis purpura . . . [etc.]

of which the well-known English version runs as follows:

> O Tree of glory, Tree most fair,
> Ordained those holy limbs to bear,
> How bright in purple robe it stood,
> The purple of a Saviour's blood!

Here, says Bethell, we have the familiar use of metaphor, leading up to *enthymeme*: *blood* is horrible, yet its color (purple) is kingly; *Regis* is used of a heavenly, yet also of an earthly, King; and so on. And therefore, just as the lowliest can be used to point to the highest within this-worldly limits, so the highest of crea-

---

[21] Dr. Bethell's article was published in a defunct periodical, *The Northern Miscellany of Literary Criticism*, No. 1 (Autumn, 1953 [Hull]).

tures can be degraded to a lowly status to point to the great origin of creation—to him who is beyond superlatives, though comparatives and superlatives must be used to indicate him. And so we are able, in Tesauro's language, to "gather from the mud the jewels of a noble art. . . . And [see that] the human mind participates in the Divine, which with the self-same Divinity dwells in the marshes and in the stars, and from the most sordid made the most divine of corporal creatures."

A study of the religious elements in English poetry over the past three hundred and more years reveals as much about the religion as it does about the poetry. A book such as H. N. Fairchild's *Religious Trends in English Poetry* should be regarded as, at the very least, a necessary companion to any ecclesiastical history.[22]

In the field of the visual arts there have been studies of the development of painting and sculpture during the past four hundred years which have suggested that a kind of artistic malnutrition has resulted from the separation of the painter from the Church, from society, and even from the deepest common instincts which unite men. In one of these studies M. Jean Mouton has called this the movement from "silence" (when the artist begins to withdraw and to speak for, and even to, himself only) to the final result, "dumbness" (when the artist cannot speak at all).[23] M. Wladimir Weidlé also, in a much earlier study, gave a similar, rather gloomy picture of the "decay of style" in the arts during the last four hundred years in Europe.[24] If there is any truth in these diagnoses, the effect is bound to be two-way: society, and "religion," certainly theology, will suffer from a complementary malnutrition.

These are only a few of the many possible themes all of which show a vital interconnection between theology and the study of the arts.

[22] Four vols. (New York: Columbia University Press, 1939–57).

[23] *Du Silence au Mutism* (Paris: Desclée de Brouwer, 1959).

[24] *Les Abeilles d'Aristée*, published in English as *The Dilemma of the Arts*, M. Jarrett-Kerr, trans. (London: SCM Press, 1948). A revised and enlarged edition published in France (Paris: Nouvelle Revue Française, 1952) has not been translated.

VI

But most of these suggested themes have concerned the relationship of theology to the arts—the molding influence of theological conceptions upon the forms of writing, painting, and so on, even if sometimes it has been an influence of repulsion rather than either attraction or "co-naturality." But what about the influence in the reverse direction? May there not, in fact, be certain *aperçus*, arrived at through study of the arts, which throw a light upon the state of theology itself? Indeed, might it not be true that the reluctance among theologians to acknowledge the validity of art study comes, not merely from incapacity or busyness, but from a hidden fear that it might show them too much?

We saw (in IV above) that the old grandiose way of speaking about the poet has been challenged in our time. Is not the same challenge issued to grandiose notions of the theologian's task? It seems to me to have been insufficiently realized, even by some of our more adventurous theologians, that the real "secular" revolution has been in the deposing of the queen of the sciences. Even where Theology no longer makes the faintest overt claims to such a position, she still often assumes that it must be her very *raison d'être* one day to recover it. For after all, if Theology is talk about God, and God is Maker of Heaven and Earth and of all things visible and invisible, how should we claim anything less than this ruling place for her? Hence even in Protestantism (more sensitive as a rule to the danger of titanic ambitions in the Church) we hear talk about the need to replace autonomy and heteronomy by theonomy. Of course we all admit that Theology doesn't *look* like a queen today; that, if allowed in at all, she has to consider herself lucky to be able to sneak into a modern university faculty as a subdepartment of, say, "General Arts." But most of us secretly cherish the hope that, though now disguised as a commoner, and perhaps having even contracted a morganatic marriage with one of the other departments of "arts" (e.g., Philosophy, Psychology, or "History of Religions") she may quietly and modestly so commend her claims that one day she will get her title back. But let's face it—we know she won't! And one of the results of studying (say) contemporary literature is to make this clear once and for all.

One literary critic has put it thus: During the past four hundred years there have been, roughly, five phases. First (1), society was generally speaking "Christian," in however broad a sense. Then (2), the community was divided into warring factions. The Church was replaced by "the Churches"; philosophy, science, and literature became unrelated to her. But then (3) came the age of compromise: the Counter Reformation and its typical product, baroque art. But soon (4) literature divides off into "religious" and "secular": and the Christian writer becomes a member of a minority. Finally (5) today that minority becomes "the opposition," and there results within it, and within the Christian artist, an internal conflict between artistic experience and a religion which is held, largely, intellectually.[25]

If that, or some similar division and analysis, is near the truth, then clearly our theology itself will not be in some magic way immune from the general infection of society and man. There is a striking image in a novel which appeared some years ago—not a great novel, though it had a great temporary success and was translated into many languages: C. Virgil Gheorgiu's *Le Vingt-cinquième Heure* (it was written in Romanian, but translated from the French as *The Twenty-fifth Hour*). Traian Koruga, the writer, is speaking:

I once went on a cruise in a submarine. I stayed under water for about forty-five days. In submarines there is a special apparatus for indicating the exact moment when the air has to be renewed. But a long time ago there was no such apparatus, and the sailors took white rabbits on board instead. The moment the atmosphere became poisonous the rabbits died, and the sailors knew then that they had only five or six hours more to live. . . . In the submarine I went in there were no white rabbits, but there was a detector. The captain noticed that I could sense every diminution of the quantity of oxygen. At first he pooh-poohed my sensitiveness, but in the end he did not use the detectors: he only had to look at me. . . . It is a gift which we have—the white rabbits and I—to

25 Turnell, *op. cit.*, pp. 2–3.

feel six hours before the rest of human beings the moment when the atmosphere becomes un-breathable.[26]

This is not to reinstate Shelley's "unacknowledged legislators": a detector—or perhaps it would be equally relevant to say a seismographer—is a more humble occupation than the romantic's ambition for the artist. I believe the image is valid: and it means that a study of the arts should act as a detector of theological "deoxygenization" (or plain fug).

Language is the simplest element to start with. Jacques Barzun, the American critic, has said in his hard-hitting book *The House of Intellect*, "The state of the mother tongue is in fact the index of our control over destiny."[27] Let us apply this at what may seem a crude level, to put this argument as nakedly as possible. Literary criticism could tell us that the sort of prose produced by the team of translators responsible for the *New English Bible* is in many places (not all) a clear indication that, however theoretically impeccable their theology, their understanding of God's Word speaking in the modern world is defective. For if you assess the life of a rosebush by its growing tips, so you may assess the life of man best when you are most sensitive to its points of creative development—i.e., its language. The English language is very alive today in some places (not least in some of the "younger" countries which use it wildly and inaccurately, yet like a new and exciting thing: I am thinking of some of the prose and verse that is being written in parts of Africa today). It is also very dead in other places; especially in editorials, commercial journals, the Houses of Commons and Lords, committee minutes, and most Church periodicals. The main gravamen against the *New English Bible* translators (or against most of them, since there are evidently exceptions) is that they seem to have been unaware which place is which: i.e., unable to distinguish life from death.[28]

Again, it may be a salutary thing for Theology to learn that

[26] C. Virgil Gheorgiu, *The Twenty-fifth Hour*, Rita Eldon, trans. from the French translation (New York: Alfred A. Knopf, 1950).
[27] New York: Harper & Brothers, 1959, p. 27.
[28] These oracular and dogmatic judgments I have tried to substantiate, with the necessary qualifications, elsewhere.

her methods are neither unique nor privileged. To take one example: the sequence, "source-criticism," "form-criticism," and
"biblical typology," can be fairly closely paralleled in literary
fields, e.g., Shakespearean criticism. The older anecdotal writings
about the author are like the "Lives of the Prophets," or "Personalities of the Old Testament," or "Women in the Bible" which
used to appear as theological belles-lettres. Close textual criticism
was followed by thematic studies (e.g., Prof. G. Wilson Knight's
early Shakespearean criticism), and by examinations of Shakespeare's imagery. The effect has been to show the "wholeness"
of Shakespeare's work, much in the way that "biblical theology"
has used critical tools to show the unity of the Bible. To work
out the parallels would be a study in itself.[29]

The relativity of Christian history, and especially the history
of theological thought, can be most clearly seen by setting art
studies beside it. Thus, in the department of Theology and Literature, within the Federated Theological Faculty of the University
of Chicago, the history of drama is treated in precisely this way.
It is shown that there are three main periods, the Greek period,
which was "serious by virtue of the tragic conjunctions between
finiteness and fate that it disclosed"; the Christian period, which
was "serious by virtue of redemptive relationships between sin
and grace or the Law and the Gospel which it has revealed"; and
the modern period, which is "serious by virtue of pathetic connections between the meaninglessness and the despair it exhibits." But
it is pointed out that the three periods are not so sharply contrasted as that brief characterization suggests. For, e.g., within the
Greek period, Sophocles' Oedipus "is represented as being wil-
fully proud in something like the Christian sense and emotionally
insecure in something approaching the modern sense, as well as
intellectually blind in a strictly Greek sense." And Christian
drama "has expressed at least two interpretations of guilt and sin
—the Christian orthodox and the Christian humanist versions":

[29] Hints toward such a study were provided in Helen Gardner's Riddell
Lectures, *The Limits of Literary Criticism* (London and New York: Ox-
ford University Press, 1956), reprinted in her *The Business of Criticism*
(New York: Oxford University Press, 1959).

the example given being *King Lear*, in which Lear is more sinned against than sinning, in Greek terms, on the point of madness in modern terms, and yet also "in the midst of expiation and rebirth in Christian terms." And modern drama, too, holds all three elements: the Freudian-psychological, the Marxist-sociological, and the existentialist-theological. (Arthur Miller's *Death of a Salesman* is analyzed from this point of view.) And, to bring all this more directly into the theological realm, it is shown that

The contrast between the right and the left wing understandings of the Christian faith which appears . . . in the form of a controversy between Christian orthodoxy and Christian humanism about what really happens at the beginning, the middle, and the end of a Christian play, must also appear in . . . [studies of] the Bible, Church History, and Christian Thought in the form of controversies about Christology, the doctrine of the Church and theological method.

And there is a final piece of study which shows the relevance of these topics in yet another realm.

The question whether the contemporary conflict between the religions and cultures of the East and the West may not have been foreshadowed by this internal conflict within the West itself between Greek, Christian, and modern insights; and the question whether either kind of conflict—the conflict within or the conflict without—can be resolved by any simple reference to what Tillich has called "the God of theism."[30]

But Gheorgiu's image of the "atmosphere detector" in the submarine is specially relevant to contemporary problems. And I would say that it is in the study of the twentieth-century novels, plays—and, for those qualified, the art of a Picasso contrasted with that of a Rouault—that the theologian should be able to develop his sensitivity to issues of growth and decay; should be able to

[30] These quotations are taken from a mimeographed syllabus for the "Sequence in Religion and Art" in the Theological Faculty at Chicago, by Prof. Preston T. Roberts, Chairman of Religion and Art, October 1955. Published by permission.

train his ears to hear the speech of the Lord of history. French novelists have, perhaps, been more ready than English-speaking novelists to open their works to the play of philosophical-existential issues; witness the following summary of the work of the philosopher-novelist Maurice Blanchot:

His novels evoke a curious middle-world, or rather middle-void. The noble assumption of the Renaissance, that man is a late creation, standing between heaven and earth and sharing the attributes of both orders, is held to but modified. Man is not a mixed mode, though having the seeds of all life in himself, but one *who keeps the realms apart*, who avoids the contamination of both earth and heaven. Art helps him to find a "between" and to preserve it as the sphere of his liberty. This is a new and hard concept of mediation, which defines man purely by the quality of the void in him, and the arts by a resistance to symbols, human or divine, that would fill this void. Standing in the midst of things, and specifically in the midst of the treachery of words, the artist bears the curse of mediacy. [Emphasis supplied.][31]

But some of our young English playwrights, leaning heavily on the French (on the political realism of Sartre, the warm stoicism of Camus, as well as the defiant nihilism of Beckett) have more to say about philosophy, ethics, and theology than they are aware of. (See a beautiful demolition of the "argument from design," of Paley-ism, in N. F. Simpson's *A Resounding Tinkle*.) The examples are endless, and the main problem for study would be one of limitation. But the fact that this should be so is immensely significant, and it points me to my conclusion.

In Section I above I asked the question: under what theological topic could a study of the arts be situated. And I think the answer should not be in doubt: under anthropology. Today that word is taken as a sibling of sociology, social anthropology, social psychology, social geography, and the comparative study of religion; formerly it meant the theological analysis of man. We can no

---

[31] Geoffrey Hartman, "Maurice Blanchot," in *The Novelist as Philosopher*, J. Cruickshank, ed. (London and New York: Oxford University Press, 1962), pp. 162 f.

longer do battle for the old meaning; let us accept the new, but give it the element that is missing from the modern family of meanings: anthropology as study of man created, fallen, redeemed. And all this is but a subdepartment of a greater topic still: the Incarnation. For if the Christ shows us what true manhood is, it should also be true that a knowledge of existing manhood helps us to understand the being of the Christ. If he "took human nature" to himself, then what human nature apart from him reveals itself to be cannot be irrelevant to his stature. And in the end the study of the arts gives us an unforgettable picture of man apart from Christ—and at the same time shows us that, in another sense, there can be no such thing as man apart from Christ. There may be no *deus ex machina* waiting in the wings to lift us out of the fifth act; but the grip in which the whole play, from the opening of Act I, holds us is itself evidence of a divine concern which is all the more pure for being unacknowledged.

Appendix

We have seen that the word "art" must be broken up into various manifestations, indeed that we need a sliding scale, from the purest kind of art (decoration, abstract patterns, "the art of the fugue," pure form) to the impurest (program music, portraiture, genre painting, etc.). But also that we need a sliding scale of "theologies," according to their hostility or friendliness toward the arts. This results in a complex double relationship which perhaps can best be represented by diagrams.

Suppose, for instance, that we represent the first scale (the scale of "qualitative purity" in the arts—call it scale Q—by a line A—B—C—D—E—F—G—H: in which A is the purest forms of art, and H the least "pure." Suppose then we construct a second scale (call it scale X) for the five possible relationships between Christ and culture: a ***** b ***** c ***** d ***** e. On this scale X, a will be the first relationship (opposition); e, at the opposite end will be the second (identity); b (which is nearest to a) will be the fourth, viz., tension; c (which comes in the middle) will be conversion; and d (which is the nearest to the fifth) will be the third possible relationship, viz., fulfillment. (Thus, using Dr. Niebuhr's five positions, on scale X, $a = 1$, $b = 4$, $c = 5$, $d = 3$, and $e = 2$.)

Now if we start from the right-hand end of scale X, viz., with e: according to e there is identity, i.e., mere continuation between the Christian culture (scale X) and the arts (scale Q). This will give us the following relationship, diagrammatically represented:

$$a^{*****}b^{*****}c^{*****}d^{*****}e = A—B—C—D—E—F—G—H.$$

The whole of scale Q (i.e., A to H) will thus be furthest from a. And this is correct, since a (opposition) holds a total discontinuity between X and Q.

However, the matter is not so simple, and cannot be represented in a purely linear form. For a (opposition) will maintain that it is the most impure elements of Q which are most inimical to theology, because they may be actual rivals, and offer an alternative to Christ (culture as autonomous and as self-redemptive). Whereas the purest forms of art may be relatively harmless: as we see in the fact that historically puritanism and iconoclasm have gone together (as in the Muslim prohibition of representational art). So we shall have to put the relationship in a more subtle way, thus:

This diagram also expresses the point that d (=fulfillment, the scholastic view that *gratia naturam non destruit sed perficit*) sees least discrepancy between the various stages from A–H: it holds that basically any form of art is like any other form in so far as it is simply a "well-made thing." And this is expressed in the diagram by the fact that the whole line A–H is roughly equidistant from d.

These two diagrams, however, do not allow for the many

variant interpretations of the Q scale. For instance, if we were to accept the language about art typical of the idealist school, from Hegel to Croce, we should have to draw $A–H$ in quite a different shape. For here the essence of art is seen in some very general concept, and its expression in varying forms is then a representation of one of the modes of the self-unfolding of Spirit. Thus Q would have to become a spiral, with the essence of art (expressed most purely in its purest forms) at the center.

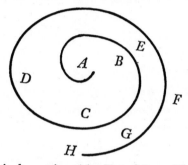

Then the theological reaction (the X scale) to this would be that e could accept this spiral development, but a would reject it most emphatically.

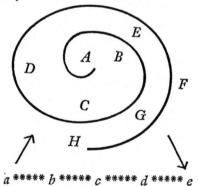

a ***** b ***** c ***** d ***** e

And even this is oversimplified: for in fact one would need to construct a separate diagram for each relationship, of a to $A–H$, of b to $A–H$, of c to $A–H$, of d to $A–H$, and of e to $A–H$; and indeed, to be complete, of the relationship of each separate point on the X-scale to each separate point on the Q-scale (i.e., to A,

B, C, D, E, F, and *G*.) The permutations are endless, and certainly enough to provide research theses for a limitless number of post-graduates in the field of theology and art for the next ten thousand years. At least this way of presenting them should drive home the point that the relationship of theology to the arts is doubly complex: complex from the theological side because of the varieties of "theologies," and complex from the aesthetic side because of the different ways of speaking about "art."

12. Theology and Education

Robert McAfee Brown

The specialized problem of "theology and education" is a kind of case study in the over-all problem of theology and culture, and the approach one adopts toward the latter problem will inevitably influence his attitude toward the former. It is, of course, immensely difficult to say anything original in either area, for both problems have been with the Church since its inception, and in one way or another all the old "solutions" keep cropping up in new dress to confront successive generations.

The ways of getting at the over-all problem range between two extremes, each of which can be illustrated from the New Testament. On the one hand there is the position exemplified in Paul's Corinthian correspondence (I Cor. 1:18-31), wherein he describes the Christ-event as "foolishness to the Greeks," i.e., incomprehensible to the cultural milieu of the time. On the other hand, there is the speech attributed to Paul on Mars Hill (Acts 17:16-34), wherein he describes the Christian proclamation as the fulfillment of those insights foreshadowed by the Stoic and Epicurean philosophers, i.e., as consonant with the cultural milieu of the time.[1]

Although he does not use the above examples specifically, H. Richard Niebuhr, in his typology of the various possible rela-

[1] Further examples of both of these attitudes in early Christian history can be found in W. W. Jaeger, *Early Christianity and Greek Paideia* (Cambridge, Mass.: Belknap Press of the Harvard University Press, 1961), esp. pp. 3–45. The book is an invaluable one for studying the modes of relationship established between the early Church and Greek culture.

tionships between Christ and culture, suggests three closely interrelated but distinguishable positions that range between the above extremes of "Christ against culture" and the "Christ of culture." These are, very briefly, a view which sees *Christ above culture*, a position represented by Thomas Aquinas, in which a synthesis is effected between the two, culture leading men toward Christ, grace perfecting nature rather than negating it; a view which sees *Christ and culture in paradox*, a position represented by Martin Luther, in which the allegiance men owe to both Christ and Caesar leaves them in an inevitable tension from which no easy escape is possible, but in which no easy capitulation to irrelevance or compromise is possible, either; and finally a view which sees *Christ as the transformer of culture*, a position represented by Augustine and Calvin (as well as latterly by F. D. Maurice), in which the cultural goods of this world can be offered up to God and converted by the power of Christ, so that creation, however much it may have fallen away from the Creator, is always open to the possibility and power of redemption.[2]

It should be clear even from this brief summary that, as Dr. Niebuhr acknowledges, there is something a little arbitrary about so tidy a classification of either men or ideas, and that there is, as Dr. Niebuhr also acknowledges, a sense in which the positions are not mutually exclusive but mutually enriching. One would be hard put indeed to cast his lot with one of these positions exclusively, for there are insights from each of the others that need to be preserved in any Christian view of the relationship of Christ and culture, let alone theology and education, and Dr. Niebuhr himself (although his greatest sympathies seem to lie with the last position) is unwilling to make a definitive choice between them.

Now while there is a problem in being sure just what is meant when the word "Christ" is used, there is as great if not a greater problem in being sure what is meant when the word "culture" is used, and this is a question to which Dr. Niebuhr's otherwise full analysis does not give sufficient attention. For even if we

---

[2] Cf. further, H. Richard Niebuhr, *Christ and Culture* (New York: Harper & Brothers, 1951), esp. 39–44 and chaps. 4–6.

can arrive at some kind of satisfactory, if arbitrary, definition of culture, we must face the fact that in the history of Christendom the Church has never been confronted simply by culture-in-general, but always and quite specifically by a *given* culture, and it has often proved true that one man's culture is another man's barbarism.

The attitude the Church takes toward a given culture will, to a large extent, be informed not only by general considerations, but by the quite specific considerations of the nature of the particular culture. It is therefore not possible to write off "culture" as the work of Antichrist, any more than it is possible to affirm that "culture" leads inevitably toward the principle of Incarnation. Some cultures *may* be the work of Antichrist, while other cultures may furnish tools by means of which the Incarnation can be made more, rather than less, intelligible. The attitude the Church takes toward Communist culture or Nazi culture or medieval culture or Ceylonese culture or Mississippi culture will consequently vary in each instance. If it can affirm none unqualifiedly, it may have to deny some absolutely. But no easy formula will cover all cases.

Enough has perhaps been said to suggest that when we are talking about "theology and . . ." or even "Christianity and . . ." the traffic is going to proceed along a two-way, rather than a one-way, street. While Christianity will judge or affirm the particular culture in which it happens to find itself, it will in turn be judged or affirmed by the culture, and in this reciprocity alone will some kind of relationship between the two be established. In a culture, for example, such as the Nazi culture, wherein the Church is denied the right even to preach the gospel, it may be the Church's primary duty to fight for that right, believing that when it is secured all other things will be added unto it; whereas in a culture such as the American culture, where Christian preaching is not regarded as dangerous but merely as irrelevant, a quite different tactic may be called for.[3] Thus the

[3] A less explosive example might be the philosophical milieu of a culture. Jaeger (*op. cit.*, pp. 31, 121) cites Justin Martyr's *Dialogue with Trypho*, in which a Jew meets a Greek philosopher and assumes that because he is a philosopher he must *therefore* be concerned with God and with problems of theology. Such an assumption could surely not be made today if one

attitude that Christianity takes toward a given culture will be partly determined by the nature of the culture and by the attitude taken by that culture toward Christianity.

THE IMPACT OF THE CULTURAL SITUATION ON EDUCATION AND THEOLOGY

Although the above introduction may appear tangential to the theme of theology and education, it should be clear by now that it lays down the guidelines by means of which the more particularized topic may be approached. The main lesson to be learned is that, just as the nature of a particular culture helps to determine the appraisal the Christian makes of it, so the nature of that culture, as it is reflected in its educational philosophy and practices, will be at least partly determinative of the strategy appropriate for dealing with the relationship of theology and education. This means that what may be appropriate strategy today in Britain or America may be inappropriate today in South India, let alone tomorrow in Britain or America. For while the over-all condition of man certainly remains fairly constant in human history, there are also specific problems and specific needs with which a given period of history confronts man, and these must be taken into account by the theologian if he proposes to speak relevantly about the impingement of his discipline on education.

To make Generalizations About Western Culture is, of course, an exceedingly dangerous business, but for our purposes it will be worth risking the following three descriptive comments, after elaborating which we can examine their implications for theology and education. Our Western culture, then, is characterized (1) by pluralism, (2) by a high degree of technological specialization, and, perhaps consequently, (3) by a lack of clear discernment of direction or meaning.

Since theology cannot proceed in a vacuum, a consideration of the impact of these cultural characteristics on both education and a theological understanding of education must be our first task,

---

were to meet a contemporary philosopher, particularly if he were representative of the current stream of philosophy regnant on most university campuses.

after which it will be proper to turn the tables and argue from certain theological considerations to their impact on the cultural and educational scene.

1. The Christian (and particularly in America the Protestant Christian) is loath to acknowledge the reality of cultural *pluralism*. To assert, for example, that "America is no longer a Protestant nation," is to open oneself, if one is a Protestant, to the charge of defeatism or worse. But Will Herberg and others have argued persuasively that America, to whatever extent it once was a Protestant nation, is now a nation in which three allegiances, at least, are recognized as interchangeable in the public eye— one need no longer be a Protestant to be "in," one can be a Protestant or a Catholic or a Jew.[4] Father John Courtney Murray, S.J., has suggested that a fourth allegiance ought also to be acknowledged, that of the "secularist." Whether the secularists are to be found largely outside the churches and synagogues, or whether they inhabit these façades, it is clear that they do represent a fourth "faith," a fourth way of organizing life, and it is progressively being acknowledged that they have just as legitimate claims on the public domain as the more strictly denominated "religionists" have had in the past. We can thus no longer speak of a Christian culture, or even a Protestant culture; we must speak of a pluralistic culture.

What does this fact mean for education? It means, quite simply, that the term "university" is becoming more and more of a misnomer.[5] There was a time, indeed, when a university was just that, a "universitas," a place where there was sung "one song," where there was a single overarching frame of reference in the light of which the pursuit and the transmission of knowledge was effected. But this can no longer be presupposed in the modern

[4] Cf. Herberg, *Protestant-Catholic-Jew* (New York: Doubleday & Co., 1959).

[5] For convenience' sake, the ensuing discussion will focus largely on theology in the university, although it should be clear that the issues raised in a university context can easily be transposed by the reader to fit other situations. On the history of the relationship of theology to higher education, cf. George H. Williams, *The Theological Idea of the University* (New York: Commission on Higher Education of the National Council of Churches, 1958), pp. 1–95, and more briefly Alexander Miller, *Faith and Learning* (New York: Association Press, 1960), esp. chap. 2.

university in the modern pluralistic culture. The university has become a "multiversity," in which a variety of songs are sung, in which a variety of pursuits are conducted in a variety of ways, and in which a single overarching frame of reference is no longer discernible.

This is not to say that the field lacks contestants for the role of providing a unifying principle for all educational activity; there are various aspirants for the position, not the least of these being the familiar, if now less confident, assertion that only methods of empirical investigation can be trusted to produce sound knowledge and learning. But the point of immediate concern is that, whereas theology was once the integrative science in the university, denominated the "queen of the sciences," it certainly is so no longer. In almost every situation it has been forced to abdicate its once-preferred status, save perhaps in the occasional denominational college where it reigns by administrative fiat rather than by the common conviction and consent of the academic community.

The question, then, which the pluralistic situation of our culture (mirrored in the pluralistic situation of the "multiversity") forces upon us is, what shall be the strategy of theology in this situation? A number of possible answers suggest themselves.

Theology could, for example, simply acquiesce in this displacement, retire from the university as gracefully as possible, and cultivate its own garden in sequestered halls of divinity.[6] To do so would certainly be to spell its death, however, for a theology withdrawn from the constant stimulus and challenge of the free give-and-take of the entire academic market place would be a theology in process of going to seed, lacking the power to germinate itself for succeeding generations.

On the other hand theology, nostalgic for the glorious past when it was indisputably queen, could seek to regain the throne from which that upstart, modern science, has displaced it, and fight to regain a now lost supremacy. In addition to being ut-

---

[6] This would seem to be the solution Morton White advocates; cf. his *Religion, Politics, and the Higher Learning* (Cambridge, Mass.: Harvard University Press, 1959), chaps. 8–9. At all events, the book deserves a careful reading as presenting a thesis quite the opposite of that argued here.

terly unrealistic (as anyone who has ever examined the power
structure of a modern university will recognize), such an attitude of academic imperialism can only lead to similarly im-
perialistic claims on the part of other disciplines, each of which
will feel compelled to affirm *its* right to be at the top of the
heap. Thus the physicists or psychologists may be persuaded to
say of theology, "The Queen is dead," but they are quite unlikely
to be persuaded to continue, ". . . Long live the Queen!" They
are more likely to join forces in giving her a decent burial.

Rather than espousing the tactics of acquiescence or aggres-
siveness, it would seem that the posture of theology in the pluralistic situation of culture and university must be both more radical
and more daring. In an image suggested by H. Richard Niebuhr,
it may be that theology must reconceive its task, and instead of
claiming to be *queen* of the sciences, must accept the more modest
but more exacting role of being their *servant*.[7] This would mean
that, rather than trying to dominate the other sciences, as it often
tried to do in the past with uniformly unhappy results, theology
would try to assist the other sciences to achieve their own true
ends, and that its task would be to bring about educational liberation rather than enslavement.

This would mean recognizing, for example, that the unin-
hibited and unabashed search for truth on the part of the most
sceptical or unbelieving laboratory technician could be a genuinely religious act, whether acknowledged as such by the technician or not, and far more pleasing to God than a theologian's
misguided attempt to preserve his own sphere of knowledge
inviolate from possible disruption by psychology or history. The
point is that the theologian must learn to see the honest scientist,
for example—the man who is willing to acknowledge mistakes,
learn from colleagues, and be humble in the face of new and
disturbing information—not as an enemy to be feared, not even
as one whose theological significance is negligible, but as a
comrade-in-arms; as one who in his own sphere of technical

[7] Cf. H. Richard Niebuhr, *Radical Monotheism and Western Culture*
(New York: Harper & Brothers, 1960), pp. 93–99. (The chapter was
originally published as "Theology—Not Queen but Servant" in *JR* [January,
1955].)

competence is striving to learn and to transmit that learning. As
Niebuhr has put it:

> . . . [The theologian] finds many colleagues in the university
> who will not or cannot speak his language in whom the essential
> elements of what he calls "life in faith" are present. They practice,
> without confessing, a universal loyalty; they count upon the vic-
> tory of universal truth and justice; they exercise a constant
> repentance, a *metanoia*, in self-examination and the search for
> disinterestedness; their scientific humility seems to have a religious
> quality.[8]

At whatever point theology can assist the other disciplines it
must do so. This may mean a joint investigation with the political
scientist about the nature of man, in which the theologian will
learn as well as contribute; but it will not mean telling the political
scientist how to organize his curriculum. It may mean exploring
with the clinical psychologist the implications of his discoveries
about the pervasive fact of human guilt; but it will not mean
dictating to him the way he is to conduct his experiments. It may
mean examining with the historian the claims of nineteenth-
century historiography to see whether or not a Christian view
of history can do more justice to more facts; but it will not mean
insisting that the historian emerge from the encounter with a
biblical eschatology. The theologian, in other words, should be
trying to help the political scientist be a better political scientist,
the clinical psychologist a more penetrating clinical psychologist,
the historian a more profound historian. He will offer help but
not impose it, and he will be willing to receive help as well. He
will explain his claims, but not seek to enforce them. He will
hold his ground in debate, but not try to expand his academic
acreage by annexing the holdings of his colleagues.

Now to some the notion of theology as servant may seem sheer
abdication, or at least a sign of unwarranted retreat. But I suggest
that the theologian who adopts this stance has not compromised
his understanding of the Christian faith or become strategically
humble merely for the purpose of making a noble virtue out of
a painful necessity. For behind such a stance is the conviction

[8] *Ibid.*, p. 96.

that all that is true can and will be used by God, and that since the world is his and he made it, whatever men know about that world is finally knowledge to the glory of God and not against it. One can, indeed, cite Calvin, not one to be accused of theological timidity, in one's defense at this point: "If we believe that the Spirit of God is the only fountain of truth, we shall neither reject nor despise the truth wherever it shall appear, unless we wish to insult the Spirit of God."[9] And as Richard Niebuhr has commented in somewhat the same vein, "Resistance to new knowledge about our earthly home and the journey of life is never an indication of faith in the revealed God but almost always an indication that our sense of life's worth rests on the uncertain foundations of confidence in our humanity, our society, or some other evanescent idol."[10] The one who is fearful, in other words, that so-called "secular knowledge" will destroy his faith betrays the fact that his faith is weak rather than strong. Believing, therefore, that all truth is one and that all truth is of God, the theologian can urge upon every department of learning simply that it be true to itself, and he can do this with a kind of serene confidence, believing that neither he nor the faith to which he is committed need fear any discovery of any truth, and believing also that even though the interrelationship and interconnection of the discoveries of the various disciplines may be momentarily hidden, there is behind it all, discernible at least by faith, a pattern of coherence and unity. Bishop Stephen Bayne has made the point graphically:

Brotherhood and the table of atomic weights and the Lord's Prayer and the history of the Hittites and the discovery of gunpowder and the Creed and the multiplication table and Heisenberg's principle of uncertainty and the Agnus Dei—all of this and all truth comes to us in one magnificent, tumbling hodge-podge, because it is all God's, and God is one.[11]

[9] *Institutes of the Christian Religion*, II. ii. 15–16.
[10] *The Meaning of Revelation* (New York: The Macmillan Co., 1941), p. 173.
[11] In Edmund Fuller, ed., *The Christian Idea of Education* (New Haven: Yale University Press, 1957), p. 257. The entire book is a worthwhile symposium on the themes being examined in this essay.

To argue, therefore, that theology should be servant rather than queen, is not to argue from weakness but from strength, and it is, moreover, to pattern theology's stance on the stance of him whom theology exists to serve, the One who came, indeed, as a king, but as a king in the form of a servant.

2. The second characteristic of Western culture is that it possesses *a high degree of technological specialization.* On the one hand, a stress on *specialization* confirms our analysis of the pluralistic nature of the culture, for the specialization proceeds in many directions: the chemist no longer has time to learn what the physicist is doing; the historian of the seventeenth century is ignorant of the history of Phoenicia; the medical school and the law school have little common ground on which to converse, save possibly about malpractice suits; and (perhaps most tragic for the university) the sciences and the humanities find that they no longer share common interests, let alone common vocabularies.[12] On the other hand, however, the stress on *technological* specialization may seem to challenge the pluralistic dimension of the culture, for it suggests (as was hinted a few pages back) that there is an ethos emerging both in the culture and in the university in which learning is put at the service of technology. One does not have to visit many universities to be aware that the humanities are on the defensive, that the large government grants and the large new buildings go to the sciences, and that the exciting breakthroughs in knowledge are more likely to be observable through microscopes or on radar screens than in the English Department. The number of top university brains that are engaged in the project to get a man to the moon *first* is only a symbol of where the priorities in modern culture and modern education have come to lie.

But it is important to note that the two claims are not incompatible. This *is* a pluralistic culture, and it *is* a culture dominated by stress on technological specialization. In broader terms, we live in an age dominated by the sciences, but the point is that

---

[12] On this theme of the disparities between the scientists and the humanities, cf. the highly controversial monograph of C. P. Snow, *The Two Cultures and the Scientific Revolution* (New York: Cambridge University Press, 1959).

the word "sciences" is in the plural. Just as we cannot really talk of "Christianity and culture" but only of Christianity and cultures, so we cannot really talk of "religion and science" but only of religion and the sciences—sciences that in this day and age exist more and more to serve technological ends. We are past the time when we can talk of scientific method, as though such a term described a set of fixed principles or procedures uniformly employed by all scientists. We now see that each science must employ methods of investigation appropriate to the subject matter being investigated. Indeed, theologians otherwise as far apart as Alan Richardson and Karl Barth have argued that theology is itself a science, in the strict meaning of the word, and has equal right to employ the categories of investigation appropriate to an examination of *its* subject matter. However that may be, the modern university is a place in which the sciences (still in the plural) are leading to greater and greater technological specialization, just as in modern culture men more and more tend to think in terms borrowed, whether consciously or not, from the sciences.

Now in this situation, which is "new" only in virtue of its being now so widespread and intense, what is to be the role and concern of theology? If we have learned the lesson of the preceding pages, the first remark must be the obvious one that theology is not only to be servant of the sciences in general, but of the modern sciences as well, and of technology in particular. One may, indeed, doubt the political wisdom of the race for the moon, and wonder if the vast sums being expended on its hasty attainment could not better be spent on housing, hospitals, and race relations, but one cannot doubt the inherent rightness of man's concern to know more of the unknown. This is not modern Prometheanism (although the scientist is in danger of being exploited by the politician for nationalistic Promethean ends), but a quite proper concern and curiosity about the created order. The scientist must be free to explore that created order, and the theologian must help to guarantee him that freedom.

This point being established, it must next be said that theology and technology need to begin a more extensive dialogue than has yet taken place. Such a dialogue is only beginning to take shape in rudimentary form, and its development may be the most crucially important thing theology does in the next half-century. Theology has long since entered into dialogue with the humanities; it must now begin in strenuous fashion the more difficult dialogue with the technological sciences.

For the danger, of course, in an era of technological specialization, is that technology may shift, unknowingly but no less disastrously, from being a means to becoming an end. The machines man makes with his technological skill may cease to be his servants and become his masters—the platitude still, unfortunately, bears repeating. One is impressed at the astounding things electronic computors can do, and the number of activities of the human brain they can reproduce. And it is beneficial to man that computors can eliminate from human life much sheer drudgery of thought, and solve problems in seconds that would take a team of human brains weeks or years to work out. But if this leads men to decide that the problems worth solving are only those that a computor can be built to solve, then the computors are becoming the masters, not the servants.

Analogously, machines can be designed to do certain manual tasks more quickly and efficiently than men can do them. We can suppose that before long machines will be able to build houses in a fraction of the time and cost that it takes human labor to do the same thing. But if this means that we design only the kinds of houses that machines can build, we will have taken another step toward letting the machine dictate how we shall live.

These are only contemporary (and on the whole rather mild) examples of the new way in which technological specialization and a technologically oriented culture enhance the older problem of the depersonalization bequeathed to us by the industrial revolution. And this is surely the point at which the theologian should be engaging in an ongoing discussion with the technological experts. For, refusing to believe that man is a machine, or that he can serve a machine without doing violence to his uniqueness, theology must take issue with views of man that deny this uniqueness. In none of this dialogue should it be insinuated that the technicians are villains or scheming plotters; they are for the most part high-minded men who are engaged in the noble task of eliminating drudgery and meaningless repetition from human life. But they are often devoted with such singleness of purpose to the perfection of new devices that they have not stopped to consider the consequences for human existence of their creations. And in a dialogue about these consequences theology, if it is to be a proper servant, must engage them. To revert to an earlier example, while theology may have little or nothing to contribute to the development of proper rocket thrust for overcoming gravitational pull, it may have a great deal to contribute to the understanding of the man who must be in the rocket, and the fears and anxieties and hopes that will motivate him, as well as to the question of the kind of use to which the rockets are put—i.e., whether they will propel a man to the moon and back, or nuclear warheads to Omsk, or electronic equipment to outer space that will help us harness solar energy to keep children warm in wintertime.

A further task of theology as servant of the scientists must be the insistence that the other scientists are servants also. Only if theology is genuinely prepared to be servant and not queen, can it insist that other disciplines exercise the same humility.

It can be gratefully acknowledged that most scientists themselves are well aware of the limitations of the methods they use, and are not likely to advocate the wholesale transfer of those methods into, say, the realm of human relations. The comment of an eminent chemist, Prof. Eric Hutchison of Stanford University, is appropriate evidence of this fact.

I can predict with only the most trifling risk of error what will happen to 6×10^{23} molecules of hydrogen when I mix them with oxygen and pass them over a platinum catalyst. God made molecules so small, and He made so many of them, that as far as molecules are concerned statistics becomes a matter of almost complete exactitude. Moreover, so far as we know, the idiosyncrasies to which molecules are liable are extremely limited.

In contrast, I fail miserably to predict how I, or my 180 million fellow citizens, will react tomorrow toward a neighbor who does something to irk us. My personality, and yours, are so complex that our emotions are not susceptible to any deep statistical treatment. It is, therefore, unjustifiably optimistic to assume that the successes of science should be transferable to other human activities by following the methodologies of science.[13]

But although this kind of humility exists within the ranks of the scientists themselves, it is not so apparent that it has made its way through all the ranks of the modern educators. The point must therefore still be urged, not so much against the physical scientists as against the social scientists, that the persistent claims of modern culture and modern education that "science" provides the methodology and the means for solving all of man's problems is an extremely suspect one, and that those who make it are making as dogmatic a "faith assumption" as ever entered into the head of any theologian to declare. That the theologian can enlist the chemist in making this point means that he is more likely to be heard, so great is the current authority of the "scientific" as opposed to the "theological" voice. But if the theologian does not make pretentious claims for his own language or viewpoint, as though it were the one system to encompass all reality, he is in a much stronger position to urge a like modesty on the part of his academic colleagues in other disciplines. He is asking them, indeed, to do no more than avoid the sin of academic *hubris* of which they have so rightly convicted theology in the past, and which makes them (one hopes unjustifiably) apprehensive about the theological revival in the present. The older scientist quite properly recoiled against the older theologian who arrogantly demanded that science either demit its field or agree with the answers to scientific questions that had presumably been given to the theologian by divine revelation. Theology today, however, in its proper and long overdue recognition of the element of mystery that remains after all human wisdom and intuition have been exhausted, can with greater justice demand a like recognition of mystery on the part of those who have uncovered another bit of information about the universe in which we live. That each new discovery, rather than further limiting the area of mystery actually widens it and opens new doors of unexplored possibility, is a lesson the physical scientists seem to have learned

[13] Eric Hutchison, "Technology Is Not Enough," *SR* (March-April, 1963), p. 46.

well. It must be hoped that educators in other fields will learn this fact from them.[14]

3. But when we turn to the third major characteristic of our culture, *its lack of clear discernment of direction or meaning*, we discover that such polemics as the above may have been flailing a dying, if not quite dead, horse. For the formerly confident equation of salvation with technological advance is sounded these days on a muted trumpet. The mood is less likely to be expressed by the jaunty assertion that "science can solve all our problems —just give us a little more time," but rather by the resigned admission, "Not even science can solve our problems—now we *are* in a fix."

This does not mean that a sense of direction or meaning must be forever denied to modern man, but that, for the moment at least, it is not apparent. In some, this state of affairs induces a sense of fearful insecurity, in others a kind of stoic indifference, a determination to make the best of things but not to expect too much from them. Still others are likely to rush frantically from this proposed "solution" to that, swaying to and fro with every wind of doctrine and creating an impression very like that of the man who jumped on his horse and rode off in all directions. The mood today, then, is less likely to be "See, we've got a solution" (whether it be religion or science or nationalism) than "Sorry, there is no solution" (not even religion or science or nationalism).

It is in the midst of this kind of vacuum that any theology worth its salt is going to have some definite things to say, for it claims to point to One who offers meaning and purpose and direction. For the fact that theology is a servant means that it acknowledges a Master, and it is the nature and purposes of that

[14] It should be clear that an acknowledgment of mystery is not a covert appeal for a "gap theology," e.g., a view that consigns to theology merely those areas about which we are still ignorant, but which we shall presumably one day know all about. The job of theology is not so much to give guesses about the unknown as it is to give insight and meaning to the known—to creation, the place of man within creation, the possibilities for the redemption of creation, and so forth. No theology based on the central affirmation that "the Word was made flesh and dwelt among us" will knowingly abdicate central responsibility for interpreting the world in which the Word was incarnate.

Master that it is called upon to proclaim. It will not be enough for theology to protest against false masters that reduce men to bondage, for this essentially negative task can never be more than preparation for the proclaiming of the true Master, whose service is not bondage but freedom. As Richard Niebuhr, once more, puts it,

. . . the protest is only the negative side of the positive conviction which such theology seeks to demonstrate. This is the conviction that there is an ultimate word, a word of God; that there is a universal Sovereignty, or better, that the universal power, whence come life and death, is good; it is the conviction that man when he is right in any way—right in inquiry, right in thought, right in conduct, right in belief—is right by faith, right by virtue of his reliance upon and his loyalty to the last word and the universal Sovereign. Such theology does not undertake to be the science of God for it knows that the Transcendent Universal is known or acknowledged only in acts of universal loyalty and in transcending confidence, precedent to all inquiry and action. Loyalty and confidence of that sort, it knows, are not demonstrated more in so-called religious acts of mind or body than in so-called secular activities. Hence it calls attention to the way in which every individual, group, and institution is directly related to the Transcendent—whether positively in trust and loyalty or negatively in distrust and disloyalty.[15]

This suggests that when it comes to the matter of discovering a meaning and direction in life, the issue is not an issue between those who "have faith" and those who do not. It is an issue between competing faiths—faith in man, faith in God, faith in science, faith in the John Birch Society—no one "provable" in advance, each one involving risk, all demanding a depth of commitment and involvement far beyond anything that the evidence can guarantee. In this sense everyone is on Kierkegaard's abyss, everyone is confronted with the necessity of making a "leap."

Just how theology enables one to discern true meaning and direction in life is the subject matter of other essays besides the present one. But one comment may be permitted: however the

[15] Niebuhr, *Radical Monotheism*, p. 95.

claim of direction and meaning is proclaimed within the university, it must be done in terms that affirm, rather than deny, the total life of the mind. Theology, to revert to an earlier example, has no right to "condemn" technology; it can only seek for ways in which technology may be used for the glory of God and consequently the good of man. Theology, indeed, may not "condemn" anything in the created order; it can only seek for ways in which all that has been given in the created order, and which may have been perverted from its true end, can be redeemed so as to glorify the Creator. It may cry out mightily against the abuse of reason, but it can never cry out against reason itself. It may caution against the destructive consequences of overweening pride in human achievement, but it can only glory in whatever human achievements God permits his children by grace. Those who acknowledge that God can use the wrath of man to praise him need sometimes to remember that so great is his power that he can even use the achievements of man to the same end.

THE IMPACT OF THEOLOGY ON EDUCATION

Thus far we have been considering some of the things that the situation tells us about theology. But a number of further problems can be unstuck if we reverse our tracks and consider some of the things that theology can tell us about the situation. The procedure to be followed will be to isolate the area of the teaching of theology in the university setting as another case study, and examine some of the conditions that must obtain if the job is to be done with integrity. In most instances, the teaching of theology poses problems that may be different in degree from the teaching of other disciplines, but are not usually different in kind. At all events, problems posed in the teaching of theology serve to highlight similar problems confronting the other disciplines, and can thus be used to cast light on the whole span of the academic endeavor.

1. *Theology must insist on the right to define its own methodology.* It must not allow itself to be maneuvered into a defensively reductionist position, by responding to the plea, "We'll give you a right to a hearing so long as you argue only on the basis of

empirically demonstrable evidence, or employ categories drawn from the prevailing philosophical outlook, or stay clear of out-moded biblical terminology." On the contrary, theology must insist on its right to employ categories and methods consonant with the nature of its subject matter. Since that subject matter is the living God who has revealed himself in the history of Israel, then whatever categories and methods can best illumine *that* con-tention are appropriate for the theologian. This means that he must not be afraid to talk about revelation or grace or vicarious suffering.[16] He has an obligation, of course, to make as clear as he can what he means by such terms, but he must not fall into the trap of assuming that he has done his job only when he has so diluted the terms that nobody takes offense at them.

One corollary of this contention is that if the theologian is to determine the methods of investigation appropriate to his subject matter, he must accord a similar privilege to other areas of the curriculum. We do not have many theologians still insisting on a "Christian physics" or a "Christian mathematics" (though there are some who claim to know about "Christian economics"), but there has been enough of this in the past so that there is still fear abroad that the theologian is somehow out to stifle freedom of inquiry in other disciplines, particularly if the conclusions of those inquiries seem inimical to revealed Christian truth. For-tunately, theology learned some chastening truths about itself during the older controversy over *time* (e.g., the meaning of evolution), and it must be prepared to learn some further truths about itself during the newer controversy over *space* (e.g., the meaning of the new physics and the implications of space ex-ploration).[17]

The further corollary of the proposition that theology has the right to define its own methodology is that the theologian is permitted to demand from his colleagues in other disciplines the

[16] Cf. further George A. Buttrick, *Biblical Thought and the Secular University* (Baton Rouge, La.: Louisiana State University Press, 1960), esp. chap. 2.

[17] A courageous attempt to raise some of these issues in a preliminary way is contained in J. A. T. Robinson, *Honest to God* (Philadelphia: Westminster Press, 1963 [paperback]). The uproar this volume has oc-casioned in the theological world is only a slight foretaste of things to come.

willingness to learn a rudimentary theological vocabulary. The modern physicist quite rightly insists that we learn a few things about his discipline before he can hope to tell us much about quantum physics. The professor of physiology can tell us very little about blood circulation until we are willing to master the distinctions between such terms as aorta, ventricle, corpuscle, and artery. Surely the theologian is similarly entitled to ask for some willingness to grapple with terms like covenant, justification, eschatology, and sacrament. He must not be put in the position of representing a discipline that people presume they know "all about" simply by instinct.[18]

2. *Theology must see itself in relation to the rest of the curriculum.* By itself, this may be a dangerous half-truth, for the study of theology cannot be solely a prolegomena to "relevance." There is a valid place for the study of theology simply as an academic exercise in attempting to find out what was once believed, or what is now believed. But the task is never done when this basic work of informing oneself has been completed. One must not only know what Pelagius believed; one must also assess how far Pelagius was right, how good or how baleful was his influence, and what are the relevant modes by which the issues Pelagius raised in his day can profitably be raised in ours. Before one has finished these latter tasks, he will have been drawn at least into the realms of psychology, philosophy, and history, and probably into linguistics as well. The present danger is perhaps not so much that the theologian will become prematurely concerned with "relevance," but that in a studied effort to demonstrate his own academic respectability, the theologian in the university will dig deeper and deeper into his own private preserve of investigation, and postpone too long the problem of how he relates his own findings to the findings of his colleagues in other departments.

[18] At a faculty luncheon at a midwestern university I was once asked a theological question which I tried to answer in theological fashion. The questioner responded, "I don't understand a word you've said." My initial reaction was one of chagrin that I had failed so miserably to communicate. I was later told, however, that the particular questioner would have considered it beneath his dignity as an educated man to "understand" anything a theologian might have tried to say.

Nothing, furthermore, is a greater betrayal of theology's subject matter than the implicit assumption that the subject matter is self-contained. A formal understanding of the doctrine of sin will have implications, for example, in an understanding of Auguste Comte, the American Constitution, Albert Camus, the relation of Church and state in the seventeenth century, the rise of modern dictatorships, the writings of Machiavelli, and the course of American foreign policy during the closing months of World War II. No one man can trace all these connections, but that there *are* connections, and that someone should trace them, it is surely the task of the theologian to insist.

In the other academic disciplines, the issue of relevance is likewise a burning one. For the baleful consequence of early specialization in graduate work and subsequently in university teaching is that the scholar, whatever his field, is more and more insulated from everyone and everything save his own narrow area of specialty, in which he probably still dreams of writing the definitive work. It may be one of the peculiar responsibilities of the discipline of theology in the current academic scene to risk forays into other areas, in the hope of eliciting reciprocal forays on the part of those who have too early and too narrowly shut themselves off.

3. *Theology must be willing to listen.* Theologians have often assumed that it was their sole task to provide answers. But it may sometimes be the initial task of the theologian to see that the right questions get asked, and to remember the dictum of Reinhold Niebuhr that there is nothing so irrelevant as the answer to an unasked question. Few things are more pathetic than the preacher in a university chapel learnedly discoursing on a problem that has not the faintest impingement upon the lives of his student hearers.

This does not mean that the only important theological issues are those raised by sophomores (though sophomores are usually better theologians than they realize), and it does not commit us to Bultmann's claim that theological questions are simply anthropological questions. But it does mean that it is crucially important for the theologian to listen before speaking, not only to learn what the questions are, but also to rephrase them so that they are the really significant questions; not only to learn something about the world, but also to learn some new things about the faith to be proclaimed to that world. When Paul Tillich says that "Picasso's 'Guernica' is a great Protestant painting,"[19] he is saying something both about the nature of Protestantism and about the nature of the culture to which Protestantism must speak. One has the feeling that many sentimental and moralistic Protestant sermons would never have been preached had the preachers taken time to study and absorb what Picasso had to say to them, before they turned to what they thought was the Christian word for our day.

It is Tillich who (along with Reinhold Niebuhr) has taken most seriously the task of listening to the questions modern man is asking. This is not the place for an exposition of Tillich's "method of correlation,"[20] but it is the place to assert that Tillich's concern to see what are the true questions man is asking, and then relate the Christian answers to those questions, is a concern that should lie at the heart of any attempt to grapple with theology and education.

This willingness to listen, if extended to the other academic disciplines as well, could do much to break down the overspecialization and compartmentalization of learning of which we have been complaining. If the specialist in seventeenth-century literature had to listen to the historian of the same period, and if both listened to the political scientist and possibly even to the theologian, a truer picture of man's situation both then and now would emerge than could possibly be discovered by any of those disciplines working in isolation.

4. It should be a truism that *theology in the university must be academically respectable and exciting.* The reminder need not be leveled so much at those who teach theology as at those who take courses in theology or who fear that the intrusion of theology into the curriculum will lead to a "lowering of academic standards." The student may assume that he can substitute piety

---

[19] *Theology of Culture,* R. C. Kimball, ed. (New York: Oxford University Press, 1959), p. 68.
[20] Cf. Tillich's *Systematic Theology,* Vol. I (Chicago: University of Chicago Press, 1951).

for performance in a religion course, and that a "feeling" for the subject matter is the most important thing. He may also feel that since "faith" is involved, the important thing is to find out what the professor believes and make that faith his own, at least for the duration of the course. It will be the task of the professor of theology to disabuse all concerned of such notions. There is a subject matter and it must be mastered; it cannot be mastered intuitively or by prayer, but only by hard work. The student may disagree and he may disbelieve; that is fair enough, so long as he understands what it is with which he disagrees, and so long as what he disbelieves is not a caricature.

This demand for academic integrity is a plea for teaching rather than for propagandizing, and for the right of disagreement as a basic right of the classroom. And it is surprising to note how vigorously this claim must be made for other classrooms than the religion classroom. The dogmatism of the undogmatic is a widespread sin in university life—as anybody will have discovered who has tried to defend metaphysics to a professor enamored of logical positivism. To the degree that theology, most suspect for lack of academic scrupulousness, can maintain genuine openness of inquiry and high academic standards, it will be making a powerful case for the retention of such virtues in other areas of the curriculum.

5. But along with academic respectability in the teaching of theology goes an apparently conflicting fact, for the very nature of the subject matter of theology is such that *the student is involved in its truth or falsity*. He takes such a course at risk—risk that proper academic investigation will involve him, as a person, in the truth or falsity of what he is investigating. He reads for the first time in his life about the "doctrine of sin," and such an exposure may drive home to him the fact that he too is a sinner. He investigates the question "What is man?"—and may find his previously held conviction that "man is the measure of all things" so challenged, and even shattered, that he has to grapple not merely with "the doctrine of grace," but with the necessity of receiving grace if his own life is to be tolerable. Paul Tillich may lead him to see that he does, in fact, have "ultimate concern," and Martin Buber may make him aware that the previous inade-

quacy of his own life has been due to his insistence on living at the level of "I-It." He may learn from Karl Barth that Christianity without Christology is travesty, or from St. Thomas that the life of reason is not a barrier to faith but an avenue to it, and have to adjust his own life accordingly.

There is no protection against the possibility that such things may happen as a result of the theology classroom. And while the professor may not, of course, insist upon their happening as a prerequisite for successful completion of the assignments, he is probably well advised to point out to students that such things are always a possibility. He must, however, make scrupulously clear that academic performance and grade are not predicated upon them. An utter nonbeliever should be able to do solid A work in a religion course, while the most existentially involved student may possibly lack the intellectual equipment to do better, academically, than a $D+$.[21]

Now it is sometimes urged that this tension between academic integrity and personal involvement is a tension peculiar to courses in religion. All that can be claimed, however, is that the tension is clearly seen in such courses, but that it is present in almost all others. It may be greatest in the humanities and least in the pure sciences. But it is hard to conceive of a person taking a course in psychology without being forced to re-examine his own psyche, or reading Thomas Hardy without having to decide whether Hardy's view of the nature of things is one that the student can accept for himself; Hardy may send the student into just as existential a tailspin as Martin Luther or Reinhold Niebuhr. There is considerably less personal involvement in, say, the study

[21] There is a difficult problem remaining, nevertheless. If it can be claimed that true understanding of the Christian faith comes only within commitment, *credere ut intellegere*, then obviously the nonbeliever will remain at a disadvantage in understanding Christian faith, until his nonbelief has by grace been transformed into belief. Nevertheless, the job of the classroom is not conversion, even though what happens in the classroom might be a step toward conversion. The job of the classroom is to inform, to expose the student to the best sources possible and also the best challenges to those sources, so that the student at least knows what "they" believe. But personal appropriation of what "they" believe so that it is transformed into what "I" believe must not, I repeat, have any bearing on the academic assessment of the student's work. See further on this point the concluding section of the present essay.

of irregular French verbs, which one either knows or does not, but it can still be argued that as progressive mastery of irregular French verbs enables the student to read Condorcet or Pascal, he will find himself once more in an area where his academic investigation will have important implications for his own life.

6. This tension between academic investigation and commitment can be further clarified by some discussion of *the role of the teacher of theology*. It is sometimes urged, though not usually by theologians, that theology should be taught "objectively," and that the committed believer cannot truly teach—since he already believes, he will therefore inevitably slant the evidence to produce a like belief on the part of his pupils.

In its crudest form the question may come from the secular educator, "How can a Catholic priest teach religion honestly? He is already committed to one particular brand of religion and cannot possibly be fair to other points of view." To which it must immediately be replied that the charge, if true, is just as damaging to a Protestant or Jewish professor of religion, since each of them likewise has a commitment to "one particular brand of religion." And—here is the point that the questioner will seldom acknowledge—such a charge is just as relevant against a "secularist" teaching religion, since he too has a bias, in this case a bias that religion is false. Will not he also be tempted to slant the evidence?

To the over-all question, however phrased, it must be urged as strongly as possible that in the teaching of theology no neutral stance is possible. Everyone teaches from *some* commitment. The important thing is not to pretend that commitment is lacking, but to lay bare the nature of the commitment so that the student can take this fact into account in his assessment of what the professor says.

This does not mean that since he has a commitment the professor is entitled to slant the evidence. He must be as scrupulously fair as possible, airing all sides of all points of view; but he must not presume, or lead his students to presume, that this is the same thing as being "objective." For the stance from which he airs all sides is crucial. More than that, he has indeed a right and an obligation, somewhere along the line, to "take sides," to make a case, to give his students something with which to take issue—provided he gives them access to the materials that can be urged against his case and in favor of another case.

All things considered, the student is probably more likely to get a real understanding of the nature of Judaism, for example, if he hears it expounded by a competent Jewish teacher, who can not only communicate facts about Judaism, but can also, by his person, his enthusiasm, and his own existential involvement in what he is describing, communicate something of the real ethos of Judaism as well. *Mutatis mutandis*, the same thing would apply to Protestantism, Catholicism, or other world religions.[22]

The crucial issue, however, is not whether or not every faith should be expounded by its own adherent, but whether or not it is appropriate that one teach from the stance of his own faith, whatever it may be. It has already been suggested that so long as the professor indicates the nature of his own stance and allows the student to take this into account, no breach of academic integrity has been committed. Indeed, the real breach of academic integrity would appear to be the opposite one, namely the effort to create the impression that the teacher *does* occupy a neutral or totally objective stance. And it must be urged with some vehemence that this posture of "academic objectivity" is perhaps the biggest fraud on the current academic market place, whether in

[22] This is not to say that only in such fashion can a point of view be communicated. Even if that were so, most university resources are not sufficient to provide such a diversity of gifts on a faculty. It can be accepted that there are teachers good enough to overcome the slant of their own perspective to such a degree that they *can* communicate, with depth and integrity, the ethos of a faith other than their own. George Foote Moore expounding Judaism though not a Jew, and Harry Austin Wolfson expounding the Church Fathers though not a Christian, are significant examples (cf. Morton White, *op. cit.*, chaps. 8–9 for a defense of this position). But such men are the exception, not the rule.

There have been occasions, indeed, when I have felt that I, a Protestant, have done reasonably tolerable justice to expounding certain facets of Roman Catholic belief—or Albert Camus's disbelief, for that matter. But I am also aware that the student realizes that these are not, in fact, my own convictions, and he is entitled to entertain the suspicion that somewhere or other a trick is being perpetrated on him.

religion courses or elsewhere. One cannot teach the Reformation, for example, without his own biases entering in, if no more than to the extent of deciding which events of that turbulent period will be described in lectures, and which primary and secondary sources will be read and discussed. The principle of selectivity in either of these matters, a principle often hidden from the student, will reveal worlds about the presuppositions the supposedly objective teacher is smuggling into his presentation.

All of these things, in their proper fashion, can be said about the other academic disciplines as well. It has often been assumed, to theology's discredit, that academic objectivity is a possibility for every discipline save theology. The truth of the matter is that the professor's commitment is just as burning an issue in the rest of the humanities, and, in varying degrees, throughout the rest of the curriculum. What must be urged upon the historian or the philosopher or the economist is not that he pretend to be without biases or presuppositions; but simply that he, too, reveal them, so that his students, too, can take them into account. A student being exposed for the first time to Plato has a right to know whether the Plato he hears expounded in class is Plato as seen through the interpretive eyes of a Platonist or an Aristotelian or a linguistic analyst. To go a step further, the student who hears Shakespeare expounded by one who loves his words and cadences is more likely to come to a true understanding of him than the student who hears him expounded by one who looks upon Shakespeare as an unwelcome intrusion into the history of English literature, decidedly inferior to both Jane Austen and George Eliot.

Thus the problem of commitment vs. academic integrity is a pseudoproblem save in the hands of the unscrupulous. The theologian must insist that in his own discipline, *and also in all the other disciplines*, there is no inconsistency between believing something and lecturing about it with integrity. Indeed, the more firmly one believes in the truth of his own position, the more open he can be to an examination of all arguments that can be urged against it. Commitment does not prejudice honest investigation, and honest investigation does not nullify commitment.

CONCLUSION: "TRUTH IS IN ORDER TO GOODNESS"

The theological discipline is one of the disciplines of Christian living. It is not the whole of it and it is not even the most important part. It is man's attempt to love God *with the mind*, and is thus that part of total Christian living most relevant to the realm of education. But man does not live by mind alone, any more than he lives by bread alone, and the full response of Christian faith includes not only loving God with one's heart and soul and strength as well as with one's mind, but also loving one's neighbor as oneself.

There is no easily charted path from education to transformation, and no way in which the shift, if desirable, can be forced; one can know that Christian faith tells him to love his neighbor and yet continue to find his neighbor most unlovable. This means that the life of the mind is only a part of the Christian's life, and that other resources than classrooms and textbooks and lectures will be needed if the full ranges of Christian living are to be experienced.

These other resources are not the primary responsibility of the university but of the Church, and it is incumbent upon the Church not to try to transform the university into a counterpart of itself. But the Church may make available within the life of the university such resources as the university is willing to accept. A university chapel, for example, may be a more important vehicle for the growth of faith than a first-rate curriculum of religious studies, though ideally both will be present. But a university chapel that does not give rigorous attention to the life of the mind as one of the conditions of its worship and prayer will be as ineffective as a religion department that studiously avoids dealing with the fact that worship and prayer can be legitimate outcomes of a study of its subject matter.

The achievement of a proper relationship between truth and goodness is not the work of man but of God, and such transformation cannot be structured or manipulated or predicted. It can occur in the chapel or the classroom or the dormitory or the local bar. Grace is not bound. For this reason, the theologian must not assume that education will produce transformation or that it will inhibit it, and he must not assume that the transition from knowing the truth to doing the truth is something over which he has control. He will therefore teach as clearly and as well as he can, and rest content in the doing of his job, willing to leave the outcome of his labors in the hands of God.

13. Theology and Other Religions

Ninian Smart

I

There are two distinct reasons for studying religion. First, religion is a striking and pervasive human phenomenon. Second, it makes a variety of important claims about reality and about values. It is convenient to label these two aspects the "scientific" and the "doctrinal" respectively.

Now it is quite obvious that for the scientific understanding of religion it would be wrong and parochial to confine our attention to the religion of our own culture. Theories about particular features of religion could well be distortions if they relied upon such a limited purview of the facts. For example, Freud's account of the father figure in the genesis of religious beliefs may have a certain plausibility as applied to the Judaeo-Christian tradition, but is rather hopeless as a means of illuminating Buddhism.

It should also be obvious that the doctrinal approach should not be culturally tribalistic. First, from the point of view of logic, it seems inadequate to make a simple appeal to revelation when there are rival claims made by the great religions on the basis of their respective revelations. It is true that today many theologians are seeing that the Christian revelation is not to be equated with a collection of scriptural propositions, but rather is the self-disclosure of God in history and human experience. But other faiths have said similar things—that the Scriptures are like fingers pointing at the moon and that what really counts is the human experience of that reality, to which they point. In short, the appeal to revelation is at least partly the appeal to experience: and what good reason can we have for ignoring the experience of other traditions? Second, it happens that the present age has seen some interpenetration of cultures—so that now, in the West, more and more people are becoming interested in and acquainted with the great faiths of the non-Christian world, notably Hinduism and Buddhism. It is worth recalling that only in the last fifty years or so have Western scholars had at their disposal the major religious texts of the East. Therefore, it is only in the twentieth century that there exist for the first time the conditions for a true dialogue of religions. Thus Christian theologians can no longer ignore the claims of the Eastern faiths. Both logic and practical exigency compel them to study religions.

Now the study of a religion outside one's own culture is necessarily comparative. For nothing is more calculated to bring distortions into the inquiry than the *unconscious* introduction of presuppositions drawn from one's own religious and cultural background. The presuppositions have to be made conscious: and the way to do this is to see clearly the differences, where they exist, between the key concepts of the alien faith and those of one's own. Indeed, this remark applies with equal force to those who have no religion, for they still are markedly affected by the image of religion presented in their own culture, and are just as likely to have unexamined thoughts about what religion, to be religion, must be like.

The clearest example of this presuppositional distortion is the way in which many Western scholars have treated Theravāda Buddhism. The concept of a spirituality which admits neither of a God nor of an eternal soul has proved difficult to grasp, and there have been persistent attempts to smuggle at least the soul back into the Theravāda.[1] Apologetic interests reinforce the dan-

[1] Recent representatives of this trend are: G. Appleton, *On the Eightfold Path* (New York: Oxford University Press, 1961); Miss I. B. Horner, "Buddhism: the Theravāda," in the *Concise Encyclopaedia of Living Faiths*, R. C. Zaehner, ed. (New York: Hawthorn Books, 1960) and R. C. Zaehner, *At Sundry Times* (New York: Humanities Press, 1958).

ger of misunderstanding, since the Christian theologian's life would seem to be easier if it could be shown that there is a God or soul in Buddhism: it would be an apologetic basis on which to build. Conversely, and paradoxically, apologists have an interest in otherness. For if you cannot get a basis to build on, or feel that it would involve too many concessions to the heathen, then why not stress the total otherness of the Christian gospel?

But quite obviously the first task of the comparative religionist is scientific. That is, he has to describe other faiths. Not only this, but the description itself must bring out the "feel" of those religions, and this necessarily involves describing them *from their own point of view*. Because human beings are conscious and have beliefs, a behavioristic and external account of their religions is inadequate; their own accounts of what they are doing and what they believe are, in a sense, authoritative, and it is useless for the outsider to try to foist other beliefs upon them in the guise of description ("What you *really* believe, my dear fellow, is that....").

It is sometimes, however, held that it is impossible to get the "feel" of an alien faith. Only those who live the life know what it is really like. There is something in this objection, but nevertheless it should be treated with suspicion. It can be the prelude to obscurantism—to a sophisticated appeal (which owes some of its glamor to its naïve appearance) to mere faith in matters of religious truth. It ignores, too, the fact that all men are human—talking to a Buddhist is not like groping amid the squeaks for communication with a Martian. Above all, it forgets that a good job, even if it is imperfect, is better than a bad one.

So far we have seen that understanding a faith outside one's own culture is necessarily comparative, to prevent presuppositional distortion. But there is a stronger sense in which the study of religions can be comparative. It is often illuminating to bring together elements from different independent histories of religion, for they may reflect a similar human phenomenon. Thus some of Prof. Mircea Eliade's work (e.g., his *Images and Symbols*) inquires whether "in addition to its own history, a symbol, a myth or a ritual, might not reveal something of the human condition

regarded in its own right as a mode of existence in the universe."[2]
By this horizontal, comparative approach as contrasted with the
vertical, historical one, it may be possible to gain insight into the
reasons for the patterns of similarity and divergence in the various systems of belief and practice.

These remarks may serve to show very roughly the rationale
for the comparative study of religion. Now although the scientific
study is the proper concern of comparative religionists, the doctrinal approach is clearly more immediately relevant to the theological attempt to give an orderly account of the truth about
ultimate Reality. I therefore wish to show how the results of the
scientific study of religions pose questions about certain influential
modern theologies.

II

1. *Barth and Kraemer.* It might have been thought that Barthian
theology could have little to say about other faiths, but Dr.
Kraemer has made a heroic attempt to apply the principles of
dialectical theology to the great religions. Despite some modifications in his attitudes since writing *The Christian Message in a
Non-Christian World*, this book is the best and most powerful
statement of one kind of Christian view about other faiths. His
thesis may be summed up in a quotation. Writing of the world
religions, he affirms: "In the illuminating light of the revelation
in Christ . . . all 'similarities' and points of contact become dis-
similarities. For the revealing function of that light is that, when
exposed to it, all religious life, the lofty and the degraded, appears
to lie under the divine judgment, because it is *misdirected*."[3]
Behind this affirmation lie two reasons. First, there is Kraemer's
espousal of dialectical theology. Second, there is his perception
(very important for comparative religionists) that every religion
is a living, indivisible entity. This view of religion he calls the
"totalitarian" approach. A better word would be "organic,"[4] in

---

[2] Mircea Eliade, *Images and Symbols* (New York: Sheed & Ward, 1961),
p. 176.
[3] Hendrik Kraemer, *The Christian Message in a Non-Christian World*
(New York and London: International Missionary Council, 1947), p. 136.
[4] See my *Reasons and Faiths* (New York: Humanities Press, 1958), pp.
11–14.

view of the unfortunate connotations of the former word in the context of politics, and because it suggests a certain exaggeration —for bits can be added to and subtracted from a religion without its losing its identity. It is not *quite* indivisible—and likewise an organism can remain viable after losing a limb or putting on fat. Still, it remains true that the doctrines and practices of a religion hang together and must be understood individually in the light of the rest. This is partly what makes the comparative study of religion a tricky and delicate business.

But does the organic thesis about religions mean that comparisons are impossible? Baseball and cricket are likewise organic in a sense, for the rules and practices of each game hang together, but we can still point to similarities and differences between the two games. One of Kraemer's reasons for his position is not, therefore, cogent. We must turn to dialectical theology.

Fortunately we do not need to decide for or against Barth in order to see the inadequacy of Kraemer's view. Let us rather concentrate upon the crucial question as to whether there can be a genuine comparison between empirical Christianity and other faiths. For if there can be, and if empirical Christianity in some way reflects the gospel, there can be no a priori reason why the gospel and other faiths should not be compared. Kraemer writes:

We have acquired the freedom to apply to empirical Christianity the same dialectical and "totalitarian" view as to other religions, and honesty requires us to do this courageously for the sake of the benefit to Christianity itself. There is only one great difference between empirical Christianity and other faiths. Empirical Christianity has stood and stands under continuous and direct influence and judgment of the revelation in Christ and is in virtue thereof in a different position from the other religions.[5]

We can neglect the *judgment* here, for all religions are equally under it. It is the *influence* that is crucial. The importance which Kraemer assigns to it implies that somehow, albeit imperfectly, empirical Christianity reflects the revelation in Christ—in its teachings, life, and worship. Consider the teachings. If the influence

[5] *Op. cit.*, p. 145.

has been at all effective, it must be possible to say such things as
"The doctrine of grace corresponds to some aspect of the revelation in Christ." But this implies in turn that the revelation in
Christ can be compared in some sense with the teachings. There
can, then, be no a priori reason to hold, if there are resemblances
between empirical Christianity and other faiths, that there can be
no resemblance between them and the revelation in Christ.

But can you so compare empirical Christianity with other
faiths? As a matter of straight fact, you can. Islām believes in a
personal Creator; Rāmānuja stresses grace; some Mahāyāna so-
teriology has some analogy to Christian atonement doctrines; Eckhart and Śankara are not totally unlike . . . and so forth (always
remembering, of course, the organic nature of religions). Certainly the concepts of grace and of a Creator are not just peripheral to the gospel.

Kraemer could evade this argument only by holding that there
is after all no correspondence between the gospel and empirical
Christianity. But this would not only make nonsense of his quite
correct insistence on the influence of the former on the latter,
but likewise it would make nonsense of the Church, Christian
devotions, and so on. For if no such correspondence exists, empirical Christianity, i.e., Church life, would have no relevance at
all to Christ, and it would be just as good for us to be Buddhists
or Muslims.

Nor is it useful to hedge by saying that revelation is nonpropositional, and so can have no correspondence (or lack of correspondence) with teachings, which *are* propositions. It is true that
Christ is not a proposition. But the facts of his life, teachings, and
identity are necessarily propositional. In any case, the claim that
revelation is nonpropositional could only be relevant to Kraemer's
thesis if revelation were entirely inexpressible in terms of doctrine. But this would lead to an absurdity. For what cannot be
expressed is equally compatible with all beliefs, facts, or propositions. Silence cannot conflict with any claim—so that on this interpretation revelation would be quite compatible with Muslim
or Hindu teachings. No doubt doctrines are often or always *inadequate* ways of expressing the revelation in Christ—but inadequacy is not the same thing as total ineptitude or falsity.

In brief, if the gospel is at all reflected in empirical Christianity, there is the possibility of comparison between it and other faiths. If Kraemer's talk of "influence" means anything, his main thesis is false.

It follows, then, that the only kind of total otherness which Christianity could have would be empirical otherness; and the facts of the comparative study of religion do not bear out this claim. Hence, the truth of Christianity implies at least the partial truth of some other faiths. But once we have said this, we are no longer in a position to appeal simply to Christian revelation, in the Barthian manner, but must extend our inquiry into the whole field of world religions. There is no good ground for an a priori theology which renders the claims of the great faiths irrelevant to the ultimate truth.

2. *Bultmann.* Bultmann's varied contributions to theology are, in truth, immense, and I only wish here to concentrate upon certain aspects of his thought which seem dubitable in the light of our knowledge of other religions. The use of existentialist categories immediately, of course, poses a question, since the highly intimate, personal, and psychological flavor of much key existentialist writing leads us to ask how far the particular, and perhaps parochial, condition of European men is what forms the basis of the existentialist description of the human predicament. In brief, if existentialism is to play the part traditionally assigned to natural theology, we may wish for assurance that it is not *simply* the outgrowth and expression of a particular stage in a particular culture.

Nor is such disquiet allayed by the fact that Bultmann's theology represents a completion and extension of the thought of Heidegger. For what special reason is there to think that the Christian direction is the most natural or convincing direction in which to move? It is true that the call for decision, for "authentic" existence, can illuminate the Christian faith, and can remind us of the danger of an intellectualist appraisal of Christian doctrine. But whether or not the story be true that Heidegger remarked, after reading Suzuki, "If I understand this man correctly, this is what I have been trying to say in all my writings,"[6] the Heideg-

---

[6] See William Barrett's "Zen for the West," in Nancy Wilson Ross, *The World of Zen: An East-West Anthology* (New York: Random House, 1960), p. 344.

gerian analysis would more naturally fit the contemplative anti-intellectualism of Zen than the Christian gospel. There is more spiritual pragmatism in Hindu and Buddhist attitudes to ultimate truth than has been the case in the Christian tradition. Doctrines are useful in so far as they lead us on to an authentic and immediate experience of ultimate Reality, and like the existentialists many Eastern teachers testify that we must transcend norms and conventions in attaining to illumination. So there is in one respect at least as important an affinity between existentialism and, say, Buddhism as there is between it and Christianity.[7]

Two courses would lie open to the existentialist theologian here. One would be to go in for a *totally* pragmatic view: the claims of Christianity amount to a means of engineering commitments and experiences. The other would be to say that there really is a kind of truth which can be seen in existential experience. If the former course is taken, the notion of any kind of theological truth would evaporate. If the latter, we are back with the challenge of other faiths and the need to take into account other traditions of religious experience. In other words, the thesis that Christian experience gives the fullest insight into what existentialism hints at would have to be considered in the light of rival claims to do this from the side of Hinduism, Buddhism, etc.

This raises further questions about history in Bultmann's thought. Christians have traditionally been faced with the problem of giving just emphasis both to the historical process of God's self-revelation, in particular to the historical Jesus, and to the continuing personal experience of Christ. In brief, there has to be a balance between the existential and the historical. But Bultmann considerably underplays the role of the historical Jesus. This no doubt is not surprising, for the difficulties created by modern scholarship over the detailed historicity of the Gospel narratives can be lightened by placing preponderant weight upon the existential experience of Christ.

This tendency, however, brings Christian faith into line with certain strands of thought in Mahāyāna Buddhism. This does not of course entail its falsity. But it does mean that we would have

[7] See also M. O'C. Walshe, *Buddhism for Today* (New York: Philosophical Library, 1963), chap. IX.

moved very far indeed from Christianity as traditionally understood. For if the historical Jesus evaporates behind the experiences
of the faithful, from the apostles onwards, then we shall have a
form of Docetism to be found in some Mahāyāna doctrines.
There, the question of the historicity of Gautama is rather unim-
portant, and the Buddha as an object of devotion and meditation
symbolizes something in human experience, but is ultimately
unreal—a manifestation of the Absolute for the sake of bringing
beings to enlightenment.

Thus, without its historical rooting, Christianity would easily
be fitted into Buddhist and Hindu categories as a religion of pure
personal experience. Hence the type of existentialist theology
exemplified by Bultmann poses important questions about the
supposed contrast between Christianity, as an "historical" faith,
and Eastern religions.

3. *Thomism.* If Barth rejects natural theology, and Bultmann
uses natural theology in a new key, St. Thomas Aquinas represents
the most impressive attempt at natural theology in the old key. The
proofs of God's existence form the basis of the whole edifice—for
it is through them that one can argue one's way out of the empirical cosmos to the Transcendent. Only thus can one have the
materials with which to reason further about the divine nature.
Now admittedly it has often been wondered whether the God
of the metaphysicians is really the God of religion. But this does
not detract from the importance of the attempted proofs. For
there must always in the nature of the case be a gap between the
conclusions of natural and those of revealed theology. If you
could get the God of religion out of metaphysics, there would be
no need for revelation. On the other hand, the God of religion
does not represent men's total apprehension of the divine Reality:
and natural theology is a sophisticated way of elucidating the fact
that God is not simply operative in history and in human experience, but sustains and enlivens the total cosmos.

Nevertheless, in the light of our knowledge of other cultures
and other religions, traditional natural theology has an air of inadequacy. In particular, those innocent-seeming concluding sentences in Aquinas' Five Ways—"This all men speak of as God"
—are suspect. For in the history of Indian philosophical theology

there are corresponding arguments for the existence of God (and counterarguments in plenty too); but quite clearly the conception of the divine Being who figures in these Indian conclusions is distinct from that of the Creator whom the Christian tradition looks to. To put it crudely: the respective natural theologies sustain very different revelations.

Nor is it sufficient to reply: "But both streams of thought flow towards a very similar concept—that of a personal God." For the role and place of this personal God can be so diversely interpreted. Śankara, for instance, holds that the personal Lord is only a secondary and illusory manifestation of the divine Absolute, sharing his illusoriness with the world which he brings into being. Thus the inevitable gap between the God of the metaphysicians and the God of religion means that there is room to graft rather different revelations onto the stem of natural theology. Moreover, both Western philosophical history and the example of agnostic or atheistic faiths in the East suggest that in view of the countervailing arguments and religious considerations the cogency of traditional natural theology will remain in question. The "proofs" may have a certain force, but are not so overwhelming as to compel the assent of all reasonable men. Thomism, in so far as it insists on the deductive validity of the Five Ways, has to depend on challengeable metaphysical premises and distinctions; while, if it is reinterpreted to mean that the proofs explicate a noninferential intuition or apprehension of God, it is open to the philosophical riposte of the Jains—that maybe the intuition of God arises from prior religious belief, and not conversely.[8]

It follows, then, that traditional natural theology would at least need to be supplemented by a new and softer variety: one in which the claims of the varying revelations are related to the experiences of men.[9] What is needed is a general "critique of religious experience": and this already presupposes that the scientific investigation of religions has been undertaken.

[8] See Dale Riepe, *The Naturalistic Tradition in Indian Thought* (Seattle, Wash.: University of Washington Press, 1961), p. 204.
[9] See I. Ramsey, *The Prospect for Metaphysics* (New York: Philosophical Library, 1961), the Introduction and my "Reason, Revelation and Religions" in that volume.

III

This brief survey of a trio of current theological positions indicates the challenge to them presented by the comparative study of religion. But such a negative harping upon the inadequacies of certain views, when they are seen in the light of the world's religions, is itself an inadequate representation of the doctrinal importance of the study of religions. For it must be remembered that the shape and substance of doctrines is in part determined apologetically: for instance, certain modern views of the Fall, as a continual process rather than as an event in time, in part result from the impact of evolutionary theory upon biblical literalism. In so far as the challenge of the great Eastern faiths gives a new form to apologetics, therefore, it will thereby involve a reformation of doctrine.

Journeying into foreign lands brings a revaluation of one's own faith. For instance, it shows wherein lies the uniqueness of Christianity. Now on this topic some twaddle is talked—as if uniqueness were a virtue, and as if Christianity were the only faith to be unique. If uniqueness means having certain properties not possessed by any other individuals in the class under consideration, then all the great religions are in fact unique. Only one religion was founded by the Buddha. Only one looks to the Veda as the central source of revelation. Only one has Muhammad as its chief Prophet. Still, despite all this, it is useful to look at the unique properties of Christianity, so that they can be evaluated, and so that their organic effects can be noted.

For example, I suspect that a reasonable conclusion from the study of religions is that, for the most part, patterns of doctrine are the product of attempts to express varying types of religious experience. Thus Theravāda Buddhism is an expression of contemplative experience with the minimum of metaphysical and religious interpretation (the experience of the Personal such as is found among the prophets and in the *bhakti* religion of India is largely wanting here). Different systems represent, as it were, varying blends of *bhakti* and contemplation, of the prophetic and the mystical. Still, Christianity, in common with the Judaism out of which it grew, stresses too the activity of God in history. Though personal experience of God, among the prophets and elsewhere, is important, history counts for a lot too. Now much analysis is needed of what "history" means here. But certainly the concept of a directional, if not necessarily progressive flow of human and humanly significant events is central to Christian thought. But it hardly has the same force east of Bombay. The belief in a cyclical cosmos and in a virtually everlasting chain of rebirth has militated against such a valuation of history.

This contrast raises some of the vital questions which are wrestled with, in another context, by existentialist theologians. For how do we relate unhistorical experience of the Transcendent with the directional flow of events? Part of the answer doubtless must be that certain forms of religious experience, and in particular the sense of God as a numinous Other, already point toward one kind of valuation of history. That is, the apprehension of a Holy Being and the sense of the contingency of the world together suggest the appropriateness of the idea that the cosmos comes into being through an act of will—almost arbitrarily. Thus is expressed the radical dependence of the world on God. But an act of will is figured as an event in time, as an historical event: so that Creation and the importance of history chime in together. If this judgment as to the relevance of religious experience to historicity has any validity, it can serve as an illustration of the type of insight that may be stimulated by the study of religions.

The situation is rather like that which we find in the use and learning of languages. Someone who knows no foreign language can no doubt speak English adequately. But a real insight is gained into the structure of the English language by learning some other: likewise, I suggest, with religions and cultures. In a way, what happens is that one's own religion begins to look *strange* again, and not something just given—as it were, a necessary feature of one's environment. We can look at it afresh, with new, perhaps more Eastern, eyes.

After all, to us, in Western culture, the scandal of particularity has been considerably attenuated. The pale Galilean swept the Roman, and so the European, world before him, and it was easy to think of Christianity as dominating the whole of civilization.

It was only by degrees, and after many years, that we began to realize the full significance of the non-European world and to see that great cultures, notably those of India and China, have been flourishing over long periods, with a leavening of noble spirituality. From their end, it is indeed scandalous that the highest truth has to be entangled with the history of the Jews. That God should be incarnate: this is intelligible. But that it should occur *only once* is scarcely credible. In this, and in other ways, the journey into alien cultures may help to freshen our perception of Christianity. It will drive us to a new and deeper analysis of what atonement means—for this is central to these issues.

There is, too, a more practical and mundane way in which the comparative study of religion has been and is of use to the theologian. It is of course a necessary background to (one shudders to use this malformed neologism) missiology. Because of historical accidents, indeed, the comparative study of religion has been much slanted to this end: for many investigators in the field were also missionaries or concerned with mission work. This was dangerous, since it tended to a systematic undervaluation of the beauty and vitality of other faiths—apologetics could too easily be disguised as description and the reader left with a curious bafflement as to why on earth the heathen should be so foolish and degraded as to remain heathen. Nevertheless, it is quite clear that it is useless training missionaries without acquainting them with the cultural and religious milieu to which they will be going. Here an objective and sympathetic presentation of the other man's faith can be of enormous value. Without this the missionary's dialogue can turn out to be a monologue.

Consider, for instance, the way in which the Christian idea of heaven may strike many Orientals. Heaven is often depicted as a kind of place, and this place is filled with a type of imagery which suggests that it is a refined and resplendent counterpart to this world. Now Buddhism describes a multiplicity of heavens and hells: but these heavens are not the final goal. They are part of the empirical cosmos: and Buddhist nirvana is genuinely transcendent to the cosmos. Likewise God and union with God in many Hindu theological writings are transcendent to the world, while heaven is not, so that liberation means going beyond heaven.

It is thus easy for the Buddhist or Hindu to think of the Christian missionary as offering a second-rate form of salvation—valid up to a point, but not the highest end of man. Consequently, there is much room for a misunderstanding of the Christian message, just because the theological categories at the receiving end are so very different, that is, until we begin to think at a very much deeper level. This, I am convinced, is one main reason why Christianity in India has made so little impact upon the educated classes. Bibliolatry has played its part here too. For the Bible, taken *tout court* and inserted into a culture which knows a great religious tradition, is wide open to misunderstanding.

For missions at home, in the West, the other faiths present a challenge too. There is now in the West a new drift of thought— the growing feeling that all religions have much to offer (which is true) and essentially say the same thing (which is false). Unable to see the truth in the dogmas of Christianity, many are turning hopefully to neo-Hinduism, as represented by modern Vedānta, or to Buddhism. Especially those who favor the former alternative think that there is a core of truth in all the main faiths; obscured, however, by priests and dogmatists, who stand between the ultimate Reality and the individual. This approach to religion is not entirely without reason, and it appeals to those who have a real feeling for the Transcendent without a conviction that Western Christianity supplies the answer. It is a result of the interpenetration of cultures in the modern world, and is thereby a movement which is almost bound to grow. The Christian pastor cannot therefore ignore it. But the movement is not to be stemmed by simply quoting the Bible. Probably this helps to encourage it: for those who quote the Bible in this apologetic context are almost bound to remind the unfaithful of that obscurantist, over-dogmatic, and fanatical brand of Christianity from which they rightly revolt. Only if the Christian faith can be seen to be true against the background of the world's faiths can this movement be countered. In short, people are interested, among other things, in the truth, and it is of no use asking people to surrender their intellects. So once again the apologetic problem is seen as central to our concern with other faiths: not apologetics with the curled lip—but instead real, down-to-fact, down-to-sensibility apologetics

—this is what is wanted. And obviously, you have to know how the other man feels and thinks if you are to communicate effectively with him. Hence once more the need for the scientific study of religions.

IV

These remarks can be concluded by saying two things. First, it is clear that in the twentieth century the study of religions is basically necessary to Christian theology. Both the scientific and the doctrinal study are inevitable. But second, it is clear that, in so far as we are interested as theologians in formulating truth, that branch of the comparative study of religion which has sometimes gone under the name of "comparative theology," i.e., the scientific comparison of doctrines, is especially vital. It is true that you cannot understand the doctrines of a religion without attending to its practices; but it is the doctrinal side which presents the real challenge to Christian theology. People are not free to believe what they will, even though they are free to take decisions. I can decide what to do now—whether to resist a temptation or no. But I cannot for the life of me, and however much I try to sweat with conviction, *believe* that there is an elephant in the room now. The logic of belief differs from the logic of action, and all the talk (some of it, happily and undoubtedly, justified) about the importance of commitment cannot add up to the conclusion that I can freely commit myself to some person or cause presupposing *any* belief you care to mention. This is why theology and that branch of it called "apologetics" is vitally important. The truth has to ring true both to my existential experience and to my intellect. And if other faiths present a different view of the world, and a view which cannot be ruled out of court, just because it springs from experience and thought, over long centuries, then we have to find out about these world-pictures. This makes life more complicated, and enriches doubt. But it is no part of Christianity to hold that complications and doubtings are to be evaded. The world is the milieu of Christ: and India and China are part of that world.

But what of Africa and the Americas? What of the ancient Middle East? If I have written nothing here about the important

scholarly studies devoted to the religion of the Incas, to the multi-
tudinous culture of tropical Africa, to the gods of Egypt and
Babylon, it is only because I believe that the important issues
concern those faiths which not only are living still, but also present a real alternative to Christianity in terms of depth and comprehensiveness of doctrine.

God works in history, and history is not merely Judaeo-
European history. While the world shrinks, our religious hori-
zons expand.

Notes on Contributors

JAMES BARR, Professor of Old Testament Literature at Princeton Theological Seminary, is the author of *Biblical Words for Time* and *The Semantics of Biblical Language*.

ROBERT McAFEE BROWN is Professor of Religion at Stanford University. Among his recent books are *The Spirit of Protestantism* and *Observer in Rome*.

JERALD C. BRAUER, Dean of the Divinity School of the University of Chicago, is the author of *Protestantism in America* and co-author of *Luther and the Reformation*.

GEORGE B. CAIRD, Lecturer and Tutor at Mansfield College, Oxford, is the author of *The Truth of the Gospel*, *The Apostolic Age*, and *The Pelican Commentary on St. Luke*.

ALEC GRAHAM has been Lecturer in Theology and Chaplain at Worcester College, Oxford, since 1958, and Fellow since 1960.

JAMES M. GUSTAFSON, Professor of Christian Ethics at Yale Divinity School, is the author of *Treasure in Earthen Vessels: The Church as a Human Community*.

MARTIN JARRETT-KERR is a member of the Anglican Community of the Resurrection, Mirfield, Yorkshire, England. Widely known for his translations from the French, he is also the author of books on D. H. Lawrence and François Mauriac. His most recent theological work is *The Secular Promise*.

DANIEL T. JENKINS, Chaplain and Senior Lecturer at the University of Sussex, is the author of *The Christian Belief in God, Beyond Religion,* and *Equality and Excellence.*

J. DAVIS McCAUGHEY is Master of Ormonde College in the University of Melbourne, Australia. He is the historian of the British Student Christian Movement.

NINIAN SMART is Professor of Theology at the University of Birmingham. His most recent books are *Philosophers and Religious Truth, Doctrine and Argument in Indian Philosophy,* and *A Dialogue of Religions.*

J. HEYWOOD THOMAS is Reader in the Philosophy of Religion at the University of Durham. He is the author of *Subjectivity and Paradox* (a study of Kierkegaard), and *Paul Tillich: An Appraisal.*

W. A. WHITEHOUSE is Master of Eliot College and Professor of Theology at the new University of Kent, Canterbury. Among his books are *The Christian Faith and the Scientific Attitude,* and *Order, Goodness, Glory.*

GIBSON WINTER, Professor of Ethics and Society at the Divinity School of the University of Chicago, is the author of *The Suburban Captivity of the Churches* and *New Creation as Metropolis.*